SAINTS' EVERLASTING REST

BY THE REV. RICHARD BAXTER,

ABRIDGED BY

BENJAMIN FAWCETT, A.M.

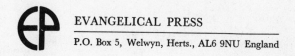

EVANGELICAL PRESS

P.O. Box 5, Welwyn, Herts., AL6 9NU England

Paperback edition issued 1978
by Evangelical Press
from the edition issued by
the American Tract Society

ISBN: 0-85234-111-3

PHOTOLITHOPRINTED BY CUSHING - MALLOY, INC.
ANN ARBOR, MICHIGAN, UNITED STATES OF AMERICA
1978

CONTENTS

PREFATORY NOTICE

RICHARD BAXTER, the author of the Saints' Rest, so well known to the world by this and many other excellent and useful writings, was a learned, laborious, and eminently holy divine of the last age. He was born near Shrewsbury in 1615, and died at London in 1691.

His ministry, in an unsettled state, was for many years employed with great and extensive success both in London and in several parts of the country; but he was nowhere fixed so long, or with such entire satisfaction to himself, and apparent advantage to others, as at Kidderminster. His abode there was indeed interrupted, partly by his bad health, but chiefly by the calamities of a civil war; yet in the whole it amounted to sixteen years; nor was it by any means the result of his own choice, or that of the inhabitants of Kidderminster, that he never settled there again, after his going from thence in 1660. Before his coming thither, the place was overrun with ignorance and profaneness; but, by the divine blessing on his wise and faithful cultivation, the fruits of righteousness sprung up in rich abundance. He at first found but a single instance or two of daily family prayer in a whole street; and on his going away but one family or two could be found in some streets that continued to neglect it. And on Lord's days, instead of the open profanation to which they had been so long accustomed, a person in passing through the town in the intervals of public worship, might overhear hun-

dreds of families engaged in singing psalms, reading the
Scriptures and other good books, or such sermons as they
had taken down while they heard them from the pulpit.
His care of the souls committed to his charge, and the
success of his labors among them, were truly remarkable; for the number of his stated communicants rose
to six hundred, of whom he himself declared there were
not twelve concerning whose sincere piety he had not
reason to entertain a good hope. Blessed be God, the
religious spirit which was thus happily introduced, is
yet to be traced in the town and neighborhood in some
degree—O that it were in a greater—and in proportion
as that spirit remains, the name of Mr. Baxter continues
in the most honorable and affectionate remembrance.

As a writer, he has the approbation of some of his
greatest contemporaries, who best knew him, and were
under no temptation to be partial in his favor. Dr. Bar-
row said, "His practical writings were never mended,
and his controversial ones seldom confuted." With a
view to his casuistical writings, the honorable Robert
Boyle declared, "He was the fittest man of the age for
a casuist, because he feared no man's displeasure, nor
hoped for any man's preferment." Bishop Wilkins observed of him, that "he had cultivated every subject he
had handled; that if he had lived in the primitive times,
he would have been one of the fathers of the church;
and that it was enough for one age to produce such a
person as Mr. Baxter." Archbishop Usher had such
high thoughts of him, that by his earnest importunity
he put him upon writing several of his practical discourses, particularly that celebrated piece, his Call to
the Unconverted. Dr. Manton, as he freely expressed it,
"thought Mr. Baxter came nearer the apostolical writ-

ings than any man in the age." And it is both as a
preacher and a writer that Dr. Bates considers him,
when, in his funeral-sermon he says, "In his sermons
there was a rare union of arguments and motives to convince the mind and gain the heart. All the fountains of
reason and persuasion were open to his discerning eye.
There was no resisting the force of his discourses, without denying reason and divine revelation. He had a
marvellous facility and copiousness in speaking. There
was a noble negligence in his style, for his great mind
could not stoop to the affected eloquence of words; he
despised flashy oratory, but his expressions were clear
and powerful; so convincing the understanding, so entering into the soul, so engaging the affections, that those
were as deaf as adders who were not charmed by so wise
a charmer. He was animated with the Holy Spirit, and
breathed celestial fire, to inspire heat and life into dead
sinners, and to melt the obdurate in their frozen tombs.
His books, for their number—which amounted to more
than one hundred and twenty—and the variety of matter
in them, make a library. They contain a treasure of controversial, casuistical, and practical divinity. His books
of practical divinity have been effectual for more numerous conversions of sinners to God than any printed in our
time; and while the church remains on earth, will be
of continual efficacy to recover lost souls. There is a
vigorous pulse in them, that keeps the reader awake and
attentive." To these testimonies may not improperly
be added that of the editors of his practical works in
four folio volumes; in the preface to which they say,
"Perhaps there are no writings among us that have
more of a true Christian spirit, a greater mixture of
judgment and affection, or a greater tendency to revive

pure and undefiled religion; that have been more esteemed abroad, or more blessed at home, for awakening the secure, instructing the ignorant, confirming the wavering, comforting the dejected, recovering the profane, or improving such as are truly serious, than the practical works of this author." Such were the apprehensions of eminent persons who were well acquainted with Mr. Baxter and his writings. It is therefore the less remarkable that Mr. Addison, from an accidental and very imperfect acquaintance, but with his usual pleasantness and candor, should mention the following incident: "I once met with a page of Mr. Baxter. Upon the perusal of it, I conceived so good an idea of the author's piety that I bought the whole book."

Whatever other causes might concur, it must chiefly be ascribed to Mr. Baxter's distinguished reputation as a preacher and a writer, that, presently after the Restoration, he was appointed one of the chaplains in ordinary to king Charles II., and preached once before him in that capacity; as also that he had an offer made him by lord-chancellor Clarendon, of the bishopric of Hereford, which, in a respectful letter to his lordship, he saw proper to decline.

The "Saints' Rest" is deservedly esteemed one of the most valuable parts of his practical works. He wrote it when he was far from home, without any book to consult but his Bible, and in such an ill state of health as to be in continual expectation of death for many months; and therefore, merely for his own use, he fixed his thoughts on this heavenly subject, "which," says he, "hath more benefited me than all the studies of my life." At this time he could be little more than thirty years old. He afterwards preached over the subject in

his weekly lecture at Kidderminster, and in 1650 published it.; indeed it appears to have been the first that
ever he published of all his practical writings.   Of this
book Dr. Bates says, "It was written by him when languishing in the suspense of life and death, but has the
signatures of his holy and vigorous mind.   To allure our
desires, he unveils the sanctuary above, and discovers
the glories and joys of the blessed in the divine presence, by a light so strong and lively, that all the glit-
tering vanities of this world vanish in the comparison,
and a sincere believer will despise them, as one of
mature age does the toys and baubles of children.   To
excite our fear, he removes the screen, and makes the
everlasting fire of hell so visible, and represents the
tormenting passions of the damned in such dreadful
colors, as, if duly considered, would check and control
the unbridled, licentious appetites of the most sensual
wretches."

Heavenly rest is a subject in its own nature so uni-
versally important and interesting, and at the same time
so truly engaging and delightful, as sufficiently accounts
for the great acceptance which this book has met with;
and partly, also, for the uncommon blessing which has
attended Mr. Baxter's manner of treating the subject,
both from the pulpit and the press.   For where are the
operations of divine grace more reasonably to be expected, or where have they, in fact, been more frequently discerned, than in concurrence with the best
adapted means?   And should it appear that persons
of distinguishing judgment and piety have expressly
ascribed their first religious impressions to the hearing
or reading the important sentiments contained in this
book; or, after a long series of years, have found it both

the counterpart and the improvement of their own divine life; will not this be thought a considerable recommendation of the book itself?

Among the instances of persons that dated their true conversion from hearing the sermons on the saints' rest when Mr. Baxter first preached them, was the Rev. Thomas Doolittle, M. A., who was a native of Kidderminster, and at that time a scholar about seventeen years old, whom Mr. Baxter himself afterwards sent to Pembroke Hall, in Cambridge, where he took his degree. Before his going to the university, he was upon trial as an attorney's clerk, and under that character, being ordered by his master to write something on a Lord's day, he obeyed with great reluctance, and the next day returned home, with an earnest desire that he might not apply himself to any thing, as the employment of life, but serving Christ in the ministry of the gospel. His praise is yet in the churches, for his pious and useful labors as a minister, a tutor, and a writer.

In the life of the Rev. John Janeway, Fellow of King's College, Cambridge, who died in 1657, we are told that his conversion was, in a great measure, occasioned by his reading the Saints' Rest. And in a letter which he afterwards wrote to a near relative, speaking with a more immediate reference to that part of the book which treats of heavenly contemplation, he says, "There is a duty which, if it were exercised, would dispel all cause of melancholy: I mean heavenly meditation and contemplation of the things to which the true Christian religion tends. If we did but walk closely with God one hour in a day in this duty, O what influence would it have upon the whole day besides, and, duly performed, upon the whole life. This duty, with its usefulness, manner, and directions, I knew in some measure before, but had it more pressed upon me by Mr. Baxter's Saints' Everlasting Rest, a book that can scarce be overvalued, and for which I have cause for ever to bless God." This excellent young minister's life is worth reading, were it only to see how delightfully he was engaged in heavenly contemplation, according to the directions in the Saints' Rest.

It was the example of heavenly contemplation, at the close of this book, which the Rev. Joseph Alleine so frequently quoted in conversation, with this solemn introduction, "Most divinely says that man of God, holy Mr. Baxter."

Dr. Bates, in his funeral-sermon, dedicated to Sir Henry Ashurst, says to that religious gentleman and most distinguished friend and executor of Mr. Baxter, "He was most worthy of your highest esteem and love; for the first impressions of heaven upon your soul were in reading his invaluable book of the Saints' Everlasting Rest."

In the life of the Rev. Matthew Henry we have the following character given us of Robert Warburton, Esq., of Grange, the son of the eminently religious Judge Warburton, and the father of Matthew Henry's second wife. "He was a gentleman that greatly affected retirement and privacy, especially in the latter part of his life: the Bible and Mr. Baxter's Saints' Everlasting Rest used to lie daily before him on the table in his parlor; he spent the greatest part of his time in reading and prayer."

In the life of that honorable and most religious knight, Sir Nathaniel Barnardiston, we are told that "he was constant in secret prayer and reading the Scriptures;

afterwards he read other choice authors; but not long before his death he took a singular delight in reading Mr. Baxter's Saints' Everlasting Rest and preparations thereunto; which was esteemed a gracious event of divine Providence, sending it as a guide to bring him more speedily and directly to that rest."

Besides persons of eminence, to whom this book has been precious and profitable, we have an instance, in the Rev. James Janeway's Token for Children, of a little boy, whose piety was so discovered and promoted by reading it, as the most delightful book to him next to the Bible, that the thoughts of everlasting rest seemed, even while he continued in health, to swallow up all other thoughts; and he lived in a constant preparation for it, and appeared more like one that was ripe for glory, than an inhabitant of this lower world. And when he was in the sickness of which he died before he was twelve years old, he said, "I pray, let me have Mr. Baxter's book, that I may read a little more of eternity before I go into it."

Nor is it less observable that Mr. Baxter himself, taking notice, in a paper found in his study after his death, what a number of persons were converted by reading his Call to the Unconverted, accounts of which he had received by letter every week, expressly adds, "This little book, the Call to the Unconverted, God hath blessed with unexpected success, beyond all that I have written, except the Saints' Rest." With an evident reference to this book, and even during the life of the author, the pious Mr. Flavel affectionately says, "Mr. Baxter is almost in heaven—living in the daily views and cheerful expectation of the saints' everlasting rest with God; and is left for a little while among us, as a great example of the life of faith." And Mr. Baxter himself says, in his preface to his Treatise of Self-Denial, "I must say, that of all the books which I have written, I peruse none so often for the use of my own soul in its daily work, as my Life of Faith, this of Self-Denial, and the last part of the Saints' Rest." On the whole, it is not without good reason that Dr. Calamy remarks concerning it, "This is a book for which multitudes will have cause to bless God for ever."

This excellent and useful book now appears in the form of an abridgment; and therefore, it is presumed, will be more likely, under the divine blessing, to diffuse its salutary influence among those that would otherwise have wanted opportunity or inclination to read over the larger volume. In reducing it to this smaller size, I have been very desirous to do justice to the author, and at the same time promote the pleasure and profit of the serious reader. And I hope these ends are in some measure answered; chiefly by dropping things of a digressive, controversial, or metaphysical nature; together with prefaces, dedications, and various allusions to some peculiar circumstances of the last age; and particularly by throwing several chapters into one, that the number of them may better correspond with the size of the volume; and sometimes by altering the form, but not the sense, of a period, for the sake of brevity; and when an obsolete phrase occurred, changing it for one more common and intelligible. I should never have thought of attempting this work, if it had not been suggested and urged by others; and by some very respectable names, of whose learning, judgment, and piety I forbear to avail myself. However defective this performance may appear, the labor of it—if it may be called a labor—has been,

I bless God, one of the most delightful labors of my life.

Certainly the thoughts of everlasting rest may be as delightful to souls in the present day, as they have ever been to those of past generations. I am sure such thoughts are as absolutely necessary now; nor are temptations to neglect them either fewer or weaker than formerly. The worth of everlasting rest is not felt, because a thousand trifles are preferred before it. But were the divine reasonings of this book duly attended to—and O that the Spirit and grace of the Redeemer may make them so!—then an age of vanity would become serious; minds enervated by sensuality would soon resume the strength of reason, and display the excellence of Christianity; the delusive names of pleasure would be blotted out by the glorious reality of heavenly joy upon earth; every station and relation in life would be filled up with the propriety and dignity of serious religion; every member of society would then effectually contribute to the beauty and happiness of the whole; and every soul would be ready for life or death, for one world or another, in a well-grounded and cheerful persuasion of having secured a title to that rest which remaineth to the people of God.

B. F.

KIDDERMINSTER, Dec. 25, 1758

THE

SAINTS' EVERLASTING REST

"THERE REMAINETH THEREFORE A REST UNTO THE
PEOPLE OF GOD."—HEBREWS 4 : 9.

CHAPTER I

INTRODUCTION—SOME ACCOUNT OF THE NATURE OF THE SAINTS' REST

The important design of the apostle in the text, to which the
author earnestly bespeaks the attention of the reader. The
saints' rest defined, with a general plan of the work. What
this rest presupposes. The author's humble sense of his
inability fully to show what this rest contains. It contains,
1. A ceasing from means of grace; 2. A perfect freedom
from all evils; 3. The highest degree of the saints' personal perfection, both in body and soul; 4. The nearest
enjoyment of God the chief good; 5. A sweet and constant
action of all the powers of soul and body in this enjoyment
of God.

IT was not only our interest in God, and actual
enjoyment of him, which was lost in Adam's fall,
but all spiritual knowledge of him, and true disposition towards such a felicity. When the Son of
God comes with recovering grace, and discoveries

of a spiritual and eternal happiness and glory, he finds not faith in man to believe it. As the poor man, that would not believe any one had such a sum as a hundred pounds, it was so far above what himself possessed, so men will hardly now believe there is such a happiness as once they had, much less as Christ hath now procured. When God would give the Israelites his Sabbaths of rest, in a land of rest, it was harder to make them believe it than to overcome their enemies and procure it for them. And when they had it, only as a small intimation and earnest of an incomparably more glorious rest through Christ, they yet believe no more than they possess, but say, with the epicure at the feast, Sure there is no other heaven but this! or, if they expect more by the Messiah, it is only the increase of their earthly felicity. The apostle aims most of this epistle against this obduracy, and clearly and largely proves that the end of all ceremonies and shadows is to direct them to Jesus Christ, the substance; and that the rest of Sabbaths and Canaan should teach them to look for *a further rest*, which indeed is their happiness. My text is his conclusion after divers arguments—a conclusion which contains the ground of all the believer's comfort, the end of all his duty and sufferings, the life and sum of all gospel promises and Christian privileges.

What more welcome to men under personal afflictions, tiring duties, disappointments, or sufferings,

than rest? It is not our comfort only, but our sta-
bility. Our liveliness in all duties, our enduring
of tribulation, our honoring of God, the vigor of
our love, thankfulness, and all our graces, yea, the
very being of our religion and Christianity, depend
on the believing, serious thoughts of our rest. And
now, reader, whoever thou art, young or old, rich or
poor, I entreat thee and charge thee, in the name of
thy Lord, who will shortly call thee to a reckoning,
and judge thee to thy everlasting, unchangeable state,
that thou give not these things the reading only,
and so dismiss them with a bare approbation; but
that thou set upon this work, and take God in Christ
for thy only rest, and fix thy heart upon him above
all. May the living God, who is the portion and
rest of his saints, make these our carnal minds so
spiritual, and our earthly hearts so heavenly, that
loving him, and delighting in him, may be the work
of our lives; and that neither I that write, nor you
that read this book, may ever be turned from this
path of life; " lest, a promise being left us of entering into his rest," we should " come short of it,"
through our own unbelief or negligence.

The saints' rest is the most happy state of a
Christian; or, it is *the perfect, endless enjoyment of
God by the perfected saints, according to the measure of their capacity, to which their souls arrive at
death, and both soul and body most fully after the
resurrection and final judgment.* According to this

definition of the saints' rest, a larger account of its
nature will be given in this chapter ; of its preparatives, chap. 2 ; its excellencies, chap. 3 ; and chap.
4, the persons for whom it is designed.   Further to
illustrate the subject, some description will be given,
chap. 5, of their misery who lose this rest ; and
chap. 6, who also lose the enjoyments of time, and
suffer the torments of hell.   Next will be shown,
chap. 7, the necessity of diligently seeking this rest ;
chap. 8, how our title to it may be discerned ; chap.
9, that they who discern their title to it should help
those that cannot ; and chap. 10, that this rest is
not to be expected on earth.   It will then be proper
to consider, chap. 11, the importance of a heavenly
life upon earth ; chap. 12, how to live a heavenly
life upon earth ; chap. 13, the nature of heavenly
contemplation, with the time, place, and temper
most fit for it ; chap. 14, what use heavenly contemplation makes of consideration, affections, soliloquy, and prayer ; and likewise, chap. 15, how heavenly contemplation may be assisted by sensible
objects, and guarded against a treacherous heart.
Heavenly contemplation will be exemplified, chap.
16, and the whole work concluded.

There are some things necessarily *presupposed* in
the nature of this rest : as,

That mortal *men* are the persons seeking it.   For
angels and glorified spirits have it already, and the
devils and damned are past hope :

That they choose *God only* for their end and happiness. He that takes any thing else for his happiness is out of the way the first step:

That they are *distant* from this end. This is the woful case of all mankind since the fall. When Christ comes with regenerating grace he finds no man sitting still, but all posting to eternal ruin, and making haste towards hell; till, by conviction, he first brings them to a stand, and then, by conversion, turns their hearts and lives sincerely to himself. This end, and its excellency, is supposed to be known, and seriously intended. An unknown good moves not to desire or endeavor. And not only a distance from this rest, but the true knowledge of this distance, is also supposed. They that never yet knew they were without God and in the way to hell, never yet knew the way to heaven. Can a man find he hath lost his God and his soul, and not cry, I am undone? The reason why so few obtain this rest is, they will not be convinced that they are, in point of title, distant from it; and, in point of practice, contrary to it. Who ever sought for that which he knew not he had lost? "They that be whole need not a physician, but they that are sick."

The influence of a superior *moving Cause* is also supposed, else we shall all stand still and not move towards our rest. If God move us not, we cannot move. It is a most necessary part of our Christian wisdom, to keep our subordination to God, and dependence on him. "We are not sufficient of ourselves to think any thing as of ourselves, but our sufficiency is of God." "Without me," says Christ, "ye can do nothing."

It is next supposed that they who seek this rest have *an inward principle of spiritual life.* God does not move men like stones, but he endows them with life, not to enable them to move without him, but in subordination to himself, the first mover.

And further, this rest supposes such an actual tendency of soul towards it as is regular and constant, *earnest and laborious.* He that hides his talent shall receive the wages of a slothful servant. Christ is the door, the only way to this rest. "But strait is the gate and narrow is the way;" and we must strive, if we will enter; for "many will seek to enter in, and shall not be able;" which implies, "that the kingdom of heaven suffereth violence." Nor will it bring us to the end of the saints, if we begin in the spirit and end in the flesh. He only "that endureth to the end shall be saved." And never did a soul obtain rest with God whose desire was not set upon him above all things else in the world. "Where your treasure is, there will your heart be also." The remainder of our old nature will much weaken and interrupt these desires, but never overcome them. And, considering the opposition to our desires, from the contrary principles in our nature, and from the weakness of our graces, together with our continued distance from the end, our tendency to that end must be laborious, and with all our might. All these things are presupposed, in order to a Christian's obtaining an interest in heavenly rest.

Now we have ascended these steps into the outward court, may we look within the veil? May we show what this rest contains as well as what it presupposes? Alas, how little know I of that glory. The glimpse which Paul had, contained what could not or must not be uttered. Had he spoken the things of heaven in the language of heaven, and none understood that language, what the better? The Lord reveal to me what I may reveal to you. The Lord open some light, and show both you and me our inheritance. Not as to Balaam only, whose eyes were opened to see the goodliness of Jacob's tents and Israel's tabernacles, where he had no portion, and from whence must come his own destruction; not as to Moses, who had only a discovery instead of possession, and saw the land which he never entered; but as the pearl was revealed to the merchant in the gospel, who rested not till he had sold all he had, and bought it; and as heaven was opened to blessed Stephen, which he was shortly to enter, and the glory showed him which should be his own possession.

The things contained in heavenly rest are such

as these: a ceasing from means of grace, a perfect freedom from all evils; the highest degree of the saints' personal perfection, both of body and soul; the nearest enjoyment of God the chief good; and a sweet and constant action of all the powers of body and soul in this enjoyment of God.

1. One thing contained in heavenly rest is, *the ceasing from means of grace.* When we have obtained the haven, we have done sailing. When the workman receives his wages, it is implied he has done his work. When we are at our journey's end, we have done with the way. Whether prophecies, they shall fail; whether tongues, they shall cease; whether knowledge, it also, so far as it had the nature of means, shall vanish away. There shall be no more prayer, because no more necessity, but the full enjoyment of what we prayed for: neither shall we need to fast, and weep, and watch any more, being out of the reach of sin and temptations. Preaching is done; the ministry of man ceases; ordinances become useless; the laborers are called in, because the harvest is gathered, the tares burned, and the work finished; the unregenerate past hope, and the saints past fear for ever.

2. There is in heavenly rest *a perfect freedom from all evils:* from all the evils that accompanied us through our course, and which necessarily follow our absence from the chief good, besides our free-

dom from those eternal flames and restless miseries
which the neglecters of Christ and grace must for
ever endure; a woful inheritance, which, both by
birth and actual merit, was due to us as well as to
them. In heaven there is nothing that defileth or
is unclean. All *that* remains without. And doubtless there is not such a thing as grief and sorrow
known there; nor is there such a thing as a pale
face, a languid body, feeble joints, helpless infancy,
decrepid age, peccant humors, painful or pining
sickness, griping fears, consuming cares, nor whatsoever deserves the name of evil. We wept and
lamented when the world rejoiced, but our sorrow
is turned to joy, and our joy shall no man take
from us.

3. Another ingredient of this rest is, *the highest
degree of the saints' personal perfection, both of body
and soul.* Were the glory ever so great, and themselves not made capable of it by a personal perfection suitable thereto, it would be little to them.
"Eye hath not seen, nor ear heard, neither have
entered into the heart of man the things which
God hath prepared for them that love him." For
the eye of flesh is not capable of seeing them, nor
this ear of hearing them, nor this heart of understanding them: but there, the eye, and ear, and
heart are made capable; else, how do they enjoy
them? The more perfect the sight is, the more
delightful the beautiful object. The more perfect

the appetite, the sweeter the food. The more musical the ear, the more pleasant the melody. The more perfect the soul, the more joyous those joys, and the more glorious to us is that glory.

4. The principal part of this rest is *our nearest enjoyment of God the chief good*. And here, reader, wonder not if I be at a loss, and if my apprehensions receive but little of that which is in my expressions. If it did not appear to the beloved disciple what we shall be, but only in general, "that when Christ shall appear we shall be like him," no wonder if I know little. When I know so little of God, I cannot much know what it is to enjoy him. If I know so little of spirits, how little of the Father of spirits, or the state of my own soul when advanced to the enjoyment of him. I stand and look upon a heap of ants, and see them all at one view: they know not me, my being, nature, or thoughts, though I am their fellow-creature : how little, then, must we know of the great Creator, though he, with one view, clearly beholds us all. A glimpse the saints behold as in a glass, which makes us capable of some poor, dark apprehensions of what we shall behold in glory. If I should tell a worldling what the holiness and spiritual joys of the saints on earth are, he cannot know; for grace cannot be clearly known without grace : how much less could he conceive it, should I tell him of this glory. But to the saints I may be somewhat more

encouraged to speak, for grace gives them a dark
knowledge and slight taste of glory.

If men and angels should study to speak the
blessedness of that state in one word, what could
they say beyond this, that it is the nearest enjoyment of God? O the full joys offered to a believer
in that one sentence of Christ, "Father, I will that
they whom thou hast given me be with me where
I am, that they may behold my glory which thou
hast given me." Every word is full of life and joy.
If the queen of Sheba had cause to say of Solomon's
glory, "Happy are thy men, happy are these thy
servants, who stand continually before thee, and
hear thy wisdom;" then, surely they that stand
continually before God, and see his glory, and the
glory of the Lamb, are more than happy. To them
will Christ give to eat of the tree of life, and to eat
of the hidden manna; yea, he will make them
pillars in the temple of God, and they shall go no
more out; and he will write upon them the name
of his God, and the name of the city of his God,
which is new Jerusalem, which cometh down out
of heaven from his God, and he will write upon
them his new name; yea, more, if more may be,
he will grant them to sit with him in his throne.
"These are they who came out of great tribulation, and have washed their robes, and made them
white in the blood of the Lamb; therefore are they
before the throne of God, and serve him day and

night in his temple; and he that sitteth on the throne shall dwell among them. The Lamb, which is in the midst of the throne, shall feed them, and shall lead them unto living fountains of water; and God shall wipe away all tears from their eyes." O blind, deceived world, can you show us such a glory? This is the city of our God, where the tabernacle of God is with men, and he will dwell with them, and they shall be his people, and God himself shall be with them, and be their God. The glory of God shall lighten it, and the Lamb is the light thereof. And there shall be no more curse; but the throne of God and of the Lamb shall be in it; and his servants shall serve him, and they shall see his face, and his name shall be in their foreheads. These sayings are faithful and true, and the things which must shortly be done.

And now we say, as Mephibosheth, let the world take all, forasmuch as our Lord will come in peace. Rejoice, therefore, in the Lord, O ye righteous, and say, with his servant David, " The Lord is the portion of mine inheritance : the lines are fallen unto me in pleasant places ; yea, I have a goodly heritage. I have set the Lord always before me ; because he is at my right hand, I shall not be moved. Therefore my heart is glad, and my glory rejoiceth; my flesh also shall rest in hope. For thou wilt not leave my soul in hell, neither wilt thou suffer thine Holy One to see corruption. Thou wilt show me

the path of life ; in thy presence is fulness of joy ;
at thy right hand there are pleasures for evermore."
What presumption would it have been once, to have
thought or spoken of such a thing, if God had not
spoken it before us. I durst not have thought of
the saints' preferment in this life, as scripture sets
it forth, had it not been the express truth of God.
How unbecoming to talk of being sons of God, speaking to him, having fellowship with him, dwelling
in him and he in us, if this had not been God's own
language. How much less durst we have once
thought of shining forth as the sun, of being joint
heirs with Christ, of judging the world, of sitting on
Christ's throne, of being one in him and the Father,
if we had not all this from the mouth and under
the hand of God. But hath he said, and shall he
not do it ? Hath he spoken, and shall he not make
it good ? Yes, as the Lord God is true, thus shall
it be done to the man whom Christ delighteth to
honor.

Be of good cheer, Christian, the time is at hand
when God and thou shalt be near, and as near as
thou canst well desire. Thou shalt dwell in his
family. Is that enough ? It is better to be a door-
keeper in the house of God, than to dwell in the
tents of wickedness. Thou shalt ever stand before
him, about his throne, in the room with him, in his
presence-chamber. Wouldst thou yet be nearer ?
Thou shalt be his child, and he thy Father ; thou

shalt be an heir of his kingdom; yea, more, the spouse of his Son. And what more canst thou desire? Thou shalt be a member of the body of his Son; he shall be thy head; thou shalt be one with him, who is one with the Father, as he himself hath desired for thee of his Father: "that they all may be one, as thou, Father, art in me, and I in thee, that they also may be one in us; and the glory which thou gavest me, I have given them, that they may be one, even as we are one; I in them, and thou in me, that they may be made perfect in one, and that the world may know that thou hast sent me, and hast loved them as thou hast loved me."

5. We must add, that *this rest contains a sweet and constant action of all the powers of the soul and body in this enjoyment of God.* It is not the rest of a stone, which ceaseth from all motion when it attains the centre. This body shall be so changed, that it shall no more be flesh and blood, which cannot inherit the kingdom of God; but a spiritual body. We sow not that body which shall be, but God giveth it a body as it hath pleased him, and to every seed his own body. If grace makes a Christian differ so much from what he was, as to say, I am not the man I was, how much more will glory make us differ. As much as a body spiritual, above the sun in glory, exceeds these frail, noisome, diseased bodies of flesh, so far shall our senses exceed

those we now possess. Doubtless, as God advances
our senses, and enlarges our capacity, so will he
advance the happiness of those senses, and fill up,
with himself, all that capacity. Certainly the body
would not be raised up and continued, if it were not
to share in the glory. As it hath shared in the
obedience and sufferings, so shall it also in the
blessedness. As Christ bought the whole man, so
shall the whole partake of the everlasting benefits
of the purchase. O blessed employment of a glorified body! to stand before the throne of God and
the Lamb, and to sound forth for ever, "Thou art
worthy, O Lord, to receive glory, and honor, and
power. Worthy is the Lamb that was slain, to
receive power, and riches, and wisdom, and strength,
and honor, and glory, and blessing; for thou hast
redeemed us to God, by thy blood, out of every
kindred, and tongue, and people, and nation; and
hast made us unto our God kings and priests. Alleluia; salvation, and glory, and honor, and power,
unto the Lord our God. Alleluia, for the Lord
God omnipotent reigneth." O Christians, this is
the blessed rest; a rest, as it were, without rest;
for "they rest not day and night, saying, Holy, holy,
holy Lord God Almighty, who was, and is, and is
to come." And if the body shall be thus employed,
O how shall the soul be taken up! As its powers
and capacities are greatest, so its actions are strongest, and its enjoyments sweetest. As the bodily

senses have their proper actions, whereby they receive and enjoy their objects, so does the soul in its own actions enjoy its own objects, by knowing, remembering, loving, and delightful joying. This is the soul's enjoyment. By these eyes it sees, and by these arms it embraces.

Knowledge, of itself, is very desirable. As far as the rational soul exceeds the sensitive, so far the delights of a philosopher, in discovering the secrets of nature, and knowing the mystery of sciences, exceed the delights of the drunkard, the voluptuary, or the sensualist. So excellent is all truth. What, then, is their delight who know the God of truth! How noble a faculty of the soul is the understanding! It can compass the earth; it can measure the sun, moon, stars, and heaven; it can foreknow each eclipse to a minute, many years before. But this is the top of all its excellency, that it can know God, who is infinite, who made all these—a little here, and more, much more hereafter. O the wisdom and goodness of our blessed Lord! He hath created the understanding with a natural bias and inclination to truth, as its object; and to the prime truth, as its prime object. Christian, when, after long gazing heavenward, thou hast got a glimpse of Christ, dost thou not sometimes seem to have been with Paul in the third heaven, whether in the body or out, and to have seen what is unutterable? Art thou not, with Peter, ready to say,

" Master, it is good to be here ?"   " O that I might
dwell in this mount !   O that I might ever see what
I now see !"   Didst thou never look so long upon
the Sun of righteousness till thine eyes were daz-
zled with his astonishing glory ?   And did not the
splendor of it make all things below seem dark and
drear to thee ?   Especially in the day of suffering
for Christ, when he usually appears most manifestly
to his people, didst thou never see one walking in
the midst of the fiery furnace with thee, like the
Son of God ?   Believe me, Christians, yea, believe
God ; you that have known most of God in Christ
here, it is as nothing to what you shall know : in
comparison of that, it scarce deserves to be called
knowledge.   For as these bodies, so that knowledge
must cease, that a more perfect may succeed.   "Knowledge shall vanish away.   For we know in part.
But when that which is perfect is come, then that
which is in part shall be done away.   When I was
a child, I spake as a child, I understood as a child,
I thought as a child ; but when I became a man,
I put away childish things.   For now we see through
a glass darkly, but then face to face ; now I know
in part, but then shall I know even as also I am
known."   Marvel not, therefore, Christian, how it
can be life eternal to know God and Jesus Christ.
To enjoy God and Christ is eternal life ; and the
soul's enjoying is in knowing.   They that savor
only of earth, and consult with flesh, think it a poor

happiness to know God. "But we know that we are of God, and the whole world lieth in wickedness; and we know that the Son of God is come, and hath given us an understanding, that we may know him that is true; and we are in him that is true, even in his Son Jesus Christ. This is the true God and eternal life."

The *memory* will not be idle, or useless, in this blessed work. From that height the saint can look behind him and before him. And to compare past with present things must raise in the blessed soul an inconceivable esteem and sense of its condition. To stand on that mount, whence we can see the wilderness and Canaan both at once—to stand in heaven and look back on earth, and weigh them together in the balance of a comparing sense and judgment, how must it needs transport the soul, and make it cry out,

"Is this the purchase that cost so dear as the blood of Christ? No wonder. O blessed price! and thrice blessed love, that invented and condescended! Is this the end of believing? Is this the end of the Spirit's workings? Have the gales of grace blown me into such a harbor? Is it hither that Christ hath allured my soul? O blessed way, and thrice blessed end! Is this the glory which the Scriptures spoke of, and ministers preached of so much? I see the gospel is indeed good tidings, even tidings of peace and good things, tidings of

great joy to all nations. Is my mourning, my fast-
ing, my sad humblings, my heavy walking, come
to this? Is my praying, watching, fearing to offend,
come to this? Are all my afflictions, Satan's temptations, the world's scorns and jeers, come to this?
O vile nature, that resisted so much, and so long,
such a blessing! Unworthy soul, is this the place
thou camest to so unwillingly? Was duty weari-
some? Was the world too good to lose? Couldst
thou not leave all, deny all, and suffer any thing
for this? Wast thou loath to die to come to this?
O false heart, thou hadst almost betrayed me to
eternal flames, and lost me this glory! Art thou
not now ashamed, my soul, that ever thou didst
question that love which brought thee hither; that
thou wast jealous of the faithfulness of thy Lord;
that thou suspectedst his love, when thou shouldst
only have suspected thyself; that ever thou didst
quench a motion of his Spirit; and that thou
shouldst misinterpret those providences, and repine
at those ways which have such an end? Now
thou art sufficiently convinced that thy blessed
Redeemer was saving thee, as well when he crossed
thy desires, as when he granted them—when he
broke thy heart, as when he bound it up. No
thanks to thee, unworthy self, for this received
crown; but to Jehovah and the Lamb be glory for
ever."

But O, the full, the near, the sweet enjoyment, is

that of *love*. " God is love ; and he that dwelleth in love dwelleth in God, and God in him." Now the poor soul complains, "O that I could love Christ more !" Then thou canst not but love him. Now, thou knowest little of his amiableness, and therefore lovest little : then, thine eyes will affect thy heart, and the continual viewing of that perfect beauty will keep thee in continual transports of love. Christians, doth it not now stir up your love, to remember all the experiences of his love ? Doth not kindness melt you, and the sunshine of divine goodness warm your frozen hearts ? What will it do then, when you shall live in love, and have all in Him, who is all ? Surely love is both work and wages. What a high favor, that God will give us leave to love him, that he will be embraced by those who have embraced lust and sin before him. But more than this, he returneth love for love ; nay, a thousand times more. Christian, thou wilt be then brimfull of love ; yet, love as much as thou canst, thou shalt be ten thousand times more beloved. Were the arms of the Son of God open upon the cross, and an open passage made to his heart by the spear ; and will not his arms and heart be open to thee in glory ? Did not he begin to love before thou lovedst, and will not he continue now ? Did he love thee, an enemy—thee, a sinner—thee, who even loathedst thyself; and own thee, when thou didst disclaim thyself ? And will he not now

immeasurably love thee, a son—thee, a perfect
saint—thee, who returnest some love for love?
He that in love wept over the old Jerusalem when
near its ruin, with what love will he rejoice over
the new Jerusalem in her glory!

Christian, believe this, and think on it: thou
shalt be externally embraced in the arms of that
love which was from everlasting, and will extend
to everlasting—of that love which brought the Son
of God's love from heaven to earth, from earth to
the cross, from the cross to the grave, from the
grave to glory—that love which was weary, hungry,
tempted, scorned, scourged, buffeted, spit upon, crucified, pierced—which did fast, pray, teach, heal,
weep, sweat, bleed, die; that love will eternally
embrace thee. When perfect created love and most
perfect uncreated love meet together, it will not be
like Joseph and his brethren, who lay upon one
another's necks weeping; it will be loving and
rejoicing, not loving and sorrowing. Yes, it will
make Satan's court ring with the news that Joseph's
brethren are come, that the saints are arrived safe
at the bosom of Christ, out of the reach of hell for
ever. Nor is there any such love as David's and
Jonathan's, breathing out its last into sad lamentations for a forced separation. Know this, believer,
to thy everlasting comfort, if those arms have once
embraced thee, neither sin nor hell can get thee
thence for ever. Thou hast not to deal with an

inconstant creature, but with Him with whom is
no variableness nor shadow of turning. His love to
thee will not be as thine was on earth to him, seldom and cold, up and down. He that would not
cease nor abate his love, for all thine enmity, unkind
neglects, and churlish resistances, can he cease to
love thee when he hath made thee truly lovely?
He that keepeth thee so constant in thy love to him,
that thou canst challenge tribulation, distress, persecution, famine, nakedness, peril, or sword, to separate thy love from Christ, how much more will he
himself be constant. Indeed thou mayest be "persuaded that neither death nor life, nor angels, nor
principalities, nor powers, nor things present, nor
things to come, nor height, nor depth, nor any other
creature, shall be able to separate us from the love
of God which is in Christ Jesus our Lord." And
now, are we not left in the apostle's admiration:
"What shall we say to these things?" Infinite
love must needs be a mystery to a finite capacity.
No wonder angels desire to look into this mystery.
And if it be the study of saints here "to know the
breadth, and length, and depth, and height of the
love of Christ, which passeth knowledge;" the
saints' everlasting rest must consist in the enjoyment of God by love.

Nor does *joy* share least in this fruition. It is
this which all we have mentioned lead to, and conclude in; even the inconceivable complacency which

the blessed feel in seeing, knowing, loving, and being loved of God. This is "the white stone which no man knoweth, saving he that receiveth it." Sure:y this is the joy with which a stranger doth not intermeddle. All Christ's ways of mercy tend to and end in the saints' joys. He wept, sorrowed, suffered, that they might rejoice; he sends the Spirit to be their comforter; he multiplies promises; he discovers their future happiness, that their joy may be full. He opens to them the fountain of living waters, that they may thirst no more, and that it may spring up in them to everlasting life. He chastens them that he may give them rest. He makes it their duty to rejoice in him always, and again commands them to rejoice. He never brings them into so low a condition that he does not leave them more cause of joy than sorrow. And hath the Lord such a care of our comfort here? O what will that joy be, where the soul being perfectly prepared for joy, and joy prepared by Christ for the soul, it shall be our work, our business, eternally to rejoice! It seems the saints' joy shall be greater than the damned's torment; for their torment is the torment of creatures, prepared for the devil and his angels; but our joy is the joy of our Lord. The same glory which the Father gave the Son, the Son hath given them, to sit with him in his throne, even as he is set down with his Father in his throne. Thou, poor soul, who prayest for joy, waitest for joy, complainest for

want of joy, longest for joy; thou then shalt have
full joy, as much as thou canst hold, and more than
ever thou thoughtest on, or thy heart desired. In
the meantime walk carefully, watch constantly, and
then let God measure out to thee thy times and
degrees of joy. It may be he keeps them until thou
hast more need. Thou hadst better lose thy comfort than thy safety. If thou shouldst die full of
fears and sorrows, it will be but a moment, and
they are all gone and concluded in joy inconceivable. As the joy of the hypocrite, so the fears of
the upright are but for a moment. God's "anger
endureth but a moment; in his favor is life; weeping may endure for a night, but joy cometh in the
morning." O blessed morning! Poor, humble,
drooping soul, how would it fill thee with joy now,
if a voice from heaven should tell thee of the love
of God, the pardon of thy sins, and assure thee of
thy part in these joys! What then will thy joy be,
when thy actual possession shall convince thee of
thy title, and thou shalt be in heaven before thou
art well aware?

And it is not thy joy only; it is a *mutual joy* as
well as a mutual love. Is there joy in heaven at
thy conversion, and will there be none at thy glorification? Will not the angels welcome thee
thither, and congratulate thy safe arrival? Yes, it
is the joy of Jesus Christ; for now he hath the end
of his undertaking, labor, suffering, dying, when we

have our joys—when he is "glorified in his saints,
and admired in all them that believe"—when he
"sees of the travail of his soul, and is satisfied."
This is Christ's harvest, when he shall reap the
fruit of his labors; and it will not repent him concerning his sufferings, but he will rejoice over his
purchased inheritance, and his people will rejoice
in him. Yea, the Father himself puts on joy, too,
in our joy. As we grieve his Spirit, and weary
him with our iniquities, so he is rejoiced in our
good. O how quickly does he now spy a returning
prodigal, even afar off! How does he run and meet
him! And with what compassion does he fall on
his neck and kiss him, and put on him the best robe,
and a ring on his hand, and shoes on his feet, and
kill the fatted calf, to eat and be merry! This is
indeed a happy meeting; but nothing to the em-
bracing and joy of that last and great meeting.
Yea, more; as God doth mutually love and joy, so
he makes this his rest, as it is our rest. What an
eternal sabbatism, when the work of redemption,
sanctification, preservation, glorification is all fin-
nished and perfected for ever! "The Lord thy God
in the midst of thee is mighty; he will save, he
will rejoice over thee with joy, he will rest in his
love, he will joy over thee with singing." Well
may we then rejoice in our God with joy, and rest
in our love, and joy in him with singing.

Alas, my fearful heart scarce dares proceed.

Methinks I hear the Almighty's voice saying to me, "Who is this that darkeneth counsel by words without knowledge?" But pardon thy servant, O Lord. I have not pried into unrevealed things. I bewail that my apprehensions are so dull, my thoughts so mean, my affections so stupid, and my expressions so low and unbecoming such a glory. I have only heard by the hearing of the ear: O let thy servant see thee, and possess these joys; then shall I have more suitable conceptions, and shall give thee fuller glory; I shall abhor my present self, and disclaim and renounce all these imperfections. "I have uttered that I understood not, things too wonderful for me, which I knew not." Yet "I believed, and therefore have I spoken." What, Lord, canst thou expect from dust, but levity; or from corruption, but defilement? Though the weakness and irreverence be the fruit of my own corruption, yet the fire is from thine altar, and the work of thy commanding. I looked not into thy ark, nor put forth my hand unto it without thee. Wash away these stains also in the blood of the Lamb. Imperfect, or none, must be thy service here. O take thy Son's excuse, "The spirit is willing, but the flesh is weak."

CHAPTER II

THE GREAT PREPARATIVES FOR THE SAINTS' REST

There are four things which principally prepare the way to enter into it: particularly, 1. The glorious appearing of Christ; 2. The general resurrection; 3. The last judgment; and, 4. The saints' coronation.

THE passage of paradise is not now so blocked up as when the law and curse reigned. Wherefore finding, beloved Christians, a new and living way consecrated for us through the vail, that is to say, the flesh of Christ, by which we may with boldness enter into the holiest, I shall draw near with fuller assurance; and, finding the flaming sword removed, shall look again into the paradise of our God. And because I know that this is no forbidden fruit, and withal that it is good for food, and pleasant to the spiritual eyes, and a tree to be desired to make one truly wise and happy, I shall, through the assistance of the Spirit, take and eat thereof myself, and give to you, according to my power, that you may eat. The porch of this temple is exceeding glorious, and the gate of it is called Beautiful. Here are four things as the four corners of this porch.

1. The *most glorious coming and appearing of the Son of God* may well be reckoned in his people's

glory. For their sake he came into the world, suf
fered, died, rose, ascended ; and for their sake it is
that he will return. To this end will Christ come
again to receive his people unto himself, that where
he is, there they may be also. The bridegroom's
departure was not upon divorce. He did not leave
us with a purpose to return no more. He hath left
pledges enough to assure us to the contrary. We
have his word, his many promises, his ordinances,
which show forth his death till he come ; and his
Spirit, to direct, sanctify, and comfort till he return.
We have frequent tokens of love from him, to show
us he forgets not his promise, nor us. We daily
behold the forerunners of his coming, foretold by
himself. We see the fig-tree putteth forth leaves,
and therefore know that summer is nigh. Though
the riotous world say, My Lord delayeth his coming,
yet let the saints lift up their heads, for their
redemption draweth nigh. Alas, fellow-Christians,
what should we do if our Lord should not return ?
What a case are we here left in ! What, leave us
in the midst of wolves, and among lions, a generation of vipers, and here forget us ! Did he buy us so
dear, and then leave us sinning, suffering, groaning,
dying daily ; and will he come no more to us ? It
cannot be. This is like our unkind dealing with
Christ, who, when we feel ourselves warm in the
world, care not for coming to him ; but this is
not like Christ's dealing with us. He that would

come to suffer, will surely come to triumph. He that would come to purchase, will surely come to possess. Where else were all our hopes? What were become of our faith, our prayers, our tears, and our waiting? What were all the patience of the saints worth to them? Were we not left of all men the most miserable? Christians, hath Christ made us forsake all the world, and to be forsaken of all the world—to hate all, and be hated of all; and all this for him, that we might have him instead of all? And will he, think you, after all this, forget us and forsake us himself? Far be such a thought from our hearts. But why staid he not with his people while he was here? Why? Was not the work on earth done? Must he not take possession of glory in our behalf? Must he not intercede with the Father, plead his sufferings, be filled with the Spirit to send forth, receive authority, and subdue his enemies? Our abode here is short. If he had staid on earth, what would it have been to enjoy him for a few days and then die? He hath more in heaven to dwell among, even the spirits of many generations. He will have us live by faith, and not by sight.

O fellow-Christians, what a day will that be, when we, who have been kept prisoners by sin, by sinners, by the grave, shall be brought out by the Lord himself! It will not be such a coming as his first was, in poverty and contempt, to be spit upon,

and buffeted, and crucified again. He will not come,
O careless world, to be slighted and neglected by
you any more. Yet that coming wanted not its
glory. If the heavenly host, for the celebration of
his nativity, must praise God, with what shoutings
will angels and saints at that day proclaim glory to
God, peace and good-will towards men. If a star
must lead men from remote parts to come to worship the child in the manger, how will the glory of
his next appearing constrain all the world to acknowledge his sovereignty. If, riding on an ass, he enter
Jerusalem with hosannas, with what peace and
glory will he come towards the new Jerusalem. If,
when he was in the form of a servant, they cry out,
"What manner of man is this, that even the winds
and the sea obey him?" what will they say when
they shall see him coming in his glory, and the
heavens and the earth obey him? "Then shall all
the tribes of the earth mourn." To think and speak
of that day with horror doth well become the im-
penitent sinner, but ill the believing saint. Shall
the wicked behold him, and cry, "Yonder is he
whose blood we neglected, whose grace we resisted,
whose counsel we refused, whose government we cast
off!" and shall not the saints, with inconceivable
gladness, cry, "Yonder is he whose blood redeemed
us, whose Spirit cleansed us, whose law governed
us; in whom we trusted, and he hath not deceived
our trust; for whom we long waited, and now we

see we have not waited in vain? O cursed corruption, that would have had us turn to the world and present things, and say, Why should we wait for the Lord any longer? Now we see, Blessed are all they that wait for him." And now, Christians, should we not put up that petition heartily, "Thy kingdom come? The Spirit and the bride say, Come: and let him that heareth," and readeth, "say, Come." Our Lord himself says, "Surely I come quickly." Amen: even so, come, Lord Jesus!

2. Another thing that leads to paradise is that great work of Jesus Christ, *in raising the body from the dust, and uniting it again unto the soul.* A wonderful effect of infinite power and love. "Yea, wonderful indeed," says Unbelief, "if it be true. What, shall all these scattered bones and dust become a man?" Let me with reverence plead for God, for that power whereby I hope to arise. What sustains the massy body of the earth? What limits the vast ocean of the waters? Whence is that constant ebbing and flowing of the tides? How many times larger than all the earth is the sun, that glorious body of light? Is it not as easy to raise the dead as to make heaven and earth, and all of nothing? Look not on the dead bones and dust and difficulty, but at the promise. Contentedly commit these bodies to a prison that shall not long contain them. Let us lie down in peace and take our rest; it will not be an everlasting

night, nor endless sleep.   If unclothing be the thing
thou fearest, it is that thou mayest have better
clothing.   If to be turned out of doors be the thing
thou fearest, remember, that when "the earthly
house of this tabernacle is dissolved, thou hast a
building of God, a house not made with hands,
eternal in the heavens."   Lay down cheerfully this
lump of corruption ; thou shalt undoubtedly receive
it again in incorruption.   Lay down freely this ter-
restrial, this natural body; thou shalt receive it
again a celestial, a spiritual body.   Though thou
lay it down with great dishonor, thou shalt receive
it in glory.   Though thou art separated from it
through weakness, it shall be raised again in mighty
power ; "in a moment, in the twinkling of an eye,
at the last trump ; for the trumpet shall sound, and
the dead shall be raised incorruptible, and we shall
be changed."   " The dead in Christ shall rise first.
Then they who are alive and remain shall be caught
up together with them in the clouds to meet the
Lord in the air."   Triumph now, O Christian, in
these promises ; thou shalt surely triumph in their
performance.   This is the day which the Lord will
make ; we shall rejoice and be glad in it.   The
grave that could not keep our Lord, cannot keep
us.   He arose for us, and by the same power will
cause us to arise.   "For if we believe that Jesus
died and rose again, even so, them also who sleep
in Jesus will God bring with him."   Let us never

look at the grave, but let us see the resurrection
beyond it. Yea, let us be " steadfast, unmovable,
always abounding in the work of the Lord, forasmuch as we know that our labor is not in vain in
the Lord."

3. Part of this prologue to the saints' rest is *the
public and solemn process at their judgment*, where
they shall first themselves be acquitted and justi
fied, and then with Christ judge the world. Young
and old, of all estates and nations, that ever were
from the creation to that day, must here come and
receive their doom. O terrible, O joyful day!—
terrible to those that have forgotten the coming of
their Lord; joyful to the saints, whose waiting and
hope was to see this day. Then shall the world
behold the goodness and severity of God: on them
who perish, severity; but to his chosen, goodness.
Every one must give an account of his stewardship.
Every talent of time, health, abilities, mercies,
afflictions, means, warnings, must be reckoned for.
The sins of youth, those which they had forgotten, and their secret sins, shall all be laid open
before angels and men. They shall see the Lord
Jesus, whom they neglected, whose word they dis-
obeyed, whose ministers they abused, whose servants they hated, now sitting to judge them. Their
own consciences shall cry out against them, and
call to their remembrance all their misdoings.
Which way will the wretched sinner look? Who

can conceive the terrible thoughts of his heart ?
Now the world cannot help him ; his old companions cannot ; the saints neither can nor will. Only
the Lord Jesus can ; but there is the misery, he will
not. Time was, sinner, when Christ would, and
you would not ; now, fain would you, and he will
not. All in vain is it to " cry to the mountains and
rocks, Fall on us, and hide us from the face of Him
that sitteth upon the throne ;" for thou hast the
Lord of mountains and rocks for thine enemy, whose
voice they will obey, and not thine. I charge thee,
therefore, before God, and the Lord Jesus Christ,
who shall judge the quick and the dead at his
appearing, and his kingdom, that thou set thyself
seriously to ponder these things.

But why tremblest thou, O humble, gracious
soul ? He that would not lose one Noah in a common deluge, nor overlook one Lot in Sodom ; nay,
that could do nothing till he went forth ; will he
forget thee at that day ? " The Lord knoweth how
to deliver the godly out of temptation, and to reserve
the unjust unto the day of judgment, to be punished." He knoweth how to make the same day
the greatest terror to his foes, and yet the greatest
joy to his people. " There is no condemnation to
them that are in Christ Jesus, who walk not after
the flesh, but after the Spirit. Who shall lay any
thing to the charge of God's elect ?" Shall the
law ? " The law of the Spirit of life in Christ

Jesus hath made them free from the law of sin and death." Or shall conscience? "The Spirit itself beareth witness with their spirit that they are the children of God. It is God that justifieth; who is he that condemneth?" If our Judge condemn us not, who shall? He that said to the adulterous woman, Hath no man condemned thee? neither do I; will say to us, more faithfully than Peter to him, Though all men deny thee, or condemn thee, I will not. Having confessed me before men, thee "will I also confess before my Father who is in heaven."

What inexpressible joy, that our dear Lord, who loveth our souls, and whom our souls love, shall be our Judge! Will a man fear to be judged by his dearest friend, or a wife by her own husband? Christian, did Christ come down and suffer, and weep, and bleed, and die for thee, and will he now condemn thee? Was he judged, condemned, and executed in thy stead, and now will he himself condemn thee? Hath he done most of the work already, in redeeming, regenerating, sanctifying, and preserving thee, and will he now undo all again? Well, then, let the terror of that day be never so great, surely our Lord can mean no ill to us in all. Let it make the devils tremble, and the wicked tremble, but it shall make us leap for joy. It must affect us deeply with the sense of our mercy and happiness, to see the most of the world tremble

with terror, while we triumph with joy; to hear
them doomed to everlasting flames, when we are
proclaimed heirs of the kingdom; to see our neigh
bors, that lived in the same town, came to the same
congregation, dwelt in the same houses, and were
esteemed more honorable in the world than ourselves, now, by the Searcher of hearts, eternally
separated. This, with the great magnificence and
dreadfulness of the day, the apostle pathetically
expresses: "It is a righteous thing with God to
recompense tribulation to them that trouble you;
and to you who are troubled, rest with us, when
the Lord Jesus shall be revealed from heaven, with
his mighty angels, in flaming fire taking vengeance
on them that know not God, and that obey not the
gospel of our Lord Jesus Christ; who shall be punished with everlasting destruction from the presence
of the Lord, and from the glory of his power; when
he shall come to be glorified in his saints, and to be
admired in all them that believe, in that day."

Yet more: we shall be so far from the dread of
that judgment, that ourselves shall become the
judges. Christ will take his people, as it were,
into commission with himself, and they shall sit
and approve his righteous judgment. "Do ye not
know that the saints shall judge the world?" Nay,
"know ye not that we shall judge angels?" 1 Cor.
6:2, 3. Were it not for the word of Christ that
speaks it, this advancement would seem incredible,

and the language arrogant. Even Enoch, the seventh from Adam, prophesied this, saying, "Behold, the Lord cometh with ten thousands of his saints, to execute judgment upon all, and to convince all that are ungodly among them, of all their ungodly deeds which they have ungodlily committed, and of all their hard speeches which ungodly sinners have spoken against him." Thus shall the saints be honored, and "the upright shall have dominion in the morning." O that the careless world "were wise, that they understood this, that they would consider their latter end;" that they would be now of the same mind as they will be when they shall see the heavens pass away with a great noise, and the elements melt with fervent heat, and the earth also, and the works that are therein, burnt up; when all shall be on fire about them, and all earthly glory consumed! "For the heavens and earth which are now, are reserved unto fire against the day of judgment and perdition of ungodly men. Seeing, then, that all these things shall be dissolved, what manner of persons ought ye to be in all holy conversation and godliness, looking for and hasting unto the coming of the day of God, wherein the heavens being on fire shall be dissolved, and the elements shall melt with fervent heat?"

4. The last preparative for the saints' rest is *their solemn coronation and receiving the kingdom*

For as Christ, their head, is anointed both King
and Priest, so under him are his people made unto
God both kings and priests, to reign, and to offer
praises for ever. The crown of righteousness which
was laid up for them, shall, by the Lord, the righteous Judge, be given them at that day. They have
been faithful unto death, and therefore he will give
them a crown of life. And according to the im
provement of their talents here, so shall their rule
and dignity be enlarged. They are not dignified
with empty titles, but real dominion. Christ will
grant them to sit with him on his throne, and will
give them power over the nations, even as he
received of his Father; and he "will give them
the morning star." The Lord himself will give
them possession, with these applauding expressions:
"Well done, good and faithful servant; thou hast
been faithful over a few things, I will make thee
ruler over many things; enter thou into the joy of
thy Lord."

And with this solemn and blessed proclamation
shall he enthrone them: " Come, ye blessed of my
Father, inherit the kingdom prepared for you from
the foundation of the world." Every word is full
of life and joy. "Come"—this is the holding forth
of the golden sceptre to warrant our approach unto
this glory. Come now as near as you will; fear
not the Bethshemites' judgment, for the enmity is
utterly abolished. This is not such a "Come" as

we were wont to hear: " Come, take up your cross and follow me." Though that was sweet, yet this is much more. " Ye blessed"—blessed indeed, when that mouth shall so pronounce us! For though the world hath accounted us accursed, and we have been ready to account ourselves so, yet certainly those that he blesseth are blessed; and those only whom he curseth are cursed; and his blessing cannot be reversed. " Of my Father"— blessed in the Father's love, as well as the Son's, for they are one. The father hath testified his love in their election, donation to Christ, and in the sending of Christ, and accepting his ransom, as the Son hath also testified his. " Inherit"—no longer bondsmen, nor servants only, nor children under age, who differ not in possession, but only in title, from servants; but now we are heirs of the kingdom, and joint-heirs with Christ. " The kingdom"—no less than the kingdom. Indeed, to be King of kings and Lord of lords is our Lord's own proper title; but to be kings, and reign with him, is ours. The enjoyment of this kingdom is as the light of the sun; each has the whole, and the rest none the less. " Prepared for you"—God is the Alpha as well as the Omega of our blessedness. Eternal love hath laid the foundation. He prepared the kingdom for us, and then prepared us for the kingdom. This is the preparation of his counsel and decree, for the execution whereof Christ was yet to make a further preparation. "For you"—not for believers only, in general, who, without individual persons, are nobody ; but for you personally. "From the foundation of the world"— not only from the promise after Adam's fall, but from eternity.

Thus we have seen the Christian safely landed in Paradise, and conveyed honorably to his rest. Now let us a little further, in the next chapter, view those mansions, consider their privileges, and see whether there be any glory like unto this glory.

CHAPTER III

THE EXCELLENCIES OF THE SAINTS' REST

1. It is the purchased possession; 2. A free gift; 3. Peculiar to saints; 4. An association with saints and angels; 5. It derives its joys immediately from God himself; 6. It will be seasonable; 7. Suitable; 8. Perfect, without sin and suffering; 9. And everlasting.

LET us draw a little nearer, and see what further excellencies this rest affordeth. The Lord hide us in the clefts of the rock, and cover us with the hands of indulgent grace, while we approach to take this view.

1. It is a most singular honor of the saints' rest, to be called *the purchased possession;* that is, the fruit of the blood of the Son of God; yea, the chief fruit, the end and perfection of all the fruits and efficacy of that blood. Greater love than this there is not, to lay down the life of the lover. And to have this our Redeemer ever before our eyes, and the liveliest sense and freshest remembrance of that dying, bleeding love, still upon our souls! How will it fill our souls with perpetual joy, to think that in the streams of this blood we have swum through the violence of the world, the snares of Satan, the seductions of flesh, the curse of the law, the wrath of an offended God, the accusations of a

guilty conscience, and the vexing doubts and fears
of an unbelieving heart, and are arrived safely at
the presence of God! Now he cries to us, "Is it
nothing to you, all ye that pass by? behold, and
see if there be any sorrow like unto my sorrow!"
And we scarce regard the mournful voice—scarce
turn aside to view the wounds. But *then* our perfected souls will feel, and flame in love for love.
With what astonishing apprehensions will redeemed
saints everlastingly behold their blessed Redeemer—
the purchaser, and the price, together with the possession! Neither will the view of his wounds of
love renew our wounds of sorrow. He, whose first
words after his resurrection were to a great sinner,
"Woman, why weepest thou?" knows how to raise
love and joy, without any cloud of sorrow or storm
of tears. If any thing we enjoy was purchased with
the life of our dearest friend, how highly should we
value it. If a dying friend deliver us but a token
of his love, how carefully do we preserve it, and
still remember him when we behold it, as if his own
name were written on it. And will not, then, the
death and blood of our Lord everlastingly sweeten
our possessed glory? As we write down the price
our goods cost us, so, on our righteousness and glory
write down the price—the precious blood of Christ.
His sufferings were to satisfy the justice that required
blood, and to bear what was due to sinners, and so
to restore them to the life they lost, and the happi-

ness from which they fell. The work of Christ's redemption so well pleased the Father, that he gave him power to advance his chosen, and give them the glory which was given to himself; and all this " according to his good pleasure and the counsel of his own will."

2. Another pearl in the saints' diadem is, that it is *a free gift*. These two, purchased and free, are the chains of gold which make up the wreaths for the tops of the pillars in the temple of God. It was dear to Christ, but free to us. When Christ was to buy, silver and gold were nothing worth ; prayers and tears could not suffice, nor any thing below his blood : but our buying is receiving ; we have it freely, without money and without price. A thankful acceptance of a free acquittance is no paying of the debt. Here is all free : if the Father freely give the Son, and the Son freely pay the debt ; and if God freely accept that way of payment, when he might have required it of the principal ; and if both Father and Son freely offer us the purchased life on our cordial acceptance ; and if they freely send the Spirit to enable us to accept ; what is here, then, that is not free ? O the everlasting admiration that must surprise the saints to think of this freeness ! " What did the Lord see in me, that he should judge me meet for such a state ; that I, who was but a poor diseased, despised wretch, should be clad in the brightness of this glory ; that I, a creeping

worm, should be advanced to this high dignity; that I, who was but lately groaning, weeping, dying, should now be as full of joy as my heart can hold ; yea, should be taken from the grave where I was decaying, and from the dust and darkness where I seemed forgotten, and be here set before his throne; that I should be taken, with Mordecai, from captivity, and be set next unto the king, and with Daniel from the den, to be made ruler of princes and provinces? Who can fathom unmeasurable love?" If worthiness were our condition for admittance, we might sit down and weep, with St. John, because no man was found worthy. But "the Lion of the tribe of Judah" is worthy, and hath prevailed ; and by that title we must hold the inheritance. We shall offer there the offering that David refused, even praise for that which cost us nothing. Here our commission runs, "Freely ye have received, freely give ;" but Christ has dearly bought, yet freely gives.

If it were only for nothing, and without our merit, the wonder were great ; but it is moreover *against* our merit, and against our long endeavoring our own ruin. What an astonishing thought it will be, to think of the immeasurable difference between our deservings and receivings—between the state we should have been in, and the state we are in ; to look down upon hell, and see the vast difference that grace hath made between us and them—to see the inheritance there to which we were born, so different from that to which we are adopted ! What pangs of love will it cause within us to think, " Yonder was the place that sin would have brought me to ; but this is it that Christ hath brought me to ! Yonder death was the wages of my sin, but this eternal life is the gift of God, through Jesus Christ my Lord. Who made me to differ ? Had I not now been in those flames if I had had my own way, and been let alone to my own will ? Should I not have lingered in Sodom till the flames had seized on me, if God had not in mercy brought me out ?" Doubtless this will be our everlasting admiration, that so rich a crown should fit the head of so vile a sinner ; that such high advancement, and such long unfruitfulness and unkindness, can be the state of the same person, and that such vile rebellions can conclude in such most precious joys. But no thanks to us, nor to any of our duties and labors, much less to our neglects and laziness; we know to whom the praise is due, and must be given for ever. Indeed, to this very end it was that infinite wisdom cast the whole design of man's salvation into this mould of purchase and freeness, that the love and joy of man might be perfected, and the honor of grace most highly advanced; that the thought of merit might neither cloud the one nor obstruct the other; and that on these two hinges the gate of heaven might turn. So then let DESERVED be written on the door of hell; but on the door of heaven and life, THE FREE GIFT.

3. This rest is *peculiar to saints*, it belongs to no other of all the sons of men. If all Egypt had been light, the Israelites would not have had the less; but to enjoy that light alone, while their neighbors lived in thick darkness, must make them more sensible of their privilege. Distinguishing mercy affects more than any mercy. If Pharaoh had passed as safely as Israel, the Red sea would have been less remembered. If the rest of the world had not been drowned, and the rest of Sodom and Gomorrah not burned, the saving of Noah had been no wonder, nor Lot's deliverance so much talked of. When one is enlightened and another left in darkness, one reformed and another by his lust enslaved, it makes the saints cry out, "Lord, how is it that thou wilt manifest thyself unto us, and not unto the world?" When the prophet is sent to one widow only of all that were in Israel, and to cleanse one Naaman of all the lepers, the mercy is more observable. That will surely be a day of passionate sense on both sides, when there shall be two in one bed, and two in the field, the one taken and the other left. The saints shall look down upon the burning lake, and in the sense of their own happiness, and in the approbation of God's just proceedings, they shall rejoice and sing, "Thou art righteous, O Lord,

who wast, art, and shalt be, because thou hast judged thus."

4. But though this rest be peculiar to the saints, yet it is *common to all the saints;* for it is an association of blessed spirits, both saints and angels— a corporation of perfected saints, whereof Christ is the head—the communion of saints completed. As we have been together in the labor, duty, danger, and distress, so shall we be in the great recompense and deliverance. As we have been scorned and despised, so shall we be owned and honored together. We who have gone through the day of sadness, shall enjoy together that day of gladness. Those who have been with us in persecution and in prison, shall be with us also in that palace of consolation. How oft have our groans made, as it were, one sound, our tears one stream, and our desires one prayer. But now all our praises shall make up one melody, all our churches one church, and all ourselves one body; for we shall be all one in Christ, even as he and the Father are one. It is true, we must be careful not to look for that in the saints which is alone in Christ. But if the forethought of sitting down with Abraham and Isaac and Jacob in the kingdom of heaven, may be our lawful joy, how much more the real sight and actual possession? It cannot but be comfortable to think of that day when we shall join with Moses in his song, with David in his psalms of praise, and with

all the redeemed in the song of the Lamb for ever; when we shall see Enoch walking with God, Noah enjoying the end of his singularity, Joseph of his integrity, Job of his patience, Hezekiah of his uprightness, and all the saints the end of their faith. Not only our old acquaintance, but all the saints of all ages, whose faces in the flesh we never saw, we shall there both know and comfortably enjoy. Yea, angels as well as saints will be our blessed acquaintance. Those who now are willingly our ministering spirits, will willingly then be our companions in joy. They who had such joy in heaven for our conversion, will gladly rejoice with us in our glorification. Then we shall truly say, as David, I am a companion of all them that fear thee; when "we are come unto mount Zion, and unto the city of the living God, the heavenly Jerusalem, and to an innumerable company of angels; to the general assembly and church of the firstborn, who are written in heaven, and to God the Judge of all, and to the spirits of just men made perfect, and to Jesus the Mediator of the new covenant." It is a singular excellence of heavenly rest, that we are "fellow-citizens with the saints, and of the household of God."

5. As another property of our rest, *we shall derive its joys immediately from God.* Now we have nothing at all immediately, but at the second or third hand; or how many, who knows? From

the earth, from man, from sun and moon, from the
ministration of angels, and from the Spirit, and
Christ. Though, in the hand of angels, the stream
savors not of the imperfection of sinners, yet it does
of the imperfection of creatures; and as it comes
from man, it savors of both. How quick and piero-
ing is the word in itself; yet many times it never
enters, being managed by a feeble arm. What
weight and worth is there in every passage of the
blessed gospel; enough, one would think, to enter
and pierce the dullest soul, and wholly possess its
thoughts and affections; and yet how oft does it
fall as water upon a stone. The things of God
which we handle are divine, but our manner of
handling is human. There is little we touch but
we leave the print of our fingers behind. If God
speaks the word himself, it will be a piercing, melt-
ing word indeed. The Christian now knows, by
experience, that his most immediate joys are his
sweetest joys; which have least of man, and are
most directly from the Spirit. Christians who are
much in secret prayer and contemplation, are men
of greatest life and joy, because they have all more
immediately from God himself. Not that we should
cast off hearing, reading, and conference, or neglect
any ordinance of God; but to live above them while
we use them, is the way of a Christian. There is
joy in these remote receivings, but the fulness of
joy is in God's immediate presence. We shall then

have light without a candle, and perpetual day without the sun, for "the city has no need of the sun, neither of the moon to shine in it, for the glory of God lightens it, and the Lamb is the light thereof: there shall be no night there, and they need no candle, neither light of the sun; and they shall reign for ever and ever." We shall then have enlightened understandings without Scripture, and be governed without a written law; for the Lord will perfect his law in our hearts, and we shall be all perfectly taught of God. We shall have joy which we drew not from the promises, nor fetched home by faith or hope. We shall have communion without ordinances, without this fruit of the vine, when Christ shall drink it new with us in his Father's kingdom, and refresh us with the comforting wine of immediate enjoyment. To have necessities, but no supply, is the state of them in hell. To have necessity supplied by means of creatures, is the state of us on earth. To have necessity supplied immediately from God, is the state of the saints in heaven. To have no necessity at all, is the prerogative of God himself.

6. A further excellence of this rest is, that it will be *seasonable*. He that expects the fruit of his vineyard at the season, and makes his people "like a tree planted by the rivers of water, that bringeth forth his fruit in his season," will also give them the crown in his season. He that will have a word of

joy spoken in season to him that is weary, will surely cause the time of joy to appear in the fittest season. They who are not weary in well-doing, shall, if they faint not, reap in due season. If God giveth rain even to his enemies, both the former and the latter in its season, and reserveth the appointed weeks of harvest, and covenants that there shall be day and night in their season, then surely the glorious harvest of the saints shall not miss its season. Doubtless, he who would not stay a day longer than his promise, but brought Israel out of Egypt on the self-same day when the four hundred and thirty years expired, neither will he fail of one day or hour of the fittest season for his people's glory. When we have had in this world a long night of darkness, will not the day-breaking and the rising of the Sun of righteousness be then seasonable? When we have passed a long and tedious journey through no small dangers, is not home then seasonable? When we have had a long and perilous war, and received many a wound, would not a peace, with victory, be seasonable? Men live in a continual weariness, especially the saints, who are most weary of that which the world cannot feel: some weary of a blind mind, some of a hard heart, some of their daily doubts and fears, some of the want of spiritual joys, and some of the sense of God's wrath. And when a poor Christian hath desired, and prayed, and waited for deliverance many years, is it not

then seasonable? We lament that we do not find
a Canaan in the wilderness, or the songs of Sion in
a strange land—that we have not a harbor in the
main ocean, nor our rest in the heat of the day, nor
heaven before we leave the earth; and would not
all this be very unseasonable?

7. As this rest will be seasonable, so it will be
suitable. The new nature of the saints doth suit
their spirits to this rest. Indeed, their holiness is
nothing else but a spark taken from this element,
and by the Spirit of Christ kindled in their hearts:
the flame whereof, mindful of its own divine orig-
inal, ever tends to the place from whence it comes
Temporal crowns and kingdoms could not make a
rest for saints. As they were not redeemed with so
low a price, neither are they endued with so low a
nature. As God will have from them a spiritual
worship suited to his own spiritual being, he will
provide them a spiritual rest suitable to their spiritual nature. The knowledge of God and his Christ,
a delightful complacency in that mutual love, an
everlasting rejoicing in the enjoyment of our God,
with a perpetual singing of his high praises; this is
heaven for a saint. Then we shall live in our own
element. We are now as the fish in a vessel of
water, only so much as will keep them alive; but
what is that to the ocean? We have a little air
let in to us, to afford us breathing; but what is that
to the sweet and fresh gales upon mount Sion? We

have a beam of the sun to lighten our darkness, and a warm ray to keep us from freezing ; but then we shall live in its light, and be revived by its heat for ever. As are the natures of the saints, such are their desires; and it is the desires of our renewed nature to which this rest is suited. While our desires remain corrupted and misguided, it is a far greater mercy to deny them, yea, to destroy them, than to satisfy them ; but those which are spiritual are of his own planting, and he will surely water them, and give the increase. He quickened our hunger and thirst for righteousness, that he might make us happy in a full satisfaction. Christian, this is a rest after thy own heart ; it contains all that thy heart can wish ; that which thou longest, prayest, laborest for, there thou shalt find it all. Thou hadst rather have God in Christ than all the world ; there thou shalt have him. What wouldst thou not give for assurance of his love ? There thou shalt have assurance without suspicion. Desire what thou canst, and ask what thou wilt, as a Christian, and it shall be given thee, not only to half of the kingdom, but to the enjoyment both of kingdom and King. This is a life of desire and prayer, but that is a life of satisfaction and enjoyment. This rest is very suitable to the saints' necessities also, as well as to their natures and desires. It contains whatsoever they truly wanted ; not supplying them with gross, created comforts,

which, like Saul's armor on David, are more burden
than benefit. It was Christ and perfect holiness
which they most needed, and with these shall they
be supplied.

8. Still more, this rest will be *absolutely perfect*.
We shall then have joy without sorrow, and rest
without weariness. There is no mixture of corruption with our graces, nor of suffering with our comfort. There are none of those waves in that harbor, which now so toss us up and down. To-day
we are well, to-morrow sick; to-day in esteem,
to-morrow in disgrace; to-day we have friends, to-
morrow none; nay, we have wine and vinegar in
the same cup. If revelations raise us to the third
heaven, the messenger of Satan must presently
buffet us, and the thorn in the flesh fetch us down.
But there is none of this inconstancy in heaven. If
perfect love casteth out fear, then perfect joy must
cast out sorrow, and perfect happiness exclude all
the relics of misery. We shall there rest from all
the evil of sin and of suffering.

Heaven excludes nothing more directly than *sin*,
whether of nature or of conversation. "There shall
in no wise enter any thing that defileth, neither
whatsoever worketh abomination, or maketh a lie."
What need Christ at all to have died, if heaven
could have contained imperfect souls? "For this
purpose the Son of God was manifested, that he
might destroy the works of the devil." His blood

and Spirit have not done all this to leave us, after
all, defiled. "What communion hath light with
darkness? and what concord hath Christ with
Belial?" Christian, if thou be once in heaven,
thou shalt sin no more. Is not this glad news to
thee, who hast prayed and watched against sin so
long? I know, if it were offered to thy choice,
thou wouldst rather choose to be freed from sin,
than have all the world. Thou shalt have thy desire. That hard heart, those vile thoughts, which
accompanied thee to every duty, shall then be left
behind for ever. Thy understanding shall never
more be troubled with darkness. All dark scriptures shall be made plain; all seeming contradic-
tions reconciled. The poorest Christian is presently
there a more perfect divine than any here. O that
happy day, when error shall vanish for ever; when
our understanding shall be filled with God himself,
whose light will leave no darkness in us. His face
shall be the scripture where we shall read the
truth. Many a godly man here, in his mistaken
zeal, has been the means of deceiving and pervert-
ing his brethren; and, when he sees his own error,
cannot tell how to undeceive them. But there we
shall join in one truth, as being one in Him who is
the truth. We shall also rest from all the sin of
our will, affections, and conversation. We shall no
more retain this rebelling principle, which is still
drawing us from God; no more be oppressed with

the power of our corruptions, nor vexed with their presence : no pride, passion, slothfulness, insensibility, shall enter with us ; no strangeness to God, and the things of God; no coldness of affections, nor imperfection in our love ; no inconstant walking, nor grieving of the Spirit; no scandalous action, nor unholy conversation : we shall rest from all these for ever. Then shall our will correspond to the divine will, as face answers face in a glass, and from which, as our law and rule, we shall never swerve. "For he that has entered into his rest, he also hath ceased from his own works, as God did from his."

Our *sufferings* were but the consequences of our sinning, and in heaven they both shall cease together.

We shall rest from all our *doubts* of God's love. It shall no more be said that "doubts are like the thistle, a bad weed, but growing in good ground." They shall now be weeded out, and trouble the gracious soul no more. We shall hear that kind of language no more, " What shall I do to know my state ? How shall I know that God is my Father; that my heart is upright ; that my conversion is true ; that faith is sincere ? I am afraid my sins are unpardoned ; that all I do is hypocrisy ; that God will reject me ; that he does not hear my prayers." All this is there turned into praise.

We shall rest from all sense of *God's displeasure*.

Hell shall not be mixed with heaven. At times the gracious soul remembered God, and was troubled; complained, and was overwhelmed, and refused to be comforted; divine wrath lay hard upon him, and God afflicted him with all his waves. But that blessed day shall convince us, that though God hid his face from us for a moment, yet with everlasting kindness will he have mercy on us.

We shall rest from all the *temptations of Satan*. What a grief is it to a Christian, though he yield not to the temptation, yet to be solicited to deny his Lord. What a torment to have such horrid suggestions made to his soul, such blasphemous ideas presented to his imagination: sometimes cruel thoughts of God, undervaluing thoughts of Christ, unbelieving thoughts of Scripture, or injurious thoughts of Providence; to be tempted sometimes to turn to present things, to play with the baits of sin, and venture on the delights of flesh, and sometimes on atheism itself; especially when we know the treachery of our own hearts, ready as tinder to take fire as soon as one of those sparks shall fall upon them. Satan hath power here to tempt us in the wilderness, but he entereth not the holy city; he may set us on a pinnacle of the temple in the earthly Jerusalem, but the new Jerusalem he may not approach; he may take us up into an exceeding high mountain, but the mount Sion he cannot ascend; and if he could, all the kingdoms of the world, and the glory of them, would be a despised bait to the soul possessed of the kingdom of our Lord. No, it is in vain for Satan to offer a temptation more.

All our temptations from *the world and the flesh* shall also cease. Oh the hourly dangers that we here walk in. Every sense and member is a snare; every creature, every mercy, and every duty is a snare to us. We can scarce open our eyes, but we are in danger of envying those above us, or despising those below us; of coveting the honors and riches of some, or beholding the rags and beggary of others with pride and unmercifulness. If we see beauty, it is a bait to lust; if deformity, to loathing and disdain. How soon do slanderous reports, vain jests, wanton speeches, creep into the heart. How constant and strong a watch does our appetite require. Have we comeliness and beauty? what fuel for pride. Are we deformed? what an occasion of repining. Have we strength of reason and gifts of learning? O how prone to be puffed up, hunt after applause, and despise our brethren. Are we unlearned? how apt then to despise what we have not. Are we in places of authority? how strong is the temptation to abuse our trust, make our will our law, and mould all the enjoyments of others by the rules and model of our own interest and policy. Are we inferiors? how prone to envy others' preëminence, and bring their actions to the bar of our judgment. Are we rich, and not too much exalted? Are we poor, and not discontented? Are we not lazy in our duties, or make a Christ of them? Not that God hath made these things our snares; but through our own corruption they become so to us. Ourselves are the greatest snares to ourselves. This is our comfort: our rest will free us from all these. As Satan hath no entrance there, so he has nothing to serve his malice; but all things there shall join with us in the high praises of our great Deliverer.

As we rest from the temptations, so shall we rest from the *abuses and persecutions* of the world. The prayers of the souls under the altar will then be answered, and God will avenge their blood on them that dwell on the earth. This is the time for crowning with thorns; that, for crowning with glory. Now, "all that will live godly in Christ Jesus shall suffer persecution;" then, they that suffered with him, shall be glorified with him. Now, we must be hated of all men for Christ's sake; then, Christ will be admired in his saints that were thus hated. We are here made a spectacle unto the world, and to angels, and to men; as the filth of the world and the offscouring of all things, men separate us from their company, and reproach us, and cast out our names as evil: but we shall then be as much gazed at for our glory; and they will be shut out of the church of the

saints, and separated from us, whether they will or
not. We can now scarce pray in our families or
sing praises to God, but our voice is a vexation to
them : how must it torment them, then, to see us
praising and rejoicing, while they are howling and
lamenting. You, brethren, who can now attempt
no work of God without losing the love of the
world, consider, you shall have none in heaven but
will further your work, and join heart and voice
with you in your everlasting joy and praise. Till
then, possess ye your souls in patience. Bind all
reproaches as a crown to your heads. Esteem them
greater riches than the world's treasures. " It is a
righteous thing with God to recompense tribulation
to them that trouble you ; and to you who are
troubled, rest with Christ."

We shall then rest from all our sad *divisions* and
unchristian quarrels with one another. How lovingly do thousands live together in heaven, who
lived at variance upon earth. There is no contention, because none of this pride, ignorance, or other
corruption. There is no plotting to strengthen our
party, nor deep designing against our brethren. If
there be sorrow or shame in heaven, we shall then
be both sorry and ashamed to remember all this
conduct on earth, as Joseph's brethren were to
behold him, when they remembered their former
unkind usage. Is it not enough that all the world
is against us, but we must also be against one

another? O happy days of persecution, which drove us together in love, whom the sunshine of liberty and prosperity crumbles into dust by our contentions! O happy day of the saints' rest in glory, when, as there is one God, one Christ, one Spirit, so we shall have one heart, one church, one employment for ever!

We shall then rest from our participation of *our brethren's sufferings.* The church on earth is a mere hospital : some groaning under a dark understanding, some under an insensible heart, some languishing under unfruitful weakness, and some bleeding for miscarriages and wilfulness ; some crying out of their poverty, some groaning under pains and infirmities, and some bewailing a whole catalogue of calamities. But a far greater grief it is, to see our dearest and most intimate friends turned aside from the truth of Christ, continuing their neglect of Christ and their souls, and nothing will awaken them out of their security : to look on an ungodly father or mother, brother or sister, wife or husband, child or friend, and think how certainly they shall be in hell for ever, if they die in their present unregenerated state ; to think of the gospel departing, the glory taken from our Israel, poor souls left willingly dark and destitute, and blowing out the light that should guide them to salvation. Our day of rest will free us from all this, and the days of mourning shall be ended. Then thy

people, O. Lord, shall be all righteous; they shall
inherit the land for ever, the branch of thy planting, the work of thy hands, that thou mayest be
glorified.

Then we shall rest from all our own *personal
sufferings*. This may seem a small thing to those
that live in ease and prosperity, but to the daily
afflicted soul it makes the thoughts of heaven delightful. O the dying life we now live; as full of
sufferings as of days and hours! Our Redeemer
leaves this measure of misery upon us, to make us
know for what we are beholden, to remind us of
what we should else forget, to be serviceable to his
wise and gracious designs, and advantageous to our
full and final recovery. Grief enters at every sense,
seizes every part and power of flesh and spirit.
What noble part is there that suffereth its pain or
ruin alone? But sin and flesh, dust and pain, will
all be left behind together. O the blessed tranquil-
lity of that region, where there is nothing but sweet
continued peace! O healthful place, where none
are sick! O fortunate land, where all are kings!
O holy assembly, where all are priests! How free
a state, where none are servants but to their supreme
Monarch! The poor man shall no more be tired
with his labors: no more hunger or thirst, cold or
nakedness: no pinching frosts or scorching heats.
Our faces shall no more be pale or sad; no more
breaches in friendship, nor parting of friends asun-

der; no more trouble accompanying our relations, nor voice of lamentation heard in our dwellings: God shall wipe away all tears from our eyes. O my soul, bear with the infirmities of thine earthly tabernacle; it will be thus but a little while; the sound of thy Redeemer's feet is even at the door.

We shall also rest from all *the toils of duties*. The conscientious magistrate, parent, and minister cries out, " O the burden that lieth upon me !" Every relation, state, age, hath variety of duties; so that every conscientious Christian cries out, " O the burden ! O my weakness, that makes it burdensome !" But our remaining rest will ease us of the burdens.

Once more, we shall rest from all these troublesome *afflictions* which necessarily accompany our absence from God. The trouble that is mixed in our desires and hopes, our longings and waitings, shall then cease. We shall no more look into our cabinet and miss our treasure—into our hearts, and miss our Christ ; no more seek him from ordinance to ordinance ; but all be concluded in a most blessed and full enjoyment.

9. The last jewel of our crown is, that it will be an *everlasting rest*. Without this all were comparatively nothing. The very thought of leaving it would imbitter all our joys. It would be a hell in heaven, to think of once losing heaven; as it

would be a kind of heaven to the damned, had they but hope of once escaping. Mortality is the disgrace of all sublunary delights. How it spoils our pleasure to see it dying in our hands. But, O blessed eternity, where our lives are perplexed with no such thoughts, nor our joys interrupted with any such fears; where "we shall be pillars in the temple of God, and go no more out!" While we were servants, we held by lease, and that but for the term of a transitory life; "but the son abideth in the house for ever." "O my soul, let go thy dreams of present pleasure, and loose thy hold of earth and flesh. Study frequently, study thoroughly this one word— eternity. What, live and never die; rejoice, and ever rejoice?" O happy souls in hell, should you but escape after millions of ages! O miserable saints in heaven, should you be dispossessed after the age of a million of worlds! This word, *everlasting*, contains the perfection of their torment and our glory. O that the sinner would study this word; methinks it would startle him out of his dead sleep. O that the gracious soul would study it; methinks it would revive him in his deepest agony. "And must I, Lord, thus live for ever? Then will I also love for ever. Must my joys be immortal; and shall not my thanks be also immortal? Surely, if I shall never lose my glory, I will never cease thy praises. If thou wilt both perfect and perpetuate me and my glory,

as I shall be thine, and not my own, so shall my
glory be thy glory. And as thy glory was thy ultimate end in my glory, so shall it also be my end,
when thou hast crowned me with that glory which
hath no end. 'Unto the King eternal, immortal,
invisible, the only wise God, be honor and glory, for
ever and ever.'"

Thus I have endeavored to show you a glimpse
of approaching glory. But how short are my expressions of its excellency. Reader, if thou be an
humble, sincere believer, and waitest with longing
and laboring for this rest, thou wilt shortly see and
feel the truth of all this. Thou wilt then have so
high an impression of this blessed state as will make
thee pity the ignorance and distance of mortals, and
will tell thee all that is here said falls short of the
whole truth a thousand-fold. In the mean time,
let this much kindle thy desires, and quicken thy
endeavors. Up and be doing; run and strive and
fight, and hold on, for thou hast a certain glorious
prize before thee. God will not mock thee; do not
mock thyself, nor betray thy soul by delaying, and
all is thine own. What kind of men, dost thou
think, would Christians be in their lives and duties,
if they had still this glory fresh in their thoughts;
what frame would their spirits be in, if their
thoughts of heaven were lively and believing?
Would their hearts be so heavy, their countenances
so sad; or would they have need to take up their

comforts from below? Would they be so loath to suffer, so afraid to die; or would they not think every day a year till they enjoy it? May the Lord heal our carnal hearts, lest we " enter not into this rest because of unbelief."

CHAPTER IV

THE CHARACTER OF THE PERSONS FOR WHOM THIS REST IS DESIGNED

The people of God who shall enjoy this rest, are, 1. Chosen from eternity; 2. Given to Christ; 3. Born again; 4. Deeply convinced of the evil of sin, their misery by sin, the vanity of the creature, and the all-sufficiency of Christ; 5. Their will is proportionably changed; 6. They engage in covenant with Christ; 7. They persevere in their engagements. The reader invited to examine himself by these characteristics of God's people. Further testimony from Scripture, that this rest shall be enjoyed by the people of God: also that none but they shall enjoy it; and that it remains for them, and is not to be enjoyed till they come to another world. The chapter concludes with showing, that their souls shall enjoy this rest while separated from their bodies.

WHILE I was in the mount, describing the excellencies of the saints' rest, I felt it was good being there, and therefore tarried the longer; and were there not an extreme disproportion between my conceptions and the subject, much longer had I been. Can a prospect of that happy land be tedious? Having read of such high and unspeakable glory, a stranger would wonder for what rare creatures this mighty preparation should be made, and expect some illustrious sun should break forth: but, behold, only a shellful of dust, animated with an invisible rational soul, and that rectified with as unseen a restoring power of grace; and this is the creature that must possess such glory! You would think it must needs be some deserving piece, or one that brings a valuable price: but, behold one that hath nothing and can deserve nothing; yea, that deserves the contrary, and would, if he might, proceed in that deserving: but, being apprehended by love, he is brought to Him that is all; and most affectionately receiving him, and resting on him, he doth, in and through him, receive all this. More particularly, the persons for whom this rest is designed are chosen of God from eternity; given to Christ as their Redeemer; born again; deeply convinced of the evil and misery of a sinful state, the vanity of the creature, and the all-sufficiency of Christ; their will is renewed; they engage themselves to Christ in covenant; and they persevere in their engagements to the end.

1. The persons for whom this rest is designed, whom the text calls "the people of God," are "*chosen of God before the foundation of the world,* that they should be holy and without blame before him in love." That they are but a part of mankind is apparent in Scripture and experience. They are the little flock, to whom "it is their Father's good pleasure to give the kingdom." Fewer they are than the world imagines; yet not so few as some drooping spirits think, who are suspicious that God

is unwilling to be their God, when they know themselves willing to be his people.

2. These persons are *given of God to his Son*, to be by him redeemed from their lost state, and advanced to this glory. God hath given all things to his Son, but not as he hath given his chosen to him. "God hath given him power over all flesh, that he should give eternal life to as many as the Father hath given him." The difference is clearly expressed by the apostle : "He hath put all things under his feet, and gave him to be the head over all things to the church." And though Christ is, in some sense, a ransom for all, yet not in that special manner as for his people.

3. One great qualification of these persons is, that they are *born again*. To be the people of God without regeneration, is as impossible as to be the children of men without generation. Seeing we are born God's enemies, we must be new-born his sons, or else remain enemies still. The greatest reformation of life that can be attained without this new life wrought in the soul, may procure our further delusion, but never our salvation.

4. This new life in the people of God discovers itself by *conviction*, or a deep sense of divine things.

They are convinced of the *evil of sin*. The sinner is made to know and feel that the sin which was his delight, is a more loathsome thing than a toad or serpent, and a greater evil than plague or famine ; being a breach of the righteous law of the most high God, dishonorable to him, and destructive to the sinner. Now the sinner no more hears the reproofs of sin as words of course ; but the mention of his sin speaks to his very heart, and yet he is willing you should show him the worst. He was wont to marvel what made men keep up such a stir against sin—what harm it was for a man to take a little forbidden pleasure ; he saw no such heinousness in it that Christ must needs die for it, and a christless world be eternally tormented in hell. Now the case is altered ; God hath opened his eyes to see the inexpressible vileness of sin.

They are convinced of *their own misery* by reason of sin. They who before read the threats of God's law as men do the story of foreign wars, now find it their own story, and perceive they read their own doom, as if they found their own names written in the curse, or heard the law say, as Nathan, "Thou art the man." The wrath of God seemed to him before but as a storm to a man in a dry house, or as the pains of the sick to the healthful stander-by ; but now he finds the disease is his own, and feels himself a condemned man : that he is dead and damned in point of law, and that nothing is wanting but mere execution to make him absolutely and irrecoverably miserable. This is a work of the Spirit, wrought in some measure in all the regenerate. How should he come to Christ for pardon, who did not first find himself guilty and condemned; or for life, who never found himself spiritually dead? "The whole need not a physician, but they that are sick." The discovery of the remedy as soon as the misery, must needs prevent a great part of the trouble. And perhaps the joyful apprehensions of mercy may make the sense of misery sooner forgotten.

They are also convinced of *the creature's vanity and insufficiency.* Every man is naturally an idolater. Our hearts turned from God in our first fall; and, ever since, the creature hath been our god. This is the grand sin of our nature. Every unregenerate man ascribes to the creature divine prerogatives, and allows it the highest room in his soul; or, if he is convinced of misery, he flies to it as his saviour. Indeed, God and his Christ shall be called Lord and Saviour; but the real expectation is from the creature, and the work of God is laid upon it. Pleasure, profit, and honor, are the natural man's trinity; and his carnal self is these in unity. It was our first sin to aspire to be as gods; and it is the greatest sin that is propagated in our nature from generation to generation. When God should guide us, we guide ourselves; when he should be our Sovereign, we rule ourselves: the laws which he gives us, we find fault with, and would correct; and, if we had the making of them, we would have made them otherwise: when he should take care

of us—and must, or we perish—we will take care
for ourselves : when we should depend on him in
daily receiving, we had rather have our portion in
our own hands : when we should submit to his
providence, we usually quarrel with it, and think
we could make a better disposal than God hath
made. When we should study and love, trust and
honor God, we study and love, trust and honor our
carnal selves. Instead of God, we would have all
men's eyes and dependence on us, and all men's
thanks returned to us, and would gladly be the only
men on earth extolled and admired by all. Thus
we are naturally our own idols. But down falls
this Dagon when God once renews the soul. It is
the chief design of that great work to bring the
heart back to God himself. He convinceth the sinner that the creature can neither be his God, to
make him happy, nor his Christ, to recover him
from his misery and restore him to God, who is his
happiness. God does this not only by his word, but
also by his providence. This is the reason why
affliction so frequently concurs in the work of conversion. Arguments which speak to the quick, will
force a hearing when the most powerful words are
slighted. If a sinner made his credit his god, and
God cast him into the lowest disgrace, or bring him
who idolized his riches, into a condition wherein
they cannot help him, or cause them to take wing
and fly away, what a help is here to this work of

conviction! If a man made pleasure his god, whatsoever a roving eye, a curious ear, a greedy appetite, or a lustful heart could desire, and God take these from him, or turn them into gall and wormwood, what a help is here to conviction! When God casts a man into languishing sickness, and inflicts wounds on his heart, and stirs up against him his own conscience, and then, as it were, says to him, "Try if your credit, riches, or pleasures can help you. Can they heal your wounded conscience? Can they now support your tottering tabernacle? Can they keep your departing soul in your body, or save you from my everlasting wrath, or redeem your soul from eternal flames? Cry aloud to them, and see now whether these will be to you instead of God and Christ." O how this works now with the sinner! Sense acknowledges the truth, and even the flesh is convinced of the creature's vanity, and our very deceiver is undeceived.

The people of God are likewise convinced of the *absolute necessity, the full sufficiency, and perfect excellency of Jesus Christ:* as a man in famine is convinced of the necessity of food; or a man that has heard or read his sentence of condemnation, of the absolute necessity of pardon; or a man that lies in prison for debt, of his need of a surety to discharge it. Now the sinner feels an insupportable burden upon him, and sees there is none but Christ can take it off: he perceives the law proclaims

him a rebel, and none but Christ can make his
peace : he is as a man pursued by a lion, that
must perish if he finds not a present sanctuary :
he is now brought to this dilemma ; either he must
have Christ to justify him, or be eternally condemned—have Christ to save him, or burn in hell
for ever—have Christ to bring him to God, or be
shut out of his presence everlastingly ! And no
wonder if he cry as the martyr, " None but Christ,
none but Christ !" Not gold, but bread, will satisfy
the hungry ; nor will any thing but pardon comfort
the condemned.

All things are counted but dung now, that he
may win Christ ; and what was gain he counts loss
for Christ. As the sinner sees his misery, and the
inability of himself and all things to relieve him, so
he perceives there is no saving mercy out of Christ.
He sees that though the creature cannot, and himself cannot, yet Christ can help him. Though the
fig-leaves of our own unrighteous righteousness are
too short to cover our nakedness, yet the righteousness of Christ is large enough : ours is dispropor-
tionate to the justice of the law, but Christ's extends
to every tittle. If he intercede, there is no denial ;
such is the dignity of his person and the value of his
merits, that the Father grants all he desires. Before, the sinner knew Christ's excellency as a blind
man knows the light of the sun ; but now, as one
that beholds its glory.

5. After this deep conviction, the *will manifests also its change.* As, for instance, the sin which the understanding pronounces evil, the will turns from with abhorrence. Not that the sensitive appetite is changed, or any way made to abhor its object; but when it would prevail against reason, and carry us to sin against God, instead of scripture being the rule, and reason the master, and sense the servant, this disorder and evil the will abhors. The misery, also, which sin hath procured, is not only discerned, but bewailed. It is impossible that the soul should now look either on its trespass against God, or yet on its own self-procured calamity, without some contrition. He that truly discerns that he hath killed Christ, and killed himself, will surely in some measure be pricked to the heart. If he cannot weep, he can heartily groan; and his heart feels what his understanding sees. The creature is renounced as vanity, and turned out of the heart with disdain: not that it is undervalued, or the use of it condemned, but its idolatrous abuse and its unjust usurpation. Can Christ be the way, where the creature is the end? Can we seek Christ to reconcile us to God, while in our hearts we prefer the creature before him? In the soul of every unregenerate man the creature is both God and Christ. As turning from the creature to God, and not by Christ, is no true turning; so believing in Christ, while the creature hath our hearts, is no true believing. Our aversion from sin, renouncing our idols, and our right receiving Christ, is all but one work, which God ever perfects where he begins. At the same time, the will cleaves to God the Father, and to Christ. Having been convinced that nothing else can be his happiness, the sinner now finds it is in God. Convinced also that Christ alone is able and willing to make peace for him, he most affectionately accepts of Christ as his Saviour and Lord. Paul's preaching was " repentance towards God, and faith towards our Lord Jesus Christ." And life eternal consists, first in "knowing the only true God," and then " Jesus Christ, whom he hath sent." To take the Lord for our God is the natural part of the covenant; the supernatural part is, to take Christ for our Redeemer. The former is first necessary, and implied in the latter. To accept Christ without affection and love, is not justifying faith : nor does love follow as a fruit, but immediately concurs ; for faith is the receiving of Christ with the whole soul. "He that loveth father or mother more than Christ," is not worthy of him, nor is justified by him. Faith accepts him as Saviour and Lord ; for in both relations will he be received, or not at all. Faith not only acknowledges his sufferings, and accepts of pardon and glory, but acknowledges his sovereignty, and submits to his government and way of salvation.

6. As an essential part of the character of God's

people, they now *enter into a cordial covenant with Christ*. The sinner was never strictly nor comfortably in covenant with Christ till now. He is sure, by the free offers, that Christ consents; and now he cordially consents himself; and so the agreement is fully made. With this covenant Christ delivers himself up in all comfortable relations to the sinner; and the sinner delivers himself to be saved and ruled by Christ. Now the soul resolutely concludes, "I have been blindly led by flesh and lust, by the world and the devil, too long, almost to my utter destruction; I will now be wholly at the disposal of my Lord, who hath bought me with his blood, and will bring me to his glory."

7. I add, that the people of God *persevere in this covenant to the end*. Though the believer may be tempted, yet he never disclaims his Lord, renounces his allegiance, nor repents of his covenant; nor can he properly be said to break that covenant, while that faith continues which is the condition of it. Indeed, those that have verbally covenanted, and not cordially, may tread under foot the blood of the covenant, wherewith they were sanctified, as an unholy thing, by separation from those without the church; but the elect cannot be so deceived. Though this perseverance be certain to true believers, yet it is made a condition of their salvation; yea, of their continued life and fruitful-

ness, and of the continuance of their justification, though not of their first justification itself. But eternally blessed be that hand of love which hath drawn the free promise, and subscribed and sealed to that which ascertains us both of the grace which is the condition, and the kingdom which on that condition is offered.

Such are the essentials of this people of God. Not a full portraiture of them in all their excellencies, nor all the marks whereby they may be discerned. I beseech thee, reader, as thou hast the hope of a Christian, or the reason of a man, judge thyself as one that must shortly be judged by a righteous God, and faithfully answer these questions. I will not inquire whether you remember the time or the order of these workings of the Spirit; there may be much uncertainty and mistake in that. If you are sure they are wrought in you, it is not so great a matter that you should know when or how you came by them. But carefully examine and inquire, Hast thou been thoroughly convinced of a prevailing depravation through thy whole soul; and a prevailing wickedness through thy whole life; and how vile sin is; and that by the covenant thou hast transgressed, the least sin deserves eternal death? Dost thou consent to the law, that it is true and righteous, and perceive thyself sentenced to this death by it? Hast thou seen the utter insufficiency of every creature, either to be itself thy happiness, or the means of removing this thy misery? Hast thou been convinced that thy happiness is only in God, as the end, and in Christ, as the way to him; and that thou must be brought to God through Christ, or perish eternally? Hast thou seen an absolute necessity of thy enjoying Christ, and the full sufficiency in him to do for thee whatsoever thy case requires? Hast thou discovered the excellency of this pearl to be worth thy "selling all to buy it?" Have thy convictions been like those of a man that thirsts; and not merely a change in opinion, produced by reading or education? Have both thy sin and misery been the abhorrence and burden of thy soul? If thou couldst not weep, yet couldst thou heartily groan under the insupportable weight of both? Hast thou renounced all thy own righteousness? Hast thou turned thy idols out of thy heart, so that the creature hath no more the sovereignty, but is now a servant to God and Christ? Dost thou accept of Christ as thy only Saviour, and expect thy justification, recovery, and glory from him alone? Are his laws the most powerful commanders of thy life and soul? Do they ordinarily prevail against the commands of the flesh, and against the greatest interest of thy credit, profit, pleasure, or life? Has Christ the highest room in thy heart and affections, so that, though thou canst not love him as thou wouldst, yet nothing else is loved so much? Hast thou, to this end, made a hearty covenant with

him, and delivered up thyself to him? Is it **thy**
uttermost care and watchful endeavor that thou
mayest be found faithful in this covenant; and
though thou fall into sin, yet wouldst not renounce
thy bargain, nor change thy Lord, nor give up thyself to any other government for all the world? If
this be truly thy case, thou art one of "the people
of God" in my text; and as sure as the promise of
God is true, this blessed rest remains for thee.
Only see thou "abide in Christ," and "endure to
the end;" for if any man draw back, his soul shall
have no pleasure in him. But if no such work
be found within thee, whatever thy deceived heart
may think, or how strong soever thy false hopes
may be, thou wilt find to thy cost, except thorough
conversion prevent it, that the rest of the saints
belongs not to thee. "O that thou wert wise, that
thou wouldst understand this, that thou wouldst
consider thy latter end!" that yet, while thy soul
is in thy body and "a price is in thy hand," and
opportunity and hope before thee, thine ears may be
open and thy heart yield to the persuasions of God,
that so thou mayest rest among his people and
enjoy "the inheritance of the saints in light."

That this rest shall be enjoyed *by the people of
God*, is a truth which the Scripture, if its testimony
be further needed, clearly asserts in a variety of
ways; as, for instance, that they are "foreordained
to it, and it for them. God is not ashamed to be

called their God, for he hath prepared for them a
city." They are styled "vessels of mercy, afore
prepared unto glory." "In Christ they have obtained an inheritance, being predestinated according to the purpose of Him who worketh all things
after the counsel of his own will." And "whom
he did predestinate, them he also glorified." Who
can deprive his people of that rest which is designed
for them by God's eternal purpose? Scripture tells
us they are redeemed to this rest. "By the blood
of Jesus we have boldness to enter into the holiest,"
whether that entrance means by faith and prayer
here, or by full possession hereafter. Therefore the
saints in heaven sing a new song unto Him who has
"redeemed them to God by his blood, out of every
kindred and tongue and people and nation, and
made them kings and priests unto God." Either
Christ, then, must lose his blood and sufferings, and
never "see of the travail of his soul," or else "there
remaineth a rest to the people of God." In Scripture this rest is promised to them. As the firmament with stars, so are the sacred pages bespangled
with these divine engagements. Christ says, "Fear
not, little flock, for it is your Father's good pleasure to give you the kingdom." "I appoint unto
you a kingdom, as my Father hath appointed unto
me; that ye may eat and drink at my table in my
kingdom." All the means of grace, the operations
of the Spirit upon the soul, and gracious actings of

the saints, every command to repent and believe, to
fast and pray, to knock and seek, to strive and labor,
to run and fight, prove that there remains a rest for
the people of God. The Spirit would never kindle
in us such strong desires after heaven, such love to
Jesus Christ, if we should not receive what we
desire and love. He that "guides our feet into the
way of peace," will undoubtedly bring us to the
end of peace. How nearly are the means and end
conjoined. "The kingdom of heaven suffereth violence, and the violent take it by force." They that
"follow Christ in the regeneration, shall sit upon
thrones of glory." Scripture assures us, that the
saints have the "beginnings, foretastes, earnests,
and seals" of this rest here. "The kingdom of
God is within them." "Though they have not
seen Christ, yet loving him, and believing in him,
they rejoice with joy unspeakable and full of glory;
receiving the end of their faith, even the salvation
of their souls." They "rejoice in hope of the glory
of God." And does God "seal them with that
Holy Spirit of promise which is the earnest of their
inheritance," and will he deny the full possession?
The Scripture also mentions, by name, those who
have entered into this rest; as Enoch, Abraham,
Lazarus, and the thief that was crucified with
Christ. And if there be a rest for these, surely
there is a rest for all believers. But it is in vain
to bring together scripture proofs, seeing it is the

very end of Scripture to be a guide to lead us to this blessed state, and to be the charter and grant by which we hold all our title to it.

Scripture not only proves that this rest remains for the people of God, but also *that it remains for none but them;* so that the rest of the world shall have no part in it. "Without holiness no man shall see the Lord. Except a man be born again, he cannot see the kingdom of God. He that believeth not the Son, shall not see life, but the wrath of God abideth on him. No whoremonger, nor unclean person, nor covetous man, who is an idolater, hath any inheritance in the kingdom of Christ and of God. The wicked shall be turned into hell, and all the nations that forget God. They all shall be damned who believe not the truth, but have pleasure in unrighteousness. The Lord Jesus shall come, in flaming fire taking vengeance on them that know not God, and that obey not the gospel of our Lord Jesus Christ; who shall be punished with everlasting destruction from the presence of the Lord, and from the glory of his power." Had the ungodly returned before their life was expired, and been heartily willing to accept of Christ for their Saviour and their King, and to be saved by him in his way and upon his most reasonable terms, they might have been saved. God freely offered them life, and they would not accept it. The pleasures of the flesh seemed more desirable to them than

the glory of the saints.   Satan offered them the one,
and God offered them the other ; and they had free
liberty to choose which they would, and they chose
" the pleasures of sin for a season" before the everlasting rest with Christ.   And is it not a righteous
thing that they should be denied that which they
would not accept ?   When God pressed them so
earnestly, and persuaded them so importunately, to
come in, and yet they would not, where should they
be but among the dogs without ?   Though man be
so wicked that he will not yield till the mighty
power of grace prevail with him, yet still we may
truly say that he may be saved, if he will, on God's
terms.   His inability being moral, and lying in
wilful wickedness, is no more excuse to him than
it is to an adulterer that he cannot love his own
wife, or to a malicious person that he cannot but
hate his own brother : is he not so much the worse,
and deserving of so much the sorer punishment ?
Sinners shall lay all the blame on their own wills
in hell for ever.   Hell is a rational torment by
conscience, according to the nature of the rational
subject.   If sinners could but then say, It was God's
fault, and not ours, it would quiet their consciences
and ease their torments, and make hell to them to
be no hell.   But to remember their wilfulness will
feed the fire, and cause the worm of conscience
" never to die."

It is the will of God that this rest should yet

remain for his people, and *not be enjoyed till they come to another world*. Who should dispose of the creatures but he that made them? You may as well ask, why have we not spring and harvest without winter; or, why is the earth below and the heavens above? as why we have not rest on earth. All things must come to their perfection by degrees. The strongest man must first be a child. The greatest scholar must first begin with the alphabet. The tallest oak was once an acorn. This life is our infancy; and would we be perfect in the womb, or born of full stature? If our rest was here, most of God's providences must be useless. Should God lose the glory of his church's miraculous deliverances, and of the fall of his enemies, that men may have their happiness here? If we were all happy, innocent, and perfect, what use was there for the glorious work of our sanctification, justification, and future salvation? If we wanted nothing, we should not depend on God so closely, nor call upon him so earnestly. How little would he hear from us, if we had what we would have. God would never have had such songs of praise from Moses at the Red sea and in the wilderness, from Deborah and Hannah, from David and Hezekiah, if they had been the choosers of their own condition. Have not thy own highest praises to God, reader, been occasioned by thy dangers or miseries? The greatest glory and praise God has through the world, is for redemption, reconciliation, and salvation by Christ; and was not man's misery the occasion of that? And where God loses the opportunity of exercising his mercies, man must needs lose the happiness of enjoying them. Where God loses his praise, man will certainly lose his comforts. O the sweet comforts the saints have had in return for their prayers. How should we know what a tender-hearted Father we have, if we had not, as the prodigal, been denied the husks of earthly pleasure and profit? We should never have felt Christ's tender heart, if we had not felt ourselves "weary and heavy laden, hungry and thirsty, poor and contrite." It is a delight to a soldier or traveller, to look back on his escapes when they are over; and for a saint in heaven to look back on his sins and sorrows upon earth; his fears and tears, his enemies and dangers, his wants and calamities must make his joy more joyful. Therefore the blessed, in praising the Lamb, mention his "redeeming them out of every nation and kindred and tongue;" and so out of their misery and wants and sins, "and making them kings and priests to God." But if they had had nothing but content and rest on earth, what room would there have been for these rejoicings hereafter?

Besides, *we are not capable of rest upon earth.* Can a soul that is so weak in grace, so prone to sin, so nearly joined to such a neighbor as this flesh, have full content and rest in such a case? What is soul-rest but our freedom from sin and imperfections and enemies? And can the soul have rest that is molested with all these, and that continually? Why do Christians so often cry out, in the language of Paul, " O wretched man that I am, who shall deliver me?" What makes them " press toward the mark, and run that they may obtain, and strive to enter in," if they are capable of rest in their present condition? And our bodies are incapable as well as our souls. They are not now those sunlike bodies which they shall be, when this " corruptible hath put on incorruption, and this mortal hath put on immortality." They are our prisons and our burdens; so full of infirmities and defects, that we spend most of our time in repairing them and supplying their continual wants. Is it possible that an immortal soul should have rest in such a disordered habitation? Surely these sickly, weary, loathsome bodies must be refined before they can be capable of enjoying rest. The objects which we here enjoy are insufficient to afford us rest. Alas, what is there in all the world to give us rest? They that have most of it have the greatest burden. They that set most by it, and rejoice most in it, do all cry out at last of its vanity and vexation. Men promise themselves a heaven upon earth; but when they come to enjoy it, it flies from them. He that has any regard to the works of the Lord, may easily see that the very end of them is to take down our idols, to make us weary of the world, and seek our rest in him. Where does he cross us most, but where we promise ourselves most content? If you have a child you dote upon, it becomes your sorrow. If you have a friend you trust in, and judge unchangeable, he becomes your scourge. Is this a place or state of rest? And as the objects we here enjoy are insufficient for our rest, so God, who is sufficient, is here little enjoyed. It is not here that he hath prepared the presence-chamber of his glory. He hath drawn the curtain between us and him. We are far from him as creatures, and farther as frail mortals, and farthest as sinners. We hear now and then a word of comfort from him, and receive his love-tokens to keep up our hearts and hopes; but this is not our full enjoyment. And can any soul that hath made God his portion, as every one hath that shall be saved by him, find rest in so vast a distance from him, and so seldom and small enjoyment of him?

Nor are we now capable of rest, as there is a worthiness must go before it. Christ will give the crown to none but the worthy. Are we fit for the crown before we have overcome; or for the prize before we have run the race; or to receive our penny before we have wrought in the vineyard; or to be rulers of ten cities before we have improved our ten talents; or to enter into the joy of our Lord before we have well done as good and faithful servants? God will not alter the course of justice, to give you rest before you have labored, nor the crown of glory till you have overcome. There is reason enough why our rest should remain till the life to come. Take heed, then, Christian reader, how thou darest to contrive and care for a rest on earth, or to murmur at God for thy trouble and toil and wants in the flesh. Doth thy poverty weary thee; thy sickness, thy bitter enemies and unkind friends? It should be so here. Do the abominations of the times, the sins of professors, the hardening of the wicked, all weary thee? It must be so while thou art absent from thy rest. Do thy sins and thy naughty, distempered heart weary thee? Be thus wearied more and more. But, under all this weariness, art thou willing to go to God, thy rest; and to have thy warfare accomplished, and thy race and labor ended? If not, complain more of thy own heart, and get it more weary, till rest seem more desirable.

I have but one thing more to add, for the close of this chapter—that the souls of believers do enjoy inconceivable blessedness and glory, *even while they remain separated from their bodies.* What can be more plain than these words of Paul: "We are always confident, knowing that while we are at home," or rather sojourning, "in the body, we are absent from the Lord; for we walk by faith, not by

sight. We are confident, I say, and willing rather
to be absent from the body, and to be present with
the Lord." Or these: "I am in a strait betwixt
two, having a desire to depart and be with Christ,
which is far better." If Paul had not expected to
enjoy Christ till the resurrection, why should he be
in a strait, or desire to depart? Nay, should he
not have been loath to depart upon the very same
grounds? for while he was in the flesh he enjoyed
something of Christ. Plain enough are the words
of Christ to the thief, "To-day shalt thou be with
me in paradise." In the parable of Dives and
Lazarus, it seems unlikely Christ would so evidently intimate and suppose the soul's happiness or
misery presently after death, if there were no such
thing. Our Lord's argument for the resurrection
supposes, that, "God being not the God of the dead,
but of the living," therefore Abraham, Isaac, and
Jacob were then living in the soul. If the "blessedness of the dead that die in the Lord" were only
in resting in the grave, then a beast or a stone were
as blessed; nay, it were evidently a curse, and not
a blessing. For was not life a great mercy? Was
it not a greater mercy to serve God and to do good;
to enjoy all the comforts of life, the fellowship of
saints, the comfort of ordinances, and much of
Christ in all, than to lie rotting in the grave?
Therefore some further blessedness is there promised. How else is it said, "We are come to the

spirits of just men made perfect?" Surely, at the
resurrection, the body will be made perfect as well
as the spirit. The Scriptures tell us that Enoch
and Elias are taken up already. And shall we
think they possess that glory alone? Did not Peter,
James, and John see Moses also with Christ on the
mount? yet the Scripture saith Moses died. And
is it likely that Christ deluded their senses in showing them Moses, if he should not partake of that
glory till the resurrection? And is not that of
Stephen as plain as we can desire? "Lord Jesus,
receive my spirit." Surely, if the Lord receive it,
it is neither asleep, nor dead, nor annihilated, but
it is where he is, and beholds his glory. That of
the wise man is of the same import: "The spirit
shall return unto God who gave it." Why are we
said to "have eternal life;" and that to "know
God is life eternal;" and that a believer "on the
Son hath everlasting life?" Or how is "the kingdom of God within us?" If there be as great an
interruption of our life as till the resurrection, this
is no eternal life, nor everlasting kingdom. "The
cities of Sodom and Gomorrah" are spoken of as
"suffering the vengeance of eternal fire." And if
the wicked already suffer eternal fire, then no
doubt but the godly enjoy eternal blessedness.
When John saw his glorious revelations, he is said
to be "in the Spirit," and to be "carried away in
the Spirit." And when Paul was "caught up to

the third heaven," he knew not "whether in the body or out of the body." This implies that spirits are capable of these glorious things without the help of their bodies. The same is implied when John says, "I saw under the altar the souls of them that were slain for the word of God." When Christ says, "Fear not them who kill the body, but are not able to kill the soul," does it not plainly imply, that when wicked men have killed our bodies, that is, have separated the souls from them, yet the souls are still alive? The soul of Christ was alive when his body was dead, and therefore so shall be ours too. This appears by his words to the thief, "To-day shalt thou be with me in paradise;" and also by his voice on the cross, "Father, into thy hands I commend my spirit." If the spirits of those that "were disobedient in the days of Noah were in prison," that is, in a living and suffering state; then certainly, the separate spirits of the just are in an opposite condition of happiness. Therefore, faithful souls will no sooner leave their prisons of flesh but angels shall be their convoy; Christ, and all the perfected spirits of the just will be their companions; heaven will be their residence, and God their happiness. When such die, they may boldly and believingly say, as Stephen, "Lord Jesus, receive my spirit;" and commend it, as Christ did, into a Father's hands.

CHAPTER V

THE GREAT MISERY OF THOSE WHO LOSE THE SAINTS' REST

I. The loss of heaven includes, 1. The personal perfection of the saints; 2. God himself; 3. All delightful affections towards God; 4. The blessed society of angels and glorified spirits. II. The aggravations of the loss of heaven: 1. The understanding of the ungodly will then be cleared; 2. Also enlarged; 3. Their consciences will make a true and close application; 4. Their affections will be more lively; 5. Their memories will be large and strong.

IF thou, reader, art a stranger to Christ, and to the holy nature and life of his people, who have been described, and shalt live and die in this condition, let me tell thee, thou shalt never partake of the joys of heaven, nor have the least taste of the saints' eternal rest. I may say, as Ehud to Eglon, "I have a message to thee from God;" that, as the word of God is true, thou shalt never see the face of God in peace. This sentence I am commanded to pass upon thee; take it as thou wilt, and escape it if thou canst. I know thy humble and hearty subjection to Christ would procure thy escape; he would then acknowledge thee for one of his people, and give thee a portion in the inheritance of his chosen. If this might be the happy success of my message, I should be so far from repining, like

Jonah, that the threatenings of God are not executed upon thee, that I should bless the day that
ever God made me so happy a messenger.   But if
thou end thy days in thy unregenerate state, as
sure as the heavens are over thy head and the earth
under thy feet, thou shalt be shut out of the rest of
the saints, and receive thy portion in everlasting
fire.   I expect thou wilt turn upon me and say,
When did God show you the book of life, or tell you
who they are that shall be saved, and who shut
out ?   I answer, I do not name thee, nor any other ;
I only conclude it of the unregenerate in general,
and of thee, if thou be such a one.   Nor do I go
about to determine who shall repent and who shall
not ; much less, that thou shalt never repent.   I had
rather show thee what hopes thou hast before thee,
if thou wilt not sit still and lose them.   I would
far rather persuade thee to hearken in time, before
the door be shut against thee, than tell thee there
is no hope of thy repenting and returning.   But, if
the foregoing description of the people of God does
not agree with the state of thy soul, is it then a
hard question whether thou shalt ever be saved ?
Need I ascend up into heaven to know that "without holiness no man shall see the Lord ;" or, that
only "the pure in heart shall see God ;" or, that
"except a man be born again, he cannot enter into
the kingdom of God ?"   Need I go up to heaven to
inquire that of Christ which he came down to earth

to tell us, and sent his Spirit in his apostles to tell us, and which he and they have left upon record to all the world? And though I know not the secrets of thy heart, and therefore cannot tell thee by name whether it be thy state or not; yet, if thou art but willing and diligent, thou mayest know thyself whether thou art an heir of heaven or not. It is the main thing I desire, that, if thou art yet miserable, thou mayest discern and escape it. But how canst thou escape, if thou neglect Christ and salvation? It is as impossible as for the devils themselves to be saved; nay, God has more plainly and frequently spoken it in scripture of such sinners as thou art, than he has of the devils. Methinks a sight of thy case should strike thee with amazement and horror. When Belshazzar " saw the fingers of a man's hand that wrote upon the wall, his countenance was changed, and his thoughts troubled him, so that the joints of his loins were loosed and his knees smote one against another." What trembling, then, should seize on thee, who hast the hand of God himself against thee, not in a sentence or two, but in the very scope of the Scriptures, threatening the loss of an everlasting kingdom. Because I would fain have thee lay it to heart, I will show thee, first, the nature of thy loss of heaven; secondly, its aggravations.

1. *The glorious personal perfection* which the saints enjoy in heaven, is the great loss of the

ungodly. They lose that shining lustre of the body, surpassing the brightness of the sun at noonday. Though the bodies of the wicked will be raised more spiritual than they were upon earth, yet that will only make them capable of the more exquisite torments. They would be glad then if every member were a dead member, that it might not feel the punishment inflicted on it; and if the whole body were a rotten carcass, or might lie down again in the dust. Much more do they want that moral perfection which the blessed partake of; those holy dispositions of mind; that cheerful readiness to do the will of God; that perfect rectitude of all their actions: instead of these, they have that perverseness of will, that loathing of good, that love to evil, that violence of passion, which they had on earth. It is true, their understandings will be much cleared by the ceasing of former temptations, and experiencing the falsehood of former delusions, but they have the same dispositions still, and fain would they commit the same sins if they could: they want but opportunity. There will be a greater difference between these wretches and the glorified Christian, than there is between a toad and the sun in the firmament. The rich man's purple and fine linen and sumptuous fare did not so exalt him above Lazarus while at his gate, full of sores.

2. They shall have *no comfortable relation to*

God, nor communion with him. "As they did not like to retain God in their knowledge," but said unto him, "Depart from us, for we desire not the knowledge of thy ways;" so God will abhor to retain them in his household. He will never admit them to the inheritance of his saints, nor endure them to stand in his presence; but "will profess unto them, I never knew you; depart from me, ye that work iniquity." They are ready now to lay as confident claim to Christ and heaven as if they were sincere believing saints. The swearer, the drunkard, the whoremonger, the worldling can say, Is not God our Father as well as yours? But when Chris' separates his followers from his foes, and his faithful friends from his deceived flatterers, where then will be their presumptuous claim? Then they shall find that God is not their Father, because they would not be his people. As they would not consent that God, by his Spirit, should dwell in them, so the tabernacle of wickedness shall have no fellowship with him, nor the wicked inhabit the city of God. Only they that walked with God here shall live and be happy with him in heaven. Little does the world know what is the loss of that soul who loses God. What a dungeon would the earth be if it had lost the sun; what a loathsome carrion the body, if it had lost the soul! yet all these are nothing to the loss of God. As the enjoyment of God is the heaven of the saints, so the loss of God is the hell of the ungodly ; and as the enjoying of God is the enjoying of all, so the loss of God is the loss of all.

3. They also lose *all delightful affections towards God :* that transporting knowledge ; those delightful views of his glorious face ; the inconceivable pleasure of loving him ; the apprehensions of his infinite love to us ; the constant joys of his saints, and the rivers of consolation with which he satisfies them. Is it nothing to lose all this ? The employment of a king in ruling a kingdom, does not so far exceed that of the vilest slave, as this heavenly employment exceeds that of an earthly king. God suits men's employment to their natures. Your hearts, sinners, were never set upon God in your lives, never warmed with his love, never longed after the enjoyment of him ; you had no delight in speaking or hearing of him ; you had rather have continued on earth, if you had known how, than to be interested in the glorious praises of God. Is it meet, then, that you should be members of the celestial choir?

4. They shall be deprived of *the blessed society of angels and glorified saints.* Instead of being companions of those happy spirits, and numbered with those triumphant kings, they must be driven down to hell, where they shall have companions of a far different nature and quality. Scorning and abusing the saints, hating them, and rejoicing at

their calamities, was not the way to obtain their blessedness. Now, you are shut out of that company from which you first shut out yourselves, and are separated from them with whom you would not be joined. You could not endure them in your houses, or towns, or scarcely in the kingdom. You took them, as Ahab did Elijah, for the "troublers of the land;" and as the apostles were taken for "men that turned the world upside down." If any thing fell out amiss, you thought all was owing to them. When they were dead or banished, you were glad they were gone, and thought the country well rid of them. They molested you by faithfully reproving your sins. Their holy conversation troubled your consciences, to see them so far excel you. It was a vexation to you to hear them pray or sing praises in their families. And is it any wonder if you be separated from them hereafter? The day is near when they will trouble you no more. Between them and you will be a great gulf fixed. Even in this life, while the saints were "mocked, destitute, afflicted, tormented," and while they had their personal imperfections, yet, in the judgment of the Holy Ghost, they were men "of whom the world was not worthy." Much more unworthy will the world be of their fellowship in glory.

II. I know many will be ready to think they could spare these things in this world well enough, and why may they not be without them in the world to come? Therefore, to show them that this loss of heaven will then be most tormenting, let them now consider,

1. *The understanding of the ungodly will then be cleared to know the worth of that which they have lost.* Now they lament not their loss of God, because they never knew his excellence; nor the loss of that holy employment and society, for they were never sensible what they were worth. A man that has lost a jewel, and took it but for a common stone, is never troubled at his loss; but when he comes to know what he lost, then he laments it. Though the understandings of the damned will not be sanctified, yet they will be cleared from a multitude of errors. They now think that their honors, estates, pleasures, health, and life are better worth their labor than the things of another world; but when these things have left them in misery, when they experience the things of which they before but read and heard, they will be of another mind. They would not believe that water would drown, till they were in the sea; nor the fire burn, till they were cast into it: but when they feel, they will easily believe. All that error of mind which made them set light by God, and abhor his worship, and vilify his people, will then be confuted and removed by experience. Their knowledge shall be increased, that their sorrows may be increased. Poor souls! they would be comparatively

happy, if their understandings were wholly taken
from them, if they had no more knowledge than
idiots or brutes ; or, if they knew no more in hell
than they did upon earth, their loss would less
trouble them.   How happy would they then think
themselves if they did not know there is such a
place as heaven'   Now, when their knowledge
would help to prevent their misery, they will not
know, or will not read or study that they may
know ; therefore, when their knowledge will but
feed their consuming fire they shall know, whether
they will or not.   They are now in a dead sleep,
and dream that they are the happiest men in the
world ; but when death awakes them, how will
their judgments be changed in a moment ! and
they that would not see, shall then see and be
ashamed.

2. As their understanding will be cleared, so it
will be *more enlarged*, and made more capacious to
conceive the worth of that glory which they have
lost.   The strength of their apprehensions, as well
as the truth of them, will then be increased.   What
deep apprehensions of the wrath of God, the madness of sinning, the misery of sinners, have those
souls that now endure this misery, in comparison
with those on earth that do but hear of it !   What
sensibility of the worth of life has the condemned
man that is going to be executed, compared with
what he was wont to have in the time of his pros-

perity! Much more will the actual loss of eternal
blessedness make the damned exceedingly appre-
hensive of the greatness of their loss; and as a
large vessel will hold more water than a shell, so
will their more enlarged understandings contain
more matter to feed their torment than their shal-
low capacity can now do.

3. Their *consciences* also will make a truer and
closer application of this doctrine to themselves,
which will exceedingly tend to increase their torment.   It will then be no hard matter to them to
say, "This is my loss; and this is my everlasting
remediless misery!"   The want of this self-appli-
cation is the main cause why they are so little
troubled now.   They are hardly brought to believe
that there is such a state of misery; but more
hardly to believe that it is like to be their own.
This makes so many sermons lost to them, and all
threatenings and warnings in vain.   Let a minister
of Christ show them their misery ever so plainly
and faithfully, they will not be persuaded they are
so miserable.   Let him tell them of the glory they
must lose, and the sufferings they must feel, and
they think he means not them, but some notorious
sinners.   It is one of the hardest things in the
world to bring a wicked man to know that he is
wicked, or to make him see himself in a state of
wrath and condemnation.   Though they may easily
find, by their strangeness to the new birth, and

their enmity to holiness, that they never were partakers of them; yet they as verily expect to see God and be saved, as if they were the most sanctified persons in the world. How seldom do men cry out, after the plainest discovery of their state, I am the man; or acknowledge that, if they die in their present condition, they are undone for ever. But when they suddenly find themselves in the land of darkness, feel themselves in scorching flames, and see they are shut out of the presence of God for ever, then the application of God's anger to themselves will be the easiest matter in the world; they will then roar out these forced confessions, "O my misery! O my folly! O my inconceivable, irrecoverable loss!"

4. Then will their *affections* likewise be *more lively*, and no longer stupefied. A hard heart now makes heaven and hell seem but trifles. We have showed them everlasting glory and misery, and they are as men asleep; our words are as stones cast against a wall, which fly back in our faces. We talk of terrible things, but it is to dead men; we search the wounds, but they never feel it; we speak to rocks rather than to men; the earth will as soon tremble as they. But when these dead souls are revived, what passionate sensibility, what working affections, what pangs of horror, what depths of sorrow will there then be! How violently will they denounce and reproach themselves!

How will they rage against their former madness! The lamentations of the most affectionate wife for the loss of her husband, or of the tenderest mother for the loss of her children, will be nothing to theirs for the loss of heaven. O the self-accusing and self-tormenting fury of those forlorn creatures! How will they even tear their own hearts, and be God's executioners upon themselves! As themselves were the only meritorious cause of their sufferings, so themselves will be the chief executioners. Even Satan, as he was not so great a cause of their sinning as themselves, will not be so great an instrument of their torment. How happy would they think themselves then, if they were turned into rocks, or any thing that had neither passion nor sense! How happy, if they could then feel as lightly as they were wont to hear; if they could sleep out the time of execution as they did the time of the sermons that warned them of it! But their stupidity is gone: it will not be.

5. Their *memories* will moreover be as large and strong as their understanding and affections. Could they but lose the use of their memory, their loss of heaven, being forgot, would little trouble them. Though they would account annihilation a great mercy, they cannot lay aside any part of their being. Understanding, conscience, affections, memory, must all live to torment them, which should have helped to their happiness. As by these they

should have fed upon the love of God, and drawn forth perpetually the joys of his presence, so by these must they feed upon his wrath, and draw forth continually the pains of his absence. Now they have no leisure to consider, nor any room in their memories for the things of another life ; but then they shall have nothing else to do ; their memories shall have no other employment. God would have had the doctrine of their eternal state "written on the posts of their doors, on their hands and hearts :" he would have them mind it, and mention it "when they lay down and rose up, when they sat in their houses, and when they walked by the way ;" and seeing they rejected this counsel of the Lord, therefore it shall be written always before them in the place of their thraldom, that, which way soever they look, they may still behold it. It will torment them to think of the greatness of the glory they have lost. If it had been what they could have spared, or a loss to be repaired with any thing else, it had been a smaller matter. If it had been health, or wealth, or friends, or life, it had been nothing. But O, to lose that exceeding and eternal weight of glory ! It will also torment them to think of the possibility they once had of obtaining it. Then they will remember, "Time was when I was as fair for the kingdom as others. I was set upon the stage of the world ; if I had believed in Christ, I might now have had possession of the inheritance. I who am now tormented with these damned fiends, might have been among yonder blessed saints. The Lord did set before me life and death ; and having chosen death, I deserve to suffer it. The prize was held out before me : if I had run well, I might have obtained it ; if I had striven, I might have had the victory ; if I had fought valiantly, I had been crowned." It will yet more torment them to remember that their obtaining the crown was not only possible, but very probable. It will wound them to think, "I had once the gales of the Spirit ready to have assisted me. I was proposing to be another man, to cleave to Christ, and forsake the world. I was almost resolved to be wholly for God. I was once even turning away from my base, seducing lusts. I had cast off my old companions, and was associating with the godly. Yet I turned back, lost my hold, and broke my promises. I was almost persuaded to be a real Christian, yet I conquered those persuasions. What workings were in my heart when a faithful minister pressed home the truth ! O how fair was I once for heaven ! I almost had it, and yet I have lost it. Had I followed on to seek the Lord, I had now been blessed among the saints."

It will exceedingly torment them to remember their *lost opportunities.* "How many weeks and months and years did I lose, which if I had im-

proved I might now have been happy. Wretch
that I was, could I find no time to study the work
for which I had all my time ; no time among all
my labors to labor for eternity? Had I time to eat
and drink and sleep, and none to save my soul?
Had I time for mirth and vain discourse, and none
for prayer? Could I take time to secure the world,
and none to try my title to heaven? O precious
time! I had once enough, and now I must have no
more. I had once so much I knew not what to do
with it ; and now it is gone, and cannot be recalled.
O that I had but one of those years to live over
again, how speedily would I repent, how earnestly
would I pray, how diligently would I hear, how
closely would I examine my state, how strictly
would I live. But it is now too late, alas, too
late."

It will add to their calamity to remember *how
often they were persuaded to return.* "Fain would
the minister have had me escape these torments.
With what love and compassion did he beseech me,
and yet I did but make a jest of it. How oft did
he convince me, and yet I stifled all these convictions. How did he open to me my very heart, and
yet I was loath to know the worst of myself. O
how glad would he have been if he could have seen
me cordially turn to Christ. My godly friends ad-
monished me ; they told me what would become of
my wilfulness and negligence at last; but I neither

believed nor regarded them. How long did God himself condescend to entreat me. How did the Spirit strive with my heart, as if he was loath to take a denial. How did Christ stand knocking, one Sabbath after another, and crying to me, 'Open, sinner, open thy heart to thy Saviour, and I will come in and sup with thee, and thou with me. Why dost thou delay? How long shall thy vain thoughts lodge within thee? Wilt thou not be pardoned and sanctified and made happy? When shall it once be?' " O how the recollection of such divine pleadings will passionately transport the damned with self-indignation. "Must I tire out the patience of Christ? Must I make the God of heaven follow me in vain, till I have wearied him with crying to me, Repent! return! O how justly is that patience now turned into fury which falls upon me with irresistible violence. When the Lord cried to me, 'Wilt thou not be made clean? When shall it once be?' my heart, or at least my practice answered, 'Never!' And now, when I cry, 'How long shall it be till I am freed from this torment?' how justly do I receive the same answer, 'Never, never!' "

It will also be most cutting to remember *on what easy terms they might have escaped their misery.* Their work was not to remove mountains, nor conquer kingdoms, nor fulfil the law to the smallest tittle, nor satisfy justice for all their transgressions.

"The yoke was easy and the burden light" which
Christ would have laid upon them. It was but to
repent and cordially accept him for their Saviour;
to renounce all other happiness, and take the Lord
for their supreme good; to renounce the world and
the flesh, and submit to his meek and gracious government; and to forsake the ways of their own
devising, and walk in his holy delightful way.
"Ah," thinks the poor tormented wretch, "how
justly do I suffer all this, who would not be at so
small pains to avoid it! Where was my understanding when I neglected that gracious offer; when I
called 'the Lord a hard master,' and thought his
pleasant service a bondage, and the service of the
devil and the flesh the only freedom? Was I not
a thousand times worse than mad, when I censured
the holy way of God as needless preciseness; when
I thought the laws of Christ too strict, and all too
much that I did for the life to come? What would
all sufferings for Christ and well-doing have been,
compared with these sufferings that I must undergo
for ever? Would not the heaven which I have
lost have recompensed all my losses? And would
not all my sufferings have been there forgotten?
What if Christ had bid me to do some great matter—whether to live in continual fears and sorrows,
or to suffer death a hundred times over; should I
not have done it? How much more, when he only
said, 'Believe and be saved. Seek my face, and

thy soul shall live. Take up thy cross and follow
me, and I will give thee everlasting life.' O gracious offer! O easy terms! O cursed wretch, that
would not be persuaded to accept them!"

This also will be a most tormenting considera
tion, to remember *for what they sold their eterna*
welfare. When they compare the value of the
pleasures of sin with the value of "the recompense
of reward," how will the vast disproportion astonish them! To think of the low delights of the
flesh, or the applauding breath of mortals, or the
possessing heaps of gold, and then to think of everlasting glory! "This is all I had for my soul, my
God, my hopes of blessedness." It cannot possibly
be expressed how these thoughts will tear his very
heart. Then will he exclaim against his folly, "O
miserable wretch! Did I set my soul to sale for so
base a price? Did I part with my God for a little
dirt and dross; and sell my Saviour, as Judas, for
a little silver? I had but a dream of delight for
my hopes of heaven; and now I am awakened, it
is all vanished. My morsels are now turned to
gall, and my cups to wormwood. When they were
past my taste, the pleasure perished. And is this
all that I have had for the inestimable treasure?
What a mad exchange did I make! What if I had
gained all the world, and lost my soul? But, alas,
how small a part of the world was it for which I
gave up heaven." O that sinners would think of

this when they are swimming in the delights of the flesh, and studying how to be rich and honorable in the world; when they are desperately venturing upon known transgression, and sinning against the checks of conscience.

It will add yet more to their torment, when they consider that *they most wilfully procured their own destruction.* Had they been forced to sin, it would much abate the rage of their consciences; or if they were punished for another man's transgressions; or any other had been the chief author of their ruin. But to think it was the choice of their own will, and that none in the world could have forced them to sin against their will, this will be a cutting thought. "Had I not enemies enough in the world," thinks this miserable creature, "but I must be an enemy to myself? God would never give the devil, nor the world, so much power over me as to force me to commit the least transgression. They could but entice: it was myself that yielded and did the evil. And must I lay hands upon my own soul, and imbrue my hands in my own blood? Never had I so great an enemy as myself. Never did God offer any good to my soul but I resisted him. He hath heaped mercy upon me, and renewed one deliverance after another, to draw my heart to him; yea, he hath gently chastised me, and made me groan under the fruit of my disobedience; and though I promised largely in my affliction, yet never

was I heartily willing to serve him." Thus will it
gnaw the hearts of these sinners, to remember that
they were the cause of their own ruin; and that they
wilfully and obstinately persisted in their rebellion,
and were mere volunteers in the service of the devil.

The wound in their consciences will be yet deeper,
when they shall not only remember it was their
own doing, but that *they were at so much cost and
pains for their own damnation.* What great under-
takings did they engage in to effect their ruin, to
resist the Spirit of God; to overcome the power of
mercies, judgments, and even the word of God; to
subdue the power of reason and silence conscience.
All this they undertook and performed. Though
they walked in continual danger of the wrath of
God, and knew he could lay them in the dust and
cast them into hell in a moment, yet would they
run upon all this. O the labor it costs sinners to be
damned! Sobriety, with health and ease, they
might have had at a cheaper rate; yet they will
rather have gluttony and drunkenness, with poverty, shame, and sickness. Contentment they might
have, with ease and delight; yet they will rather
have covetousness and ambition, though it costs
them cares and fears, labor of body and distraction
of mind. Though their anger be self-torment, and
revenge and envy consume their spirits; though
uncleanness destroy their bodies, estates, and good
names, yet will they do and suffer all this, rather

than suffer their souls to be saved. With what rage will they lament their folly, and say, "Was damnation worth all this cost and pains? Might I not have been damned on free cost, but I must purchase it so dearly? I thought I could have been saved without so much ado, and could I not have been destroyed without so much ado? Must I so laboriously work out my own damnation, when God commanded me to 'work out my own salvation?' If I had done as much for heaven as I did for hell, I had surely had it. I cried out of the tedious way of godliness, and the painful course of self-denial; and yet I could be at a great deal more pains for Satan and for death. Had I loved Christ as strongly as I did my pleasures and profits and honors, and thought on him as often and sought him as painfully, O how happy had I now been! How justly do I suffer the flames of hell for buying them so dear, rather than have heaven when it was purchased to my hands."

O that God would persuade thee, reader, to take up these thoughts now, for preventing the inconceivable calamity of taking them up in hell as thy own tormentor! Say not that they are only imaginary. Read what Dives thought, being in torments. As the joys of heaven are chiefly enjoyed by the rational soul in its rational acting, so must the pains of hell be suffered. As they will be men still, so will they feel and act as men.

CHAPTER VI

THE MISERY OF THOSE WHO, BESIDES LOSING THE
SAINTS' REST, LOSE THE ENJOYMENTS OF TIME,
AND SUFFER THE TORMENTS OF HELL

I. The enjoyments of time which the damned lose: 1. Their
presumptuous belief of their interest in God and Christ;
2. All their hopes; 3. All their peace of conscience; 4. All
their carnal mirth; 5. All their sensual delights. II. The
torments of the damned are exceedingly great: 1. The
principal Author of them is God himself. 2. The place or
state of torment. 3. These torments are the effects of
divine vengeance. 4. God will take pleasure in executing
them. 5. Satan and sinners themselves will be God's executioners. 6. These torments will be universal; 7. Without any mitigation; 8. And eternal. The obstinate sinner
convinced of his folly in venturing on these torments; and
entreated to fly for safety to Christ.

As "godliness hath a promise of the life that
now is, and of that which is to come;" and if we
"seek first the kingdom of God and his righteousness," then all meaner "things shall be added unto
us;" so also are the ungodly threatened with the
loss both of spiritual and temporal blessings; and
because they sought not first God's kingdom and
righteousness, therefore shall they lose both it and
that which they did seek, and there shall be taken
from them that little which they have. If they
could but have kept their present enjoyments, they
would not have much cared for the loss of heaven

If they had "lost and forsaken all for Christ," they would have found all again in him; for he would have been all in all to them. But, now they have forsaken Christ for other things, they shall lose Christ and that also for which they forsook him, even the enjoyments of time, besides suffering the torments of hell.

1. They shall lose *their presumptuous belief of their interest in the favor of God and the merits of Christ*. This false belief now supports their spirits, and defends them from the terrors that would otherwise seize upon them. But what will ease their trouble when they can believe no longer, nor rejoice any longer? If a man be near to the greatest mischief, and yet strongly conceit that he is in safety, he may be as cheerful as if all were well. If no more were needed to make a man happy but to believe that he is so, or shall be so, happiness would be far more common than it is like to be. As true faith is the leading grace in the regenerate, so is false faith the leading vice in the unregenerate. Why do such multitudes sit still when they might have pardon, but that they verily think they are pardoned already? If you could ask thousands in hell what madness brought them thither, they would most of them answer, "We thought we were sure of being saved, till we found ourselves damned. We would have been more earnest seekers of regeneration and the power of godliness, but we verily

thought we were Christians already. We have
flattered ourselves into these torments, and now
there is no remedy." Reader, I must in faithfulness tell thee that the confident belief of their good
state, which the careless, unholy, unhumbled multitude so commonly boast of, will prove in the end
but a soul-damning delusion. There is none of this
believing in hell. It was Satan's stratagem, that
being blindfold, they might follow him the more
boldly; but then he will uncover their eyes, and
they shall see where they are.

2. They shall lose also *all their hopes.* In this
life, though they were threatened with the wrath
of God, yet their hope of escaping it bore up their
hearts. We can now scarce speak with the vilest
drunkard, or swearer, or scoffer, but he hopes to be
saved, for all this. O happy world, if salvation
were as common as this hope! Nay, so strong are
men's hopes, that they will dispute the cause with
Christ himself at the judgment, and plead their
"having ate and drank in his presence, and prophesied in his name, and in his name cast out devils;"
they will stiffly deny that ever they neglected
Christ, in hunger, nakedness, or in prison, till he
confutes them with the sentence of their condemnation. O the sad state of those men when they must
bid farewell to all their hopes! "When a wicked
man dieth, his expectation shall perish; and the
hope of unjust men perisheth. The eyes of the

wicked shall fail, and they shall not escape, and their hope shall be as the giving up of the ghost." The giving up of the ghost is a fit but terrible resemblance of a wicked man giving up his hopes. As the soul departeth not from the body without the greatest pain, so doth the hope of the wicked depart. The soul departs from the body suddenly, in a moment, which hath there delightfully continued so many years; just so doth the hope of the wicked depart. The soul will never more return to live with the body in this world; and the hope of the wicked takes an everlasting farewell of his soul. A miracle of resurrection shall again unite soul and body; but there shall be no such miraculous resurrection of the damned's hope. Methinks it is the most pitiable sight this world affords, to see such an ungodly person dying, and to think of his soul and his hopes departing together. With what a sad change he appears in another world. Then if a man could but ask that hopeless soul, "Are you as confident of salvation as you were wont to be?" what a sad answer would be returned. O that careless sinners would be awakened to think of this in time. Reader, rest not till thou canst give a reason of all thy hopes, grounded upon scripture promises: that they purify thy heart; that they quicken thy endeavors in godliness; that the more thou hopest the less thou sinnest, and the more exact is thy obedience. If thy hopes be such as

these, go on in the strength of the Lord, hold fast
thy hope, and "never shall it make thee ashamed."
But if thou hast not one sound evidence of a work
of grace on thy soul, cast away thy hopes.   Despair
of ever being saved, "except thou be born again;"
or of "seeing God, without holiness;" or of having
part in Christ, except thou "love him above father,
mother, or thy own life."   This kind of despair is
one of the first steps to heaven.   If a man be quite
out of his way, what must be the first means to
bring him in again?   He must despair of ever coming to his journey's end in the way that he is in.
If his home be eastward and he is going westward,
as long as he hopes he is right he will go on; and
as long as he goes on hoping, he goes further amiss.
When he despairs of coming home except he turn
back, then he will return, and then he may hope.
Just so it is, sinner, with thy soul : thou art born
out of the way to heaven, and hast proceeded many
a year; thou goest on and hopest to be saved
because thou art not so bad as many others.   Except thou throw away those hopes, and see that
thou hast all this while been quite out of the way
to heaven, thou wilt never return and be saved.
There is nothing in the world more likely to keep
thy soul out of heaven, than thy false hopes of being
saved while thou art out of the way to salvation.   See then how it will aggravate the misery
of the damned, that, with the loss of heaven, they

shall lose all that hope of it which now supports them.

3. They will lose *all that false peace of conscience which makes their present life so easy.* Who would think, observing how quietly the multitude of the ungodly live, that they must very shortly lie down in everlasting flames? They are as free from the fears of hell as an obedient believer; and for the most part have less disquiet of mind than those who shall be saved. Happy men, if this peace would prove lasting! "When they shall say, Peace and safety, then sudden destruction cometh upon them, as travail upon a woman with child; and they shall not escape." O cruel peace, which ends in such a war! The soul of every man by nature is Satan's garrison; all is at peace in such a man till Christ comes and gives it terrible alarms of judgment and hell, batters it with the ordnance of his threats and terrors, forces it to yield to his mere mercy, and take him for the governor; then doth he cast out Satan, "overcome him, take from him all his armor wherein he trusted, and divideth his spoils," and then doth he establish a firm and lasting peace. If, therefore, thou art yet in that first peace, never think it will endure. Can thy soul have lasting peace in enmity with Christ? Can he have peace against whom God proclaims war? I wish thee no greater good than that God break in upon thy careless heart, and shake thee

out of thy false peace, and make thee lie down at the feet of Christ and say, "Lord, what wouldst thou have me to do?" and so receive from him a better and surer peace, which will never be quite broken, but be the beginning of thy everlasting peace, and not perish in thy perishing as the groundless peace of the world will do.

4. They shall lose *all their carnal mirth*. They will themselves say of their "laughter, it is mad; and of their mirth, what doeth it?" It was but "as the crackling of thorns under a pot." It made a blaze for a while, but it was presently gone, and returned no more. The talk of death and judgment was irksome to them, because it damped their mirth. They could not endure to think of their sin and danger, because these thoughts sunk their spirits. They knew not what it was to weep for sin, or to humble themselves under the mighty hand of God. They could laugh away sorrow, and sing away cares, and drive away those melancholy thoughts. To meditate and pray, they fancied, would be enough to make them miserable or run mad. Poor souls, what a misery will that life be, where you shall have nothing but sorrow—intense, heart-piercing, multiplied sorrow; when you shall neither have the joys of saints nor your own former joys! Do you think there is one merry heart in hell; or one joyful countenance or jesting tongue? You now cry, "A little mirth is worth a great deal

of sorrow." But surely a little godly sorrow, which would have ended in eternal joy, had been worth much more than all your foolish mirth; for the end of such mirth is sorrow.

5. They shall also lose *all their sensual delights*. That which they esteemed their chief good, their heaven, their god, must they lose, as well as God himself. What a fall will the proud, ambitious man have from the height of his honors! As his dust and bones will not be known from the dust and bones of the poorest beggar, so neither will his soul be honored or favored more than theirs. What a number of the great, noble, and learned will be shut out from the presence of Christ! They shall not find their magnificent buildings, soft beds, and easy couches. They shall not view their curious gardens, their pleasant meadows, and plenteous harvests. Their tables will not be so furnished nor attended. The rich man is there no more "clothed in purple and fine linen, and faring sumptuously every day." There is no expecting the admiration of beholders. They shall spend their time in sadness, and not in sports and pastimes. What an alteration will they then find! The heat of their lust will then be abated. How will it even cut them to the heart to look each other in the face! What an interview will there then be, cursing the day that ever they saw one another! O that sinners would now remember and say, "Will these

delights accompany us into the other world? Will
not the remembrance of them be then our torment?
Shall we then take this partnership in vice for true
friendship? Why should we sell such lasting, incomprehensible joys for a taste of seeming pleasure?
Come, as we have sinned together, let us pray together that God would pardon us; and let us help
one another towards heaven, instead of helping to
deceive and destroy each other." O that men but
knew what they desire, when they would so earnestly have all things suited to the desires of the
flesh. It is but to desire their temptations to be
increased and their snares strengthened.

II. As the loss of the saints' rest will be aggra-
vated by losing the enjoyments of time, it will be
much more so by suffering the torments of hell.
The exceeding greatness of such torments may appear by considering,

1. The *principal author* of hell-torments is God
himself. As it was no less than God whom sinners had offended, so it is no less than God who
will punish them for their offences. He hath prepared those torments for his enemies. His continued
anger will still be devouring them. His breath of
indignation will kindle the flames. His wrath will
be an intolerable burden to their souls. If it were
but a creature they had to do with, they might
better bear it. Woe to him that falls under the
strokes of the Almighty! "It is a fearful thing to

fall into the hands of the living God." It were
nothing in comparison to this, if all the world were
against them, or if the strength of all creatures
were united in one to inflict their penalty. They
had now rather venture to displease God than displease a landlord, a customer, a master, a friend, a
neighbor, or their own flesh; but then they will
wish a thousand times, in vain, that they had been
hated of all the world, rather than have lost the
favor of God. What a consuming fire is his wrath!
If it be kindled here but a little, how do we "wither
like grass!" How soon doth our strength decay
and turn to weakness, and our beauty to deformity!
The flames do not so easily run through the dry
stubble, as the wrath of God will consume these
wretches. They that could not bear a prison, or a
gibbet, or a fire for Christ, or scarcely a few scoffs,
how will they now bear the devouring flames of
divine wrath?

2. The *place or state of torment* is purposely
ordained to glorify the justice of God. When God
would glorify his power, he made the worlds. The
comely order of all his creatures declareth his wisdom. His providence is shown in sustaining all
things. When a spark of his wrath kindles upon
the earth, the whole world, except only eight persons, are drowned; Sodom and Gomorrah, Admah
and Zeboim are burnt with fire from heaven; the
sea shuts her mouth upon some, the earth opens

and swallows up others; the pestilence destroys by
thousands.   What a standing witness of the wrath
of God is the present deplorable state of the Jews!
Yet the glorifying of the mercy and justice of God
is intended most eminently for the life to come.
As God will then glorify his mercy in a way that
is now beyond the comprehension of the saints who
must enjoy it, so also will he manifest his justice
to be indeed the justice of God.   The everlasting
flames of hell will not be thought too hot for the
rebellious ; and when they have there burned
through millions of ages, he will not repent him
of the evil which has befallen them.   Woe to the
soul that is thus the object of the wrath of the
Almighty, as a bush that must burn in the flames
of his jealousy and never be consumed!

The torments of the damned must be extreme,
because they are the *effect of divine vengeance.*
Wrath is terrible, but vengeance is implacable.
When the great God shall say, " My rebellious
creatures shall now pay for all the abuse of my
patience ; remember how I waited your leisure in
vain, how I stooped to persuade and entreat you:
did you think I would always be so slighted?"
then will he be avenged for every abused mercy,
and for all their neglects of Christ and grace.   O
that men would foresee this, and please God better
in preventing their woe.

4. Consider also, that though God had rather

men would accept of Christ and mercy, yet, when they persist in rebellion, *he will take pleasure in their execution.* He tells us, "Fury is not in me;" yet he adds, "Who would set the briars and thorns against me in battle? I would go through them, I would burn them together." Wretched creatures, when "he that made them will not have mercy upon them, and he that formed them will show them no favor. As the Lord rejoiced over them to do them good, so the Lord will rejoice over them to destroy them, and bring them to naught." Woe to the souls whom God rejoiceth to punish: "He will laugh at their calamity, he will mock when their fear cometh; when their fear cometh as desolation, and their destruction cometh as a whirlwind; when distress and anguish come upon them." Terrible thing, when none in heaven or earth can help them but God, and he shall rejoice in their calamity! Though Scripture speaks of God's laughing and mocking, not literally, but after the manner of men, yet it is an act of God in tormenting the sinner, which cannot otherwise be more fitly expressed.

5. Consider that *Satan and themselves shall be God's executioners.* He that was here so successful in drawing them from Christ, will then be the instrument of their punishment for yielding to his temptations. That is the reward he will give them for all their service; for their rejecting the

commands of God, forsaking Christ, and neglecting
their souls at his persuasion. If they had served
Christ as faithfully as they did Satan, he would
have given them a better reward. It is also most
just that they should be their own tormentors, that
they may see their whole destruction is of themselves ; and then whom can they complain of but
themselves ?

6. Consider also that their torment will be *universal*. As all parts have joined in sin, so must
they all partake in the torment. The soul, as it
was the chief in sinning, shall be the chief in suffering ; and as it is of a more excellent nature than
the body, so will its torments far exceed bodily torments ; and as its joys far surpass all sensual pleasures, so the pains of the soul exceed corporeal pains.
It is not only a soul, but a sinful soul that must
suffer. Fire will not burn, except the fuel be
combustible ; but if the wood be dry, how fiercely
will it burn. The guilt of their sins will be to
damned souls like tinder to gunpowder, to make the
flames of hell take hold upon them with fury.
The body must also bear its part. The body which
was so carefully looked to, so tenderly cherished,
so curiously dressed, what must it now endure !
How are its haughty looks now brought down !
How little will those flames regard its comeliness
and beauty ! Those eyes, which were wont to be
delighted with curious sights, must then see nothing

but what shall terrify them : an angry God above them, with those saints whom they scorned enjoying the glory which they have lost ; and about them will be only devils and damned souls. How will they look back and say, " Are all our feasts and games and revels come to this ?" Those ears which were accustomed to music and songs, shall hear the shrieks and cries of their damned companions; children crying out against their parents, who gave them encouragement and example in evil ; husbands and wives, masters and servants, ministers and people, magistrates and subjects, charging their misery upon one another, for discouraging in duty, conniving at sin, and being silent when they should have plainly foretold the danger. Thus will soul and body be companions in woe.

7. Far greater will these torments be, because *without mitigation.* In this life, when told of hell, or if conscience troubled their peace, they had comforters at hand; their carnal friends, their business, their company, their mirth. They could drink, play, or sleep away their sorrows. But now all these remedies are vanished. Their hard, presumptuous, unbelieving heart was a wall to defend them against trouble of mind. Satan was himself their comforter, as he was to our first mother : " Hath God said, ye shall not eat ? Ye shall not surely die. Doth God tell you that you shall lie in hell ? There is no such matter; God is more merciful.

Or, if there be a hell, what need you fear it? Are not you Christians? Was not the blood of Christ shed for you?" Thus as the Spirit of Christ is the Comforter of the saints, so Satan is the comforter of the wicked. Never was a thief more careful lest he should awake the people when he is robbing a house, than Satan is not to awaken a sinner. But when the sinner is dead, then Satan hath done flattering and comforting. Which way, then, will the forlorn sinner look for comfort? They that drew him into the snare and promised him safety, now forsake him, and are forsaken themselves. His comforts are gone, and the righteous God, whose forewarnings he made light of, will now make good his word against him to the last tittle.

8. But the greatest aggravation of these torments will be their *eternity*. When a thousand millions of ages are past, they are as fresh to begin as the first day. If there were any hope of an end, it would ease the damned to foresee it; but *for ever* is an intolerable thought. They were never weary of sinning, nor will God be weary of punishing. They never heartily repented of sin, nor will God repent of their suffering. They broke the laws of the eternal God, and therefore shall suffer eternal punishment. They knew it was an everlasting kingdom which they refused, and what wonder if they are everlastingly shut out of it? Their immortal souls were guilty of the trespass, and there-

fore must immortally suffer the pains. What happy men would they think themselves, if they might have lain still in their graves, or might but there lie down again! How will they call and cry, "O death, whither art thou now gone? Now come and cut off this doleful life. O that these pains would break my heart, and end my being! O that I might once at last die! O that I had never had a being!" These groans will the thoughts of eternity wring from their hearts. They were wont to think sermons and prayers long; how long then will they think these endless torments! What difference is there between the length of their pleasures and their pains! The one continued but a moment, the other endure through all eternity. Sinner, remember how time is almost gone. Thou art standing at the door of eternity; and death is waiting to open the door, and put thee in. Go, sleep out a few more nights, and stir about a few more days on earth, and then thy nights and days shall end: thy thoughts and cares and pleasures shall all be devoured by eternity; thou must enter upon the state which shall never be changed. As the joys of heaven are beyond our conception, so are the pains of hell. Everlasting torment is inconceivable torment.

But methinks I see the obstinate sinner desperately resolving, "If I must be damned, there is no remedy. Rather than I will live as the Scripture requires, I will put it to the venture; I shall escape

as well as others, and we will even bear it as well
as we can." Alas, poor creature, let me beg this
of thee before thou dost so resolve, that thou
wouldst lend me thy attention to a few questions,
and weigh them with the reason of a man. Who
art thou, that thou shouldst bear the wrath of God?
What is thy strength? Is it not as the strength
of wax or stubble to resist the fire; or as chaff to
the wind; or as dust before the fierce whirlwind?
If thy strength were as iron, and thy bones as
brass; if thy foundation were as the earth, and
thy power as the heavens, yet shouldst thou perish
at the breath of his indignation. How much more,
when thou art but a piece of breathing clay, kept
a few days from being eaten with worms by the
mere support and favor of Him whom thou art thus
resisting! Why dost thou tremble at the signs of
almighty power and wrath; at peals of thunder, or
flashes of lightning; or that unseen power which
rends in pieces the mighty oaks, and tears down
the strongest buildings; or at the plague when it
rageth around thee? If thou hadst seen the
plagues of Egypt, or the earth swallow up Dathan
and Abiram, or Elijah bring fire from heaven to
destroy the captains and their companies, would
not any of these sights have daunted thy spirit?
How then canst thou bear the plagues of hell?
Why art thou dismayed with such small sufferings
as befall thee here: a toothache, a fit of the gout

or stone, the loss of a limb, or falling into beggary and disgrace? And yet all these laid together will be one day accounted a happy state, in comparison with that which is suffered in hell. Why does the approach of death so much affright thee? O how cold it strikes to thy heart! And would not the grave be accounted a paradise, compared with that place of torment which thou slightest? Is it an intolerable thing to burn part of thy body by hold-ing it in the fire? What, then, will it be to suffer ten thousand times more for ever in hell? The thought or mention of hell occasions disquiet in thy spirit; and canst thou endure the torments themselves? Why doth the rich man complain to Abraham of his torments in hell; or thy dying companions lose their courage, and change their haughty language? Why cannot these make as light of hell as thyself? Didst thou never see or speak with a man in despair? How uncomfortable was his talk; how burdensome his life! Nothing he possessed did him good: he had no sweetness in meat or drink; the sight of friends troubled him; he was weary of life, and fearful of death. If the misery of the damned can be endured, why cannot a man more easily endure these foretastes of hell? What if thou shouldst see the devil appear to thee in some terrible shape; would not thy heart fail thee, and thy hair stand on an end? And how wilt thou endure to live for ever where thou shalt have no other company but devils and the damned, and shalt not only see them, but be tormented with them and by them? Let me once more ask, If the wrath of God be so light, why did the Son of God himself make so great a matter of it? It caused "his sweat to be as it were great drops of blood, falling down to the ground." The Lord of life cried, "My soul is exceeding sorrowful, even unto death." And on the cross, "My God, my God, why hast thou forsaken me?" Surely if any one could have borne these sufferings easily, it would have been Jesus Christ. He had another measure of strength to bear it than thou hast. Woe to thee, sinner, for thy mad security! Dost thou think to find that tolerable to thee, which was so heavy to Christ? Nay, the Son of God is cast into a bitter agony and bloody sweat, only under the curse of the law; and yet thou, feeble, foolish creature, fearest not to bear also the curse of the gospel, which requires a "much sorer punishment." The good Lord bring thee to thy right mind by repentance, lest thou buy thy wit at too dear a rate.

And now, reader, I demand thy resolution. What use wilt thou make of all this? Shall it be lost to thee, or wilt thou consider it in good earnest? Thou hast cast away many a warning of God; wilt thou do so by this also? Take heed; God will not always stand warning and threatening. The hand of vengeance is lifted up, the blow is coming, and

woe to him on whom it lighteth ! Dost thou throw
away the book, and say it speaks of nothing but
hell and damnation ? Thus thou usedst also to
complain of the preacher. But wouldst thou not
have us tell thee of these things ? Should we be
guilty of the blood of thy soul, by keeping silent
that which God hath charged us to make known ?
Wouldst thou perish in ease and silence, and have
us perish with thee, rather than displease thee by
speaking the truth ? If thou wilt be guilty of such
inhuman cruelty, God forbid we should be guilty
of such sottish folly. This kind of preaching or
writing is the ready way to be hated ; and the desire of applause is so natural that few delight in
such a displeasing way. But consider, are these
things true, or are they not ? If they were not
true, I would heartily join with thee against any
that fright people without a cause. But if these
threatenings be the word of God, what a wretch
art thou, that will not hear it and consider it !
If thou art one of the people of God, this doctrine
will be a comfort to thee, and not a terror. If
thou art yet unregenerate, methinks thou shouldst
be as fearful to hear of heaven as hell, except the
bare name of heaven or salvation be sufficient.
Preaching heaven and mercy to thee, is entreating
thee to seek them, and not reject them ; and
preaching hell is but to persuade thee to avoid it.
If thou wert quite past hope of escaping it, then it

were in vain to tell thee of hell; but as long
as thou art alive there is hope of thy recovery,
and therefore all means must be used to awake
thee from thy lethargy. Alas, what heart can
now possibly conceive, or what tongue express, the
pains of these souls that are under the wrath of
God? Then, sinners, you will be crying to Jesus
Christ, "O mercy! O pity, pity on a poor soul!"
Why, I do now, in the name of the Lord Jesus, cry
to thee, "O have mercy, have pity, man, upon thy
own soul!" Shall God pity thee, who will not be
entreated to pity thyself? If thy horse see but a
pit before him, thou canst scarcely force him in;
and wilt thou so obstinately cast thyself into hell,
when the danger is foretold thee? "Who can stand
before the indignation of the Lord, and who can
abide the fierceness of his anger?" Methinks thou
shouldst need no more words, but presently cast
away thy soul-damning sins, and wholly deliver up
thyself to Christ. Resolve on it immediately, and
let it be done, that I may see thy face in rest among
the saints. May the Lord persuade thy heart to
strike this covenant without any longer delay.
But if thou be hardened unto death, and there be
no remedy, yet say not another day but that thou
wast faithfully warned, and hadst a friend that
would fain have prevented thy damnation.

CHAPTER VII

THE NECESSITY OF DILIGENTLY SEEKING THE SAINTS' REST

The saints' rest surprisingly neglected. The author mourns the neglect, and excites the reader to diligence by considering, 1. The ends we aim at, the work we have to do, the shortness and uncertainty of our time, and the diligence of our enemies; 2. Our talents, mercies, relations to God, and our afflictions; 3. What assistance we have, what principles we profess, and our certainty never to do enough; 4. That every grace tends to diligence, and to trifle is lost labor; that much time is misspent, and that our recompense and labor will be proportionable; 5. That striving is the divine appointment; all men do or will approve it; the best Christians, at death, lament their want of it; heaven is often lost for want of it, but never obtained without it; 6. God, Christ, and the Holy Spirit are in earnest; God is so in hearing and answering prayer; ministers in their instructions and exhortations; all the creatures in serving us; sinners in serving the devil, as we were once, and now are, in worldly things, and in heaven and hell all are in earnest.

IF there be so certain and glorious a rest for the saints, why is there no more earnest seeking after it? One would think, if a man did but once hear of such unspeakable glory to be obtained, and believed what he heard, he would be transported with the vehemency of his desire after it, and would almost forget to eat and drink, and would care for nothing else, and speak of and inquire after nothing else, but how to get this treasure. And yet people who hear of it daily, and profess to believe it as a fundamental article of their faith, as little mind it, or labor for it, as if they had never heard of any such thing, or did not believe one word they hear. This reproof is applicable to the worldly-minded, to the profane multitude, to formal professors, and even to the godly themselves.

The *worldly-minded* are so taken up in seeking the things below, that they have neither heart nor time to seek this rest. O foolish sinners, "who hath bewitched you?" The world bewitches men into brute beasts, and draws them even to madness. See what riding and running, what scrambling and catching for a thing of naught, while eternal rest lies neglected. What contriving and caring to get a step higher in the world than their brethren, while they neglect the kingly dignity of the saints. What insatiable pursuit of fleshly pleasures, while they regard the praises of God, the joy of angels, as a tiresome burden. What unwearied diligence in raising their posterity, enlarging their possessions—perhaps for a poor living from hand to mouth—while judgment is drawing near ; but how it shall go with them then, never brings them to one hour's consideration. What rising early and sitting up late, and laboring from year to year to maintain themselves and children in credit till they die ; but what shall follow after they never think. Yet these men cry, "May we not be saved without so much ado?" How early do they rouse up their servants to their labor, but how seldom do they call them to prayer or reading the scriptures! What hath this world done for its lovers and friends, that it is so eagerly followed and painfully sought after, while Christ and heaven are neglected; or what will the world do for them for the time to come? The common entrance into it is through anguish and sorrow. The passage through it is with continual care and labor. The passage out of it is the sharpest of all. O unreasonable, deluded men, will mirth and pleasure stay by you; will gold and worldly glory prove fast friends to you in the time of your greatest need? Will they hear your cries in the day of your calamity? At the hour of your death, will they either answer or relieve you? Will they go along with you to the other world, and bribe the Judge and bring you off clear, or purchase you a place among the blessed? Why then did the rich man want "a drop of water to cool his tongue?" Or are the sweet morsels of present delight and honor of more worth than eternal rest? And will they recompense the loss of that enduring treasure? Can there be the least hope of any of these? Ah, vile, deceitful world, how oft have we heard thy most faithful servants at last complaining, "O, the world hath deceived me and undone me. It flattered me in my prosperity, but now it turns me off in my necessity. If I had as faithfully served Christ as I have served it, he would not have left me thus comfortless and hopeless." Thus they complain; and yet succeeding sinners will take no warning.

As for the *profane multitude*, they will not be persuaded to be at so much pains for salvation as to perform the common outward duties of religion. If they have the gospel preached in the town where they dwell, it may be they will give the hearing to it one part of the day, and stay at home the other ; or if the master come to the congregation, yet part of his family must stay at home. If they have not the plain and powerful preaching of the gospel, how few are there in a whole town who will travel a mile or two abroad to hear, though they will go many miles to the market for provisions for their bodies. They know the Scripture is the law of God, by which they must be acquitted or condemned in the judgment, and that "the man is blessed who delights in the law of the Lord, and in his law doth meditate day and night," yet will they not be at the pains to read a chapter once a day. If they carry a Bible to church, and neglect it all the week, this is the most use they make of it. Though they are commanded to pray without ceasing, and to pray always, yet they will neither pray constantly in their families nor in secret. Though Daniel would rather be cast to the lions than forbear praying three times a day in his house, where his enemies might hear him, yet these men will rather venture to be an eternal prey to Satan the roaring lion, than thus seek their own safety. Or their cold and heartless prayers invite God to a denial; for among men it is taken for granted, that he who asks but slightly and seldom, cares not much for what he asks. They judge themselves unworthy of heaven, who think it not worth their more constant and earnest requests. If every door was marked where families do not, morning and evening, earnestly seek the Lord in prayer, and his wrath were poured out upon such prayerless families, our towns would be as places overthrown by the plague, the people being dead within, and the mark of judgment without; I fear, where one house would escape, ten would be marked out for death; and the very doors, as it were, cry, "Lord, have mercy upon us," because the people would not pray themselves. But especially if we could see what men do in their secret chambers, how few would you find in a whole town that spend one quarter of an hour, morning and night, in earnest supplication to God for their souls. O how little do these men value eternal rest! Thus do they slothfully neglect all endeavors for their own welfare, except some public duty in the congregation, to which custom or credit engages them. Persuade them to read good books, learn the grounds of religion in their catechism, and sanctify the Lord's day in prayer and meditation and hearing the word, forbearing all worldly thoughts and speeches, and what a tedious life do they take this to be ; as if they thought heaven were not worth doing so much for.

Another class are *formal professors*, who will be brought to any outward duty, but to the inward work of religion they will never be persuaded. They will preach, or hear, or read, or talk of heaven, or pray in their families, and take part with the persons or causes that are good, and desire to be esteemed among the godly ; but you can never bring them to the more spiritual duties : as to be constant and fervent in secret prayer and meditation ; conscientious in self-examination ; heavenly-minded ; to watch over their hearts, words, and ways ; to mortify the flesh, and not make provision to fulfil its lusts ; to love and heartily forgive an enemy, and prefer their brethren before themselves ; to lay all they have, or do, at the feet of Christ, and prize his service and favor before all ; to prepare to die, and willingly leave all to go to Christ. Hypocrites will never be persuaded to any of these. If any hypocrite entertains the gospel with joy, it is only in the surface of his soul ; he never gives the seed any depth of earth : it changes his opinions, but never melts and new moulds his heart, nor sets up Christ there in full power and authority. As his religion lies most in opinion, so does his chief business and conversation. He is usually an ignorant, bold, conceited dealer in controversies, rather than an humble embracer of known truth with love and obedience. By his slighting the judgments and persons of others, and seldom talking with seriousness and humility of the great things of Christ, he shows his religion dwells in his brain, and not in his heart. The wind of temptation carries him away as a feather, because his heart is not established with Christ and grace. He never, in private conversation, humbly bewails his soul's imperfections, or tenderly acknowledges his unkindness to Christ; but gathers his greatest comfort from his being of such a persuasion or party. The like may be said of the worldly hypocrite, who chokes the gospel with the thorns of worldly cares and desires. He is convinced that he must be religious, or he cannot be saved; and therefore he reads and hears and prays and forsakes his former company and courses; but he resolves to keep his hold of present things. His judgment may say, God is the chief good, but his heart and affections never said so. The world has more of his affections than God, and therefore it is his god. Though he does not run after opinions and novelties like the world, yet he will be of that opinion which will best serve his worldly advantage. And as one whose spirits are enfeebled by

some pestilential disease, so this man's spirits being
possessed by the plague of a worldly disposition,
how feeble is he in secret prayer; how superficial
in examination and meditation; how poor in heart-
watchings; how nothing at all in loving and walking with God, rejoicing in him, or desiring him!
So that both these and many other sorts of hypocrites, though they will go with you in the easy
outside of religion, yet will never be at the pains of
inward and spiritual duties.

And even the *godly themselves* are too lazy seekers
of their everlasting rest.   Alas, what a disproportion
is there between our light and heat, our profession
and prosecution!   Who makes such haste as if it
were for heaven?   How still we stand; how idly
we work; how we talk and jest and trifle away
our time; how deceitfully we perform the work of
God; how we hear as if we heard not, and pray as
if we prayed not, and examine and meditate and
reprove sin as if we did it not, and enjoy Christ as
if we enjoyed him not; as if we had learned to use
the things of heaven as the apostle teacheth us to
"use the things of the world!"   What a frozen
stupidity has benumbed us!   We are dying, and we
know it, and yet we stir not; we are at the door of
eternal happiness or misery, and yet we perceive it
not; death knocks, and we hear it not; God and
Christ call and cry to us, "To-day, if ye will hear
my voice, harden not your hearts; work while it is

day, for the night cometh, when none can work."
Now ply your business, labor for your lives, lay out
all your strength and time; now or never! and yet
we stir no more than if we were half asleep. What
haste do death and judgment make; how fast do
they come on; they are almost upon us, and yet
what little haste we make! Lord, what a senseless, earthly, hellish thing is a hard heart! Where
is the man that is in earnest a Christian? Methinks men everywhere make but a trifle of their
eternal state. They look after it but a little by the
by; they do not make it the business of their lives.
If I were not sick myself of the same disease, with
what tears should I mix this ink, with what groans
should I express these complaints, and with what
heart-grief should I mourn over this universal
deadness!

Do *magistrates* among us seriously perform their
work? Are they zealous for God? Do they build
up his house? Are they tender of his honor? Do
they second the word, and oppose sin and sinners as
the disturbers of our peace, and the only cause of
all our miseries? Do they improve all their power, wealth, and honor, and all their influence, for
the greatest advantage to the kingdom of Christ,
as men that must shortly give an account of their
stewardship?

How few are the *ministers* who are serious in
their work! Nay, how grievously do the **very**

best fail in this! Do we cry out of men's disobedience to the gospel, "in the demonstration of the
Spirit," and deal with sin as the destroying fire in
our towns, and by force pull men out of it? Do
we persuade our people as those should that "know
the terrors of the Lord?" Do we press Christ and
regeneration and faith and holiness upon men,
believing that, without these, they can never have
life? Do our bowels yearn over the ignorant,
careless, obstinate multitude? When we look them
in the face, do our hearts melt over them, lest we
should never see their faces in rest? Do we, as
Paul, "tell them, weeping," of their fleshly and
earthly disposition; "and teach them publicly, and
from house to house, at all seasons, and with many
tears?" And do we entreat them as for their souls'
salvation? Or rather, do we not study to gain the
approbation of critical hearers; as if a minister's
business were of no more weight but to tell a
smooth tale for an hour, and look no more after
the people till the next sermon? Does not carnal
prudence control our fervor, and make our discourses lifeless on subjects the most piercing?
How gently do we handle those sins which will so
cruelly handle our people's souls. In a word, our
want of seriousness about the things of heaven
charms the souls of men into formality, and brings
them to this customary careless hearing, which
undoes them. May the Lord pardon the great

sin of the ministry in this thing, and, in particular, my own.

And are the *people* more serious than magistrates or ministers ? How can it be expected ? Reader, look but to thyself, and resolve the question. Ask conscience, and suffer it to tell thee truly. Hast thou set thy eternal rest before thine eyes, as the great business thou hast to do in this world ? Hast thou watched and labored with all thy might "that no man take thy crown ?" Hast thou made haste, lest thou shouldst come too late, and die before thy work be done ? Hast thou pressed on, through crowds of opposition, "towards the mark for the prize of the high calling of God in Christ Jesus," still "reaching forth unto those things which are before ?" Can conscience witness your secret cries and groans and tears ? Can your family witness that you taught them the fear of the Lord, and warned them not to "go to that place of torment ?" Can your minister witness that he has heard you cry out, "What shall I do to be saved ?" and that you have followed him with complaints against your corruptions, and with earnest inquiries after the Lord ? Can your neighbors about you witness that you reprove the ungodly, and take pains to save the souls of your brethren ? Let all these witnesses judge this day between God and you, whether you are in earnest about eternal rest. You can tell by his work whether your servant has loitered, though you did not see him; so you may, by looking at your own work. Are your love to Christ, your faith, your zeal, and other graces, strong or weak? What are your joys? What is your assurance? Is all in order with you? Are you ready to die if this should be the day? Do the souls among whom you have conversed bless you? Judge by this, and it will quickly appear whether you have been laborers or loiterers.

O blessed rest, how unworthily art thou neglected! O glorious kingdom, how art thou undervalued! Little know the careless sons of men what a state they so neglect. If they once knew it, they would surely be of another mind. I hope thou, reader, art sensible what a desperate thing it is to trifle about eternal rest, and how deeply thou hast been guilty of this thyself. And I hope, also, thou wilt not suffer this conviction to die. Should the physician tell thee, " If you will observe but one thing, I doubt not to cure your disease," wouldst thou not observe it? So I tell thee, if thou wilt observe but this one thing for thy soul, I make no doubt of thy salvation; shake off thy sloth, and put to all thy strength, and be a Christian indeed: I know not then what can hinder thy happiness. As far as thou art gone from God, seek him with all thy heart, and no doubt thou shalt find him. As unkind as thou hast been to Jesus Christ, seek him heartily, obey him unreservedly, and thy salvation is as sure as if thou hadst it already. But, full as Christ's satisfaction is, free as the promise is, large as the mercy of God is, if thou only talk of these when thou shouldst eagerly entertain them, thou wilt be never the better for them : and if thou loiter when thou shouldst labor, thou wilt lose the crown. Fall to work then speedily and seriously, and bless God that thou hast yet time to do it.

To show that I urge thee not without cause, I will here add a variety of animating considerations. Rouse up thy spirit, and, as Moses said to Israel, "Set thy heart unto all the words which I testify unto thee this day; for it is not a vain thing, because it is thy life." May the Lord open thy heart, and fasten his counsel effectually upon thee !

1. *Consider how reasonable it is that our diligence should be answerable to the ends we aim at, to the work we have to do, to the shortness and uncertainty of our time, and to the contrary diligence of our enemies.*

The *ends* of a Christian's desire and endeavors are so great that no human understanding can comprehend them. What is so excellent, so important, or so necessary as the glorifying of God, the salvation of our own and other men's souls, by escaping the torments of hell and possessing the glory of heaven? And can a man be too much affected with things of such moment? Can he desire them too earnestly, or love them too strongly,

or labor for them too diligently ?   Do not we know
that if our prayers prevail not, and our labor succeeds not, we are undone for ever ?

The *work* of a Christian here is very great and
various.   The soul must be renewed ; corruptions
must be mortified ; customs, temptations, and worldly interests must be conquered ; flesh must be subdued ; life, friends, and credit must be slighted ;
conscience, on good grounds, be quieted; and assurance of pardon and salvation attained.   Though
God must give us these without our merit, yet he
will not give them without our earnest seeking and
labor.   Besides, there is much knowledge to be
acquired, many ordinances to be used, and duties
to be performed ; every age, year, and day, every
place we come to, every person we deal with, every
change of our condition, still require the renewing
of our labor ; wives, children, servants, neighbors,
friends, enemies, all of them call for duty from us.
Judge, then, whether men that have so much business lying upon their hands should not exert themselves, and whether it be their wisdom either to
delay or loiter.

Time passeth on.   Yet a *few days*, and we shall
be here no more.   Many diseases are ready to assault us.   We, that are now preaching and hearing
and talking and walking, must very shortly be carried
and laid in the dust, and there left to the worms, in
darkness and corruption : we are almost there al-

ready; we know not whether we shall have another sermon or Sabbath or hour. How active should they be who know they have so short a space for so great a work. And we have *enemies* that are always plotting and laboring for our destruction. How diligent is Satan in all kinds of temptations! Therefore "be sober, be vigilant; because your adversary the devil, as a roaring lion, walketh about, seeking whom he may devour; whom resist, steadfast in the faith." How diligent are all the "ministers of Satan; false teachers, scoffers, persecutors," and our inbred corruptions, the most busy and diligent of all. Will a feeble resistance serve our turn? Should not we be more active for our own preservation than our enemies are for our ruin?

2. *It should excite us to diligence when we consider our talents and our mercies, our relation to God, and the afflictions he lays upon us.*

The *talents* which we have received are many and great. What people breathing on earth have had plainer instructions or more forcible persuasions or more constant admonitions, in season and out of season; sermons till we have been weary of them, and Sabbaths till we have profaned them; excellent books in such plenty that we knew not which to read? What people have had God so near them, or have seen so much of Christ crucified before their eyes, or have had heaven and hell so open unto them? What speed should such a people make for heaven; how should they fly that are thus winged; and how swiftly should they sail that have wind and tide to help them. A small measure of grace becomes not such a people, nor will an ordinary diligence in the work of God excuse them.

All our lives have been filled with *mercies*. God hath mercifully poured out upon us the riches of sea and land, of heaven and earth. We are fed and clothed with mercy. We have mercies within and without. To number them is to count the stars or the sands of the sea-shore. If there be any difference between hell and earth, yea, or heaven and earth, then certainly we have received mercy. If the blood of the Son of God be mercy, then we are engaged to God by *mercy*. Shall God think nothing too much nor too good for us, and shall we think all too much that we do for him? When I compare my slow and unprofitable life with the frequent and wonderful mercies received, it shames me, it silences me, and leaves me inexcusable.

Besides our talents and mercies, our *relations* to God are most endearing. Are we his children, and do we not owe him our most tender affections and dutiful obedience? Are we "the spouse of Christ," and should we not obey and love him? "If he be a Father, where is his honor; and if he be a Master, where is his fear? We call him Master and

Lord, and we say well;" but if our industry be not answerable to our relations, we condemn ourselves in saying we are his children or his servants. How will the hard labor and daily toil which servants undergo to please their masters, judge and condemn those who will not labor so hard for their great Master. Surely there is no master like him; nor can any servants expect such fruit of their labors as his servants. And if we wander out of God's way, or loiter in it, how is every creature ready to be his rod to bring us back or urge us on. Our sweetest mercies will become our sorrows. Rather than want a rod, the Lord will make us a scourge to ourselves; our diseased bodies shall make us groan; our perplexed minds shall make us restless; our conscience shall be as a scorpion in our bosom. And is it not easier to endure the labor than the spur? Had we rather be still afflicted, than be up and doing? And though they that do most, meet also with afflictions, yet surely, according to their peace of conscience and faithfulness to Christ, the bitterness of their cup is abated.

3. *To quicken our diligence in our work, we should also consider what assistance we have, what principles we profess, and our certainty that we can never do too much.*

For our assistance in the service of God, all the world are our servants. The sun, moon, and stars attend us with their light and influence. The earth, with all its furniture of plants and flowers, fruits, birds, and beasts; the sea, with its inhabitants; the air, the wind, the frost and snow, the heat and fire, the clouds and rain, all wait upon us while we do our work. Yea, "the angels are all our ministering spirits." Nay more, the patience of God doth wait upon us; the Lord Jesus Christ waiteth in the offers of his blood; the Holy Spirit waiteth by striving with our backward hearts; besides the ministers of the gospel, who study and wait, preach and wait, pray and wait upon careless sinners. And is it not an intolerable crime for us to trifle, while angels and men, yea, the Lord himself, stand by and look on, and as it were hold us the candle while we do nothing? I beseech you, Christians, whenever you are praying, or reproving transgressors, or upon any duty, remember what assistance you have for your work, and then judge how you ought to perform it.

The *principles* we profess are, that God is the chief good; that all our happiness consists in his love, and therefore it should be valued and sought above all things; that he is our only Lord, and therefore chiefly to be served: that we must love him with all our heart and soul and strength; that our great business in the world is to glorify God and obtain salvation. Are these doctrines seen in our practice; or rather, do not our works deny what our words confess?

But, however our assistance and principles excite us to our work, we are sure *we can never do too much.* Could we "do all, we are unprofitable servants;" much more when we are sure to fail in all. No man can obey or serve God too much. Though all superstition, or service of our own devising, may be called a "being righteous overmuch," yet, as long as we keep to the rule of the word, we can never be righteous too much. The world are mad with malice when they think that faithful diligence in the service of Christ is foolish singularity. The time is near when they will easily confess that God could not be loved or served too much, and that no man can be too earnest to save his soul. We may easily do too much for the world, but we cannot for God.

4. Let us further consider *that it is the nature of every grace to promote diligence, that trifling in the way to heaven is lost labor, that much precious time is already misspent, and that in proportion to our labor will be our recompense.*

See *the nature and tendency* of every grace. If you loved God, you would think nothing too much that you could possibly do to serve him and please him. Love is quick and impatient, active and observant. If you loved Christ, you would keep his commandments, nor accuse them of too much strictness. If you had faith, it would quicken and encourage you. If you had the hope of glory, it would, as the spring in the watch, set all the wheels of your souls agoing. If you had the fear of God, it would rouse you out of your slothfulness. If you had zeal, it would inflame and "eat you up." In what degree soever thou art sanctified, in the same degree thou wilt be serious and laborious in the work of God.

They that trifle lose their labor. Many who, like Agrippa, are but almost Christians, will find, in the end, they shall be but almost saved. If two be running in a race, he that runs slowest loses both prize and labor. A man that is lifting at a weight, if he put not sufficient strength to it, had as good put none at all. How many duties have Christians lost for want of doing them thoroughly. "Many will seek to enter in, and shall not be able," who, if they had striven, might have been able. Therefore, put to a little more diligence and strength, that all you have done already be not in vain.

Besides, is not *much precious time already lost?* With some of us childhood and youth are gone; with some their middle age also; and the time before us is very uncertain. What time have we slept, talked, and played away, or spent in worldly thoughts and cares! How little of our work is done! The time we have lost cannot be recalled; should we then not redeem and improve the little which remains? If a traveller sleep or trifle most of the day, he must travel so much faster in the evening, or fall short of his journey's end.

Doubt not but the *recompense will be according to your labor.* The seed which is buried and dead will bring forth a plentiful harvest. Whatever you do or suffer, everlasting rest will pay for all. There is no repenting of labors or sufferings in heaven. There no one says, "Would I had spared my pains, and prayed less, or been less strict, and done as the rest of my neighbors." On the contrary, it will be their joy to look back upon their labors and tribulations, and to consider how the mighty power of God brought them through all. We may all say, as Paul, "I reckon that the sufferings" and labors "of this present time are not worthy to be compared with the glory which shall be revealed in us." We labor but for a moment; we shall rest for ever. Who would not put forth all his strength for one hour, when for that hour's work he may be a prince while he lives? "God is not unrighteous to forget our work and labor of love" Will not "all our tears be wiped away," and all the sorrow of our duties be then forgotten?

5. Nor does it less deserve to be considered, that *striving is the divinely appointed way of salvation; that all men either do, or will approve it; that the best Christians, at death, lament their negligence; and that heaven itself is often lost for want of striving, but is never had on easier terms.*

The sovereign wisdom of God has made *striving* necessary to salvation. Who knows the way to heaven better than the God of heaven? When men tell us we are too strict, whom do they accuse, God or us? If it were a fault, it would lie in him that commands, and not in us who obey. These are the men that ask us whether we are wiser than all the world besides; and yet they will pretend to be wiser than God. How can they reconcile their language with the laws of God? "The kingdom of heaven suffereth violence, and the violent take it by force. Strive to enter in at the strait gate; for many will seek to enter in, and shall not be able. Whatsoever thy hand findeth to do, do it with thy might; for there is no work, nor device, nor knowledge, nor wisdom in the grave, whither thou goest. Work out your own salvation with fear and trembling. Give diligence to make your calling and election sure. If the righteous scarcely be saved, where shall the ungodly and the sinner appear?" Let them bring all the seeming reasons they can against the holy violence of the saints; this sufficeth me to confute them all, that God is of another mind, and that he hath commanded me to do much more than I do; and though I could see no other reason for it, his will is reason enough. Who should make laws for us, but he that made us; and who should point out the way to heaven, but he that must bring us thither; and who should fix

the terms of salvation, but he that bestows the gift
of salvation? So that, let the world, the flesh, or
the devil speak against a holy, laborious life, this is
my answer, God hath commanded it. Nay, there
never was, nor ever will be, a man but will *approve*
such a life, and will one day justify the diligence
of the saints. And who would not go that way
which every man shall finally applaud? True, it
is now a way "everywhere spoken against." But
let me tell you, most that speak against it, in their
judgments approve of it; and those that are now
against it will shortly be of another mind. If they
come to heaven, their mind must be changed before
they come there. If they go to hell, their judgment will then be altered whether they will or not.
Remember this, you that love the opinion and way
of the multitude. Why then will you not be of the
opinion that all will be of? Why will you be of a
judgment which you are sure, all of you, shortly to
change? O that you were but as wise in this as
those in hell.

Even *the best of Christians, when they come to
die, exceedingly lament their negligence.* They
then wish, "O that I had been a thousand times
more holy, more heavenly, more laborious for my
soul! The world accuses me for doing too much,
but my own conscience accuses me for doing too
little. It is far easier bearing the scoffs of the
world than the lashes of conscience. I had rather

be reproached by the devil for seeking salvation, than reproved of God for neglecting it." How do their failings thus wound and disquiet those who have been the wonder of the world for their heavenly conversation.

It is *for want of diligence that heaven itself is lost.* When they that have "heard the word, and anon with joy received it, and have done many things, and heard" the ministers of Christ gladly, shall yet perish, should not this rouse us out of our security? How far hath many a man followed Christ, and yet forsaken him when all worldly interests and hopes were to be renounced. God hath resolved that heaven shall not be had on easier terms. Rest must always follow labor. "Without holiness no man shall see the Lord." Seriousness is the very thing wherein consists our sincerity. If thou art not serious, thou art not a Christian. It is not only a high degree in Christianity, but the very life and essence of it. As fencers upon a stage differ from soldiers fighting for their lives, so hypocrites differ from serious Christians. If men could be saved without this serious diligence, they would never regard it; all the excellencies of God's ways would never entice them. But when God hath resolved that, without serious diligence here, we shall not rest hereafter, is it not wisdom to exert ourselves to the uttermost?

6. But to persuade thee, if possible, reader,

to be serious in thy endeavors for heaven, let me add more considerations : as, for instance, consider,

God is in earnest with you, and why should you not be so with him? In his commands, his threatenings, his promises, he means as he speaks. In his judgments he is serious. Was he not so when he drowned the world, when he consumed Sodom and Gomorrah, and when he scattered the Jews ? Is it time, then, to trifle with God ? Jesus Christ was serious in purchasing our redemption. In teaching, he neglected his meat and drink : in prayer, he continued all night : in doing good, his friends thought him beside himself : in suffering, he fasted forty days, was tempted, betrayed, spit upon, buffeted, crowned with thorns, sweat drops of blood, was crucified, pierced, died. There was no jesting in all this. And should we not be serious in seeking our own salvation ?

The Holy Spirit is serious in soliciting us to be happy. His motions are frequent, pressing, and importunate. "He striveth with us." He is grieved when we resist him ; and should we not be serious, then, in obeying and yielding to his motions ? God is serious in hearing our prayers and bestowing his mercies. He is afflicted with us. He "regardeth every groan and sigh, and puts every tear into his bottle." The next time thou art in trouble thou wilt beg for a serious regard of thy prayers. And shall we expect real mercies, when we are slight and superficial in the work of God?

The ministers of Christ are serious in exhorting and instructing you. They beg of God, and of you; and long more for the salvation of your souls than for any worldly good. If they kill themselves by their labor, or suffer martyrdom for preaching the gospel, they think their lives are well bestowed, so that they prevail for the saving of your souls. And shall other men be so careful and self-denying for your salvation, and you be so careless and negligent of your own?

How diligent and serious are all the creatures in serving you! What haste makes the sun to compass the world. The fountains are always flowing for thy use; the rivers still running; spring and harvest keep their times. How hard does thy ox labor for thee from day to day; how speedily does thy horse travel with thee. And shalt thou only be negligent? Shall all these be so serious in serving thee, and thou so careless in thy service to God?

The servants of the world and the devil are serious and diligent. They work as if they could never do enough; they make haste, as if afraid of coming to hell too late; they bear down ministers, sermons, and all before them. And shall they be more diligent for damnation than thou for salvation? Hast thou not a better Master, sweeter employment, greater encouragements, and a better reward? Time was when thou wast serious thyself in serving Satan and the flesh, if it be not so yet. How eagerly didst thou follow thy sports, thy evil company, and sinful delights. And wilt thou not now be as earnest and violent for God? You are to this day in earnest about the things of this life. If you are sick or in pain, what serious complaints do you utter. If you are poor, how hard do you labor for a livelihood. And is not the business of your salvation of far greater moment?

There is no jesting in heaven or hell. The saints have a real happiness, and the damned a real misery. There are no remiss or sleepy praises in heaven, nor such lamentations in hell. All there are in earnest. When thou, reader, shalt come to death and judgment, O what deep, heart-piercing thoughts wilt thou have of eternity! Methinks I foresee thee already astonished to think how thou couldst possibly make so light of these things. Methinks I even hear thee crying out of thy stupidity and madness.

And now, reader, having laid down these undeniable arguments, I do, in the name of God, *demand thy resolution:* wilt thou yield obedience or not? I am confident thy conscience is convinced of thy duty. Darest thou now go on in thy common, careless course, against the plain evidence of reason and commands of God, and against the light of thy own conscience? Darest thou live as loosely, sin as boldly, and pray as seldom as before? Darest thou profane the Sabbath, slight the service of God, and think of thine everlasting state as carelessly as before? Or dost thou not rather resolve to "gird up the loins of thy mind," and set thyself wholly to the work of thy salvation, and break through the oppositions, and slight the scoffs and persecutions of the world, and "lay aside every weight and the sin which doth so easily beset thee, and run with patience the race that is before thee?" I hope these are thy full resolutions. Yet, because I know the obstinacy of the heart of man, and because I am solicitous that thy soul should live, I entreat thy attention to the following questions: and I command thee from God, that thou stifle not thy conscience nor resist conviction; but answer them faithfully, and obey accordingly.

If, by being diligent in godliness, you could grow rich, get honor or preferment in the world, be recovered from sickness, or live for ever in prosperity on earth, what lives would you lead, and what pains would you take in the service of God? And is not the saints' rest a more excellent happiness than all this? If it were felony to break the Sabbath, neglect secret or family worship, or be loose in your lives, what manner of persons would you then be? And is not eternal death more terrible than temporal? If God usually punished with

some present judgment every act of sin, as he did
the lie of Ananias and Sapphira, what kind of lives
would you lead? And is not eternal wrath far
more terrible? If one of your acquaintance should
come from the dead and tell you that he suffered
the torments of hell for those sins you are guilty of,
what manner of persons would you be afterwards?
How much more should the warnings of God affright
you. If you knew that this were the last day you
had to live in the world, how would you spend it?
And you know not but it may be your last, and are
sure your last is near. If you had seen the general
dissolution of the world, and all the pomp and glory
of it consumed to ashes, what would such a sight
persuade you to do? Such a sight you shall certainly see. If you had seen the judgment-seat and
the books opened, and the wicked stand trembling
on the left hand of the Judge, and the godly rejoicing on the right hand, and their different sen-
tences pronounced, what persons would you have
been after such a sight? This sight you shall one
day surely see. If you had seen hell open, and all
the damned there in their endless torments; also
heaven opened, as Stephen did, and all the saints
there triumphing in glory, what a life would you
lead after such sights? These you will see before
it be long. If you had lain in hell but one year, or
one day or hour, and there felt the torments you
now hear of, how seriously would you then speak

of hell, and pray against it. And will you not take God's word for the truth of this, except you feel it? Or, if you had possessed the glory of heaven but one year, what pains would you take rather than be deprived of such incomparable glory.

Thus I have said enough, if not to stir up the sinner to a serious working out his salvation, yet at least to silence him, and leave him inexcusable at the judgment of God. Only as we do by our friends when they are dead, and our words and actions can do them no good, yet to testify our affection for them we weep and mourn, so will I also do for these unhappy souls. It makes my heart tremble to think how they will stand before the Lord confounded and speechless. When he shall say, "Was the world or Satan a better friend to you than I, or had they done for you more than I had done? Try now whether they will save you, or recompense you for the loss of heaven, or be as good to you as I would have been"—what will the wretched sinner answer to any of this? But though man will not hear, we may hope in speaking to God:

"O thou that didst weep and groan in spirit over a dead Lazarus, pity these dead and senseless souls, till they are able to weep and groan in pity to themselves. As thou hast bid thy servants speak, so speak now thyself. They will hear thy voice speaking to their hearts, who will not hear mine speaking to their ears. Lord, thou hast knocked long at these hearts in vain ; now break the doors and enter in."

To show the godly why they, above all men, should be laborious for heaven, I desire to ask them, What manner of persons should those be whom God hath chosen to be vessels of mercy ; who have felt the smart of their negligence in their new birth, in their troubles of conscience, in their doubts and fears, and in other sharp afflictions ; who have often confessed their sins of negligence to God in prayer ; who have bound themselves to God by so many covenants ? What manner of persons should they be who are near to God as the children of his family ; who have tasted such sweetness in diligent obedience ; who are many of them so uncertain what shall everlastingly become of their souls ? What manner of persons should they be in holiness, whose sanctification is so imperfect ; whose lives and duties are so important to the saving or destroying a multitude of souls ; and on whom the glory of the great God so much depends ? Since these things are so, I charge thee, Christian, in thy Master's name, to consider and resolve the question, "What manner of persons ought we to be in all holy conversation and godliness ?" And let thy life answer the question as well as thy tongue.

CHAPTER VIII

HOW TO DISCERN OUR TITLE TO THE SAINTS' REST

Self-examination urged, 1. From the possibility of arriving
at a certainty; 2. From the hinderances which will be
thrown in our way by Satan, sinners, our own hearts, and
many other causes; 3. From considering how easy, common, and dangerous it is to be mistaken; that trying will
not be so painful as the neglect; that God will soon try
us, and that to try ourselves will be profitable. 4. Directions how to try ourselves. 5. Marks for trial, particularly,
Do we make God our chief good? Do we heartily accept
of Christ for our Lord and Saviour?

Is there such a glorious rest so near at hand,
and shall none enjoy it but the people of God?
What mean most of the world, then, to live so contentedly without assurance of their interest in this
rest, and neglect the trying of their title to it?
When the Lord has so fully opened the blessedness
of that kingdom which none but obedient believers
shall possess, and so fully expressed those torments
which the rest of the world must eternally suffer,
methinks they that believe this to be certainly true
should never be at any quiet in themselves till they
are fully assured of their being heirs of the kingdom.
Lord, what a strange madness is this, that men who
know they must presently enter upon unchangeable
joy or pain, should yet live as uncertain what shall

be their doom as if they had never heard of any
such state ; yea, and live as quietly and merrily in
this uncertainty as if all were made sure, and there
were no danger ! Are these men alive or dead ;
are they awake or asleep ? What do they think
on ? Where are their hearts ? If they have but a
weighty suit at law, how careful are they to know
whether it will go for or against them. If they
were to be tried for their lives at an earthly bar,
how careful would they be to know whether they
should be saved or condemned, especially if their
care might surely save them. If they be danger-
ously sick, they will inquire of the physician,
"What think you, sir ; shall I escape or not ?"
But in the business of their salvation they are content to be uncertain.

If you ask of most men "a reason of the hope
that is in them," they will say, "Because God is
merciful, and Christ died for sinners," and the like
general reasons, which any man in the world may
give as well as they ; but put them to prove their
interest in Christ and in the saving mercy of God,
and they can say nothing to the purpose. If God
or man should say to one of them, "Friend, what
is the state of thy soul ? Is it regenerate, sanctified,
and pardoned, or not ?" He would say as Cain of
Abel, "I know not ; am I my soul's keeper ? I
hope well ; I trust God with my soul ; I shall speed
as well as other men do ; I thank God I never made

any doubt of my salvation." Thou hast cause **to**
doubt because thou didst never doubt, and yet more
because thou hast been so careless in thy confidence.
What do thy expressions discover but a wilful neglect of thy own salvation; as a shipmaster that
should let his vessel alone, and say, "I will venture it among the rocks and waves and winds; I
will trust God with it; it will speed as well as
other vessels." What horrible abuse of God is this,
to pretend to trust God to cloak their own wilful
negligence. If thou didst really trust God, thou
wouldst also be ruled by him, and trust him in his
own appointed way. He requires thee to give
"diligence to make thy calling and election sure,"
and so trust him. He hath marked out a way in
Scripture by which thou art charged to search and
try thyself, and mayest arrive at certainty. Were
he not a foolish traveller that would hold on his
way when he does not know whether he be right
or wrong, and say, "I hope I am right; I will go
on, and trust in God?" Art thou not guilty of
this folly in thy travel to eternity; not considering that a little serious inquiry whether thy way
be right might save thee a great deal of labor,
which thou bestowest in vain, and must undo
again, or else thou wilt miss of salvation and undo
thyself?

How canst thou think or speak of the great God
without terror, as long as thou art uncertain wheth-

er he be thy father or thy enemy, and knowest
not but all his perfections may be employed against
thee; or of Jesus Christ, when thou knowest not
whether his blood hath purged thy soul, whether
he will condemn or acquit thee in judgment; or
whether he be the foundation of thy happiness, or
a stone of stumbling to break thee and grind thee
to powder? How canst thou open the Bible and
read a chapter, but it should terrify thee? Methinks every leaf should be to thee as Belshazzar's
writing on the wall, except only that which draws
thee to try and reform. If thou readest the promises, thou knowest not whether they shall be fulfilled to thee. If thou readest the threatenings, for
any thing thou knowest thou readest thy own sentence. No wonder thou art an enemy to plain
preaching, and sayest of the minister, as Ahab of
the prophet, "I hate him; for he doth not prophesy
good concerning me, but evil." How canst thou
without terror join in prayer? When thou receivest the Lord's supper, thou knowest not whether it
be thy bane or bliss. What comfort canst thou
find in thy friends and honors and houses and lands,
till thou knowest thou hast the love of God with
them, and shalt have rest with him when thou
leavest them? Offer a prisoner, before he knows
his sentence, either music, or clothes, or preferment;
what are they to him till he knows he shall escape
with his life? for if he knows he must die the next

day, it will be small comfort to die rich or honorable. Methinks it should be so with thee till thou
knowest thy eternal state. When thou liest down
to take thy rest, methinks the uncertainty of thy
salvation should keep thee waking, or amaze thee
in thy dreams and trouble thy sleep. Doth it not
grieve thee to see the people of God so comfortable
in their way to glory, when thou hast no good hope
of ever enjoying it thyself? How canst thou think
of thy dying hour? Thou knowest it is near, and
there is no avoiding it, nor any remedy found out
that can prevent it. If thou shouldst die this day—
and who knows "what a day may bring forth?"—
thou art not certain whether thou shalt go to heaven
or hell. And canst thou be merry till thou hast
escaped from this dangerous state? What shift dost
thou make to preserve thy heart from horror, when
thou rememberest the great judgment day, and
everlasting flames? When thou hearest of it, dost
thou not tremble as Felix? If the "keepers shook,
and became as dead men, when they saw the angel
come and roll back the stone from Christ's sepulchre," how canst thou think of living in hell with
devils, till thou hast some well-grounded assurance
that thou shalt escape it? Thy bed is very soft,
or thy heart is very hard, if thou canst sleep soundly
in this uncertain case.

If this general uncertainty of the world about
their salvation were remediless, then must it be

borne as other unavoidable miseries. But alas, the common cause is wilful negligence. Men will not be persuaded to use the remedy. The great means to conquer this uncertainty is self-examination, or the serious and diligent trying of a man's heart and state by the rule of Scripture. Either men understand not the nature and use of this duty, or else they will not be at the pains to try. Go through a congregation of a thousand men, and how few of them will you find that ever bestowed one hour in all their lives in a close examination of their title to heaven. Ask your own conscience, reader, when was the time, and where was the place, that ever you solemnly took your heart to task, as in the sight of God, and examined it by Scripture whether it be renewed or not; whether it be holy or not; whether it be set most on God or the creatures, on heaven or earth. And when did you follow on this examination till you had discovered your condition, and pass sentence on yourself accordingly?

But since this is a work of so high importance, and so commonly neglected, I will show that it is possible, by trying, to come to a certainty; then show what hinders men from trying and knowing their state; and then offer motives to examine, and directions, together with some marks out of Scripture by which men may try, and certainly know whether they are the people of God or not.

1. Scripture shows that *the certainty of salvation*

may be attained, and ought to be labored for, when
it tells us so frequently that the saints before us
have known their justification and future salvation ; when it declares that "whosoever believeth
in Christ shall not perish, but have everlasting
life ;" which it would be vain to declare, if we cannot know ourselves to be believers or not ; when it
makes such a wide difference between the children
of God and the children of the devil ; when it bids
us "give diligence to make our calling and election
sure ;" and earnestly urges us to "examine, prove,
know our own selves, whether we be in the faith,
and whether Jesus Christ be in us, or we be repro-
bates ;" also, when its precepts require us to rejoice
always, to call God our Father, to live in his
praises, to love Christ's appearing, to wish that he
may come quickly, and to comfort ourselves with
the mention of it. But who can do any of these
heartily, that is not, in some measure sure that he
is the child of God ?

2. Among the many *hinderances* which keep
men from self-examination, we cannot doubt but
Satan will do his part. If all the power he hath,
or all the means and instruments he can employ
can do it, he will be sure, above all duties, to keep
you from this. He is loath that the godly should
have the joy, assurance, and advantage against
corruption, which the faithful performance of self-
examination would procure them. As for the

ungodly, he knows if they should once earnestly examine, they would find out his deceits and their own danger, and so be very likely to escape him. How could he get so many millions to hell willingly, if they knew they were going thither? And how could they avoid knowing it, if they did but thoroughly examine, having such a clear light and sure rule in the Scripture to discover it? If the snare be not hid, the bird will escape it. Satan knows how to angle for souls better than to show them the hook and line, or fright them away with a noise, or with his own appearance. Therefore he labors to keep them from a searching ministry; or to keep the minister from helping them to search; or to take off the edge of the word, that it may not pierce and divide; or to turn away their thoughts; or to possess them with prejudice. Satan knows when the minister has provided a searching sermon, fitted to the state and necessity of a hearer; and therefore he will keep him away that day, if it be possible, or cast him into a sleep, or steal away the word by the cares and talk of the world, or some way prevent its operation.

Another great hinderance to self-examination arises from wicked men. Their example, their merry company and discourse, their continually insisting on worldly concerns, their raillery and scoffs at godly persons; also their persuasions, allurements, and threats, are all of them exceed-

ingly great temptations to security. God doth
scarcely ever open the eyes of a poor sinner to see
that his way is wrong, but presently there is a multitude of Satan's apostles ready to deceive and
settle him again in the quiet possession of his
former master.

"What," say they, "do you make a doubt of
your salvation, who have lived so well, and done
nobody any harm? God is merciful; and if such
as you shall not be saved, God help a great many.
What do you think of all your forefathers? And
what will become of all your friends and neighbors
that live as you do? Will they all be damned?
Come, come, if you hearken to these preachers they
will drive you out of your senses. Are not all men
sinners, and did not Christ die to save sinners?
Never trouble your head with these thoughts, and
you shall do well."

O, how many thousands have such charms kept
asleep in deceit and security till death and hell
have awakened them. The Lord calls to the sinner,
and tells him, "The gate is strait, the way is narrow, and few find it; try and examine yourself;
give diligence to make sure." The world cries,
"Never doubt, never trouble yourself with these
thoughts." In this strait, sinner, consider it is
Christ, and not your forefathers, or neighbors, or
friends, that must judge you at last; and if Christ
condemn you, these cannot save you; therefore

common reason may tell you that it is not from the words of ignorant men, but from the word of God, you must gain your hope of salvation. When Ahab would inquire among the multitude of flattering prophets, it was his death. They can flatter men into the snare, but they cannot tell how to bring them out. " Let no man deceive you with vain words ; for because of these things cometh the wrath of God upon the children of disobedience : be not ye therefore partakers with them."

But the greatest hinderances are in men's own hearts. Some are so ignorant that they know not what self-examination is, nor what a minister means when he persuades them to try themselves ; or they know not that there is any necessity for it, but think every man is bound to believe that his sins are pardoned, whether it be true or false, and that it is a great fault to make any question of it ; or they do not think that assurance can be attained ; or that there is any great difference between one man and another, but that we are all Christians, and therefore need not trouble ourselves any further ; or at least they know not wherein the difference lies. They have as gross an idea of regeneration as Nicodemus had. Some will not believe that God will ever make such a difference between men in the life to come, and therefore will not search themselves whether they differ here. Some are so stupefied, say what we can to them, that they lay it not to heart, but give us the hearing, and there is the end. Some are so possessed with self-love and pride, that they will not so much as suspect they are in danger : like a proud tradesman, who scorns the prudent advice of casting up his books ; or like fond parents, who will not believe or hear any evil of their children. Some are so guilty that they dare not try themselves, and yet they dare venture on a more dreadful trial. Some are so in love with sin, and so dislike the way of God, that they dare not try their ways, lest they be forced from the course they love to that which they loathe. Some are so resolved never to change their present state, that they neglect examination as a useless thing. Before they will seek a new way, when they have lived so long and gone so far, they will put their eternal state to hazard, come of it what will. Many men are so busy in the world that they cannot set themselves to the trying of their title to heaven. Others are so clogged with slothfulness of spirit that they will not be at the pains of an hour's examination of their own hearts. But the most common and dangerous impediment is that false faith and hope, commonly called presumption, which bears up the hearts of the greatest part of the world, and so keeps them from suspecting their danger.

And if a man should break through all these hinderances, and set upon the duty of self-examination, yet assurance is not presently attained. Too many deceive themselves in their inquiries after it, through one or other of the following causes: there is such confusion and darkness in the soul of man, especially of an unregenerate man, that he can scarcely tell what he does, or what is in him. As in a house where nothing is in its proper place, it will be difficult to find what is wanted, so it is in the heart where all things are in disorder. Most men accustom themselves to be strangers at home, and too little observe the temper and motions of their own hearts. Many are resolved what to judge before they try; like a bribed judge, who examines as if he would judge uprightly, when he is previously resolved which way the cause shall go. Men are partial in their own cause; ready to think their great sins small, and their small sins none; their gifts of nature to be the work of grace, and to say, "All these have I kept from my youth;" "I am rich, and increased in goods, and have need of nothing." Most men search but by the halves. If it will not easily and quickly be done, they are discouraged, and leave off. They try themselves by false marks and rules, not knowing wherein the truth of Christianity consists; some looking beyond, and some short of the scripture standard. And frequently they fail in this work by attempting it in their own strength. As some expect the Spirit should do it without them, so others attempt it themselves, without seeking or expecting the help of the Spirit. Both these will certainly fail of assurance.

Some other hinderances keep even true Christians from comfortable certainty. As, for instance, *the weakness of grace.* Small things are hardly discerned. Most Christians content themselves with a small measure of grace, and do not follow on to spiritual strength and manhood. The chief remedy for such would be to follow on in duty till their graces be increased. Wait upon God in the use of his prescribed means, and he will undoubtedly bless you with increase. O that Christians would bestow most of that time in getting more grace, which they bestow in anxious doubtings whether they have any or none ; and lay out those serious affections in praying for more grace, which they bestow in fruitless complaints. I beseech thee, Christian, take this advice as from God; and then, when thou believest strongly, and lovest fervently, thou canst no more doubt of thy faith and love, than a man that is very hot can doubt of his warmth, or a man that is strong and vigorous can doubt of his being alive.

Christians hinder their own comfort by looking more at signs which tell them *what they are*, than at precepts which tell them *what they should do :* as if their present must needs be their everlasting state ; and if they be now unpardoned, there were no remedy. Were he not mad that would lie weeping because he is not pardoned, when his prince stands by all the while offering him a pardon, and persuading him to accept of it? Justifying faith, Christian, is not thy persuasion of God's special love to thee, but thy accepting Christ to make thee lovely. It is far better to accept Christ as offered, than spend so much time in doubting whether we have Christ or not.

Another cause of distress to Christians is their mistaking *assurance* for the *joy* that sometimes accompanies it: as if a child should think himself a son no longer than while he sees the smiles of his father's face, or hears the comfortable expressions of his mouth; and as if the father ceased to be a father whenever he ceased those smiles and speeches.

The trouble of souls is also increased by their not knowing *the ordinary way of God's conveying comfort*. They think they have nothing to do but to wait when God will bestow it. But they must know that the matter of their comfort is in the promises, and thence they must draw it as often as they expect it, by daily and diligently meditating upon the promises; and in this way they may expect the Spirit will communicate comfort to their souls. The joy of the promises and the joy of the Holy Ghost are one: add to this their expecting a greater measure of assurance than God usually bestows. As long as they have any doubting, they think they have no assurance. They consider not that there are many degrees of certainty. While they are here, they shall "know but in part." Add also their deriving their comfort at first from insufficient grounds. This may be the case of a gracious soul, who hath better grounds, but doth not see them. As an infant hath life before he knoweth it, and many misapprehensions of himself and other things, yet it will not follow that he hath no life. So when Christians find a flaw in their first comforts, they are not to judge it a flaw in their safety.

Many continue doubting through the exceeding weakness of their natural powers. Many honest hearts have weak heads, and know not how to perform the work of self-trial. They will acknowledge the premises, and yet deny the apparent conclusion. If God do not some other way supply the defect of their reason, I see not how they should have clear and settled peace.

One great and too common cause of distress is the secret maintaining of *some known sin*. This abates the degree of our graces, and so makes them more undiscernible. It obscures that which it destroys not; for it bears such sway that grace is not in action, nor seems to stir, nor is scarce heard speak, for the noise of this corruption. It puts out or dims the eye of the soul, and stupefies it, that it can neither see nor feel its own condition. But especially it provokes God to withdraw himself, his comforts, and the assistance of his Spirit, without which we may search long enough before we have assurance. God hath made a separation between sin and peace. As long as thou dost cherish thy pride, thy love of the world, the desires of the flesh, or any unchristian practice, thou expectest comfort in vain. If a man "setteth up his idols in his heart, and putteth the stumbling-block of his iniquity before his face, and cometh" to a minister, or to God, "to inquire" for comfort, instead of comforting him, God "will answer him that cometh according to the multitude of his idols."

Another very great and common cause of the want of comfort is, that grace is not kept in *constant* and lively exercise. The way of painful duty is the way of fullest comfort. Peace and comfort are Christ's great encouragements to faithfulness and obedience; and therefore, though our obedience does not merit them, yet they usually rise and fall with our diligence in duty. As prayer must have faith and fervency to procure it success, besides the blood and intercession of Christ, so must all other parts of our obedience. If thou growest seldom and formal and cold in duty, especially in thy secret prayers to God, and yet findest no abatement in thy joys, I cannot but fear thy joys are either carnal or diabolical. Besides, grace is never apparent and sensible to the soul but while it is in action; there-

fore want of action must cause want of assurance.
And the action of the soul upon such excellent
objects naturally bringeth consolation with it. The
very act of loving God, in Christ, is inexpressibly
sweet. The soul that is best furnished with grace,
when it is not in action is like a lute well stringed
and tuned, which, while it lieth still, maketh no
more music than a common piece of wood; but
when it is handled by a skilful musician, the melody
is delightful. Some degree of comfort follows every
good action, as heat accompanies fire, and as beams
and influence issue from the sun. A man that is
cold should labor till heat be excited; so he that
wants assurance must not stand still, but exercise
his graces till his doubts vanish.

The want of consolation in the soul is also very
commonly owing to *bodily melancholy*. It is no
more strange for a conscientious man, under melancholy, to doubt and fear and despair, than for a
sick man to groan, or a child to cry when it is chastised. Without the physician in this case, the labors
of the divine are usually in vain. You may silence,
but you cannot comfort such persons. You may
make them confess they have some grace, and yet
cannot bring them to the comfortable conclusion.
All the good thoughts of their state which you can
possibly help them to, are seldom above a day or
two old. They cry out of sin and the wrath of
God, when the chief cause is in their bodily disease.

3. As *motives* to the duty of self-examination, I entreat you to consider the following.

To be deceived about your title to heaven is very *easy*. Many are now in hell that never suspected any falsehood in their hearts, that excelled in worldly wisdom, that lived in the clear light of the gospel, and even preached against the negligence of others. To be mistaken in this great point is also very *common*. It is the case of most in the world. In the old world, and in Sodom, we find none that were in any fear of judgment. Almost all men among us verily expect to be saved; yet Christ tells us, "there be few that find the strait gate and narrow way which leadeth unto life." And if such multitudes are deceived, should we not search the more diligently, lest we should be deceived as well as they? Nothing is more dangerous than to be thus mistaken. If the godly judge their state worse than it is, the consequences of this mistake will be sorrowful; but the mischief flowing from the mistake of the ungodly is unspeakable. It will exceedingly confirm them in the service of Satan. It will render ineffectual the means that should do them good. It will keep a man from compassionating his own soul. It is a case of the greatest moment, where everlasting salvation or damnation is to be determined. And if you mistake till death, you are *undone for ever*. Seeing then the danger is so great, what wise man would not follow the search

of his heart both day and night till he were assured
of his safety? Consider how small the labor of
this duty in comparison with that sorrow which follows its neglect. You can endure to toil and sweat
from year to year to prevent poverty; and why not
spend a little time in self-examination, to prevent
eternal misery? By neglecting this duty you can
scarce do Satan a greater pleasure, or yourself a
greater injury. It is the grand design of the devil,
in all his temptations, to deceive you, and keep you
ignorant of your danger till you feel the everlasting
flames; and will you join with him to deceive yourself? If you do this for him, you do the greatest
part of his work. And hath he deserved so well of
you, that you should assist him in such a design as
your damnation? The time is nigh when God will
search you. If it be but in this life by affliction, it
will make you wish that you had tried and judged
yourself, that you might have escaped the judgment
of God. It was a terrible voice to Adam, "Where
art thou? Hast thou eaten of the tree?" And to
Cain, "Where is thy brother?" Men "consider not
in their hearts that I," saith the Lord, "remember
all their wickedness; now their own doings have
beset them about; they are before my face."

Consider also what would be *the sweet effects* of
this self-examination. If thou be upright and
godly, it will lead thee straight towards assurance
of God's love; if thou be not, though it will trouble

thee at the present, yet it will tend to thy happiness, and at length lead thee to the assurance of that happiness. Is it not a desirable thing to know what shall befall us hereafter; especially what shall befall our souls, and what place and state we must be in for ever? And as the very knowledge itself is desirable, how much greater will the comfort be of that certainty of salvation. What sweet thoughts wilt thou have of God. All that greatness and justice which is the terror of others will be thy joy. How sweet may be thy thoughts of Christ, and the blood he hath shed, and the benefits he hath procured. How welcome will the word of God be to thee, and how beautiful the very feet of those that bring it. How sweet will be the promises when thou art sure they are thine own. The very threatenings will occasion thy comfort, to remember that thou hast escaped them. What boldness and comfort mayest thou then have in prayer, when thou canst say, "Our Father," in full assurance. It will make the Lord's supper a refreshing feast to thy soul. It will multiply the sweetness of every common mercy. How comfortably mayest thou then undergo all afflictions. How will it sweeten thy forethoughts of death and judgment, of heaven and hell. How lively will it make thee in the work of the Lord, and how profitable to all around thee. What vigor will it infuse into all thy graces and affections. How will it kindle thy repentance, inflame thy love, quicken thy desires, and confirm thy faith; be a fountain of continual rejoicing, overflow thy heart 'with thankfulness, raise thee high in the delightful work of praise, help thee to be heavenly-minded, and render thee persevering in all. All these sweet effects of assurance would make thy life a heaven upon earth.

Though I am certain these motives have weight of reason in them, yet I am jealous, reader, lest you lay aside the book as if you had no more to do, and never set yourself to the practice of the duty. The case in hand is of the greatest moment—whether thou shalt everlastingly live in heaven or hell. I here request thee, in behalf of thy soul, nay, I charge thee, in the name of the Lord, that thou defer no longer, but take thy heart to task in good earnest, and think with thyself, "Is it so easy, so common, and so dangerous to be mistaken? Are there so many wrong ways? Is the heart so deceitful? Why then do I not search into every corner till I know my state? Must I shortly undergo the trial at the bar of Christ, and do I not now try myself? What a case were I in, should I then fail of salvation. May I know by a little diligent inquiry now, and do I refuse the labor?"

But perhaps you will say, "I know not how to do it." In that I am now to give thee directions; but, alas, it will be in vain, if thou art not resolved to practise them. Wilt thou, therefore, before thou goest any further, here promise, before the Lord, to set thyself upon the speedy performance of the duty, according to the directions. I shall lay down from the word of God? I demand nothing unreasonable or impossible: it is but to bestow a few hours to know what shall become of thee for ever. If a neighbor or a friend desired but an hour's time of thee, in conversation or business, or any thing in which thou mayest be of service, surely thou wouldst not deny it; how much less shouldst thou deny this to thyself in so great a matter. I pray thee to take from me this request as if, in the name of Christ, I presented it to thee on my knees; and I will betake me on my knees to Christ again, to beg that he will persuade thy heart to the duty.

4. The *directions how to examine thyself* are such as these: Empty thy mind of all other cares and thoughts, that they may not distract or divide thy mind. This work itself will be enough without joining others with it. Then fall down before God in hearty prayer, desiring the assistance of his Spirit to discover to thee the plain truth of thy condition, and to enlighten thee in the whole progress of this work. Make choice of the most convenient time and place. Let the place be the most private, and the time when you have nothing to interrupt you; and, if possible, let it be the present time. Have in readiness, either in memory or writing,

some scriptures, containing the descriptions of the saints and the gospel terms of salvation; and convince thyself thoroughly of their infallible truth. Proceed then to put the question to thyself. Let it not be, whether there be any good in thee at all, nor whether thou hast such or such a degree and measure of grace; but whether such or such *a saving grace* be in thee in sincerity or not. If thy heart draw back from the work, force it on. Lay thy command upon it. Let reason interpose, and use its authority. Yea, lay the command of God upon it, and charge it to obey, upon the pain of his displeasure. Let conscience also do its office, till thy heart be excited to the work. Nor let thy heart trifle away the time, when it should be diligently at the work. Do as the psalmist: "My spirit made diligent search." He that can prevail with his own heart shall also prevail with God. If, after all thy pains, thou art still in doubt, then seek out for help. Go to one that is godly, experienced, able, and faithful, and tell him thy case, and desire his best advice. Use the judgment of such a one as that of a physician for thy body: though this can afford thee no full certainty, yet it may be a great help to stay and direct thee. But do not make it a pretence to put off thy own self-examination. Only use it as one of the last remedies, when thy own endeavors will not serve. When thou hast discovered thy true state, pass sentence on thyself accordingly; either that thou art a true Christian, or that thou art not. Pass not this sentence rashly, nor with self-flattery nor with melancholy terrors; but deliberately, truly, and according to thy conscience, convinced by Scripture and reason. Labor to get thy heart affected with its condition, according to the sentence passed on it. If graceless, think of thy misery ; if renewed and sanctified, think what a blessed state the Lord hath brought thee into. Pursue these thoughts till they have left their impression on thy heart. Write this sentence at least in thy memory : "At such a time, upon thorough examination, I found my state to be thus or thus." Such a record will be very useful to thee hereafter. Trust not to this one discovery, so as to try no more ; nor let it hinder thee in the daily search of thy ways; neither be discouraged if the trial must be often repeated. Especially take heed, if unregenerate, not to conclude of thy future state by the present. Do not say, "Because I am ungodly, I shall die so ; because I am a hypocrite, I shall continue so." Do not despair. Nothing but thy unwillingness can keep thee from Christ, though thou hast hitherto abused him and dissembled with him.

5. Now let me add some *marks* by which you may try your title to the saints' rest. I will only mention these two : taking God for thy chief good, and heartily accepting Christ for thy only Saviour and Lord.

Every soul that hath a title to this rest *places his chief happiness in God.* This rest consists in the full and glorious enjoyment of God. He that makes not God his chief good and ultimate end is in heart a pagan and a vile idolater. Let me ask, then, dost thou truly account it thy chief happiness to enjoy the Lord in glory, or dost thou not? Canst thou say, "The Lord is my portion? Whom have I in heaven but thee? and there is none upon earth that I desire besides thee." If thou be an heir of rest, it is thus with thee. Though the flesh will be pleading for its own delights, and the world will be creeping into thine affections, yet in thy ordinary, settled, prevailing judgment and affections, thou preferrest God before all things in the world. Thou makest him the very end of thy desires and endeavors. The very reason why thou hearest and prayest, and desirest to live on earth, is chiefly this, that thou mayest seek the Lord, and make sure of thy rest. Though thou dost not seek it so zealously as thou shouldst, yet it hath the chief of thy desires and endeavors, so that nothing else is desired or preferred before it. Thou wilt think no labor or suffering too great to obtain it. And though the flesh may sometimes shrink, yet thou art resolved and ready to go through all. Thy esteem for it will also be so high, and thy affection to it so great, that thou wouldst not exchange thy title to it, and hopes of it, for any worldly good whatsoever. If God should set before thee an eternity of earthly pleasure on the one hand, and the saints' rest on the other, and bid thee take thy choice, thou wouldst refuse the world and choose this rest. But if thou art yet unsanctified, then thou dost in thy heart prefer thy worldly happiness before God; and though thy tongue may say that God is thy chief good, yet thy heart doth not so esteem him, for the world is the chief end of thy desires and endeavors. Thy very heart is set upon it. Thy greatest care and labor is to maintain thy credit or fleshly delights. But the life to come hath little of thy care or labor. Thou didst never perceive so much excellency in the unseen glory of another world, as to draw thy heart after it, and bring thee to labor heartily for it. The little pains thou bestowest for it is but a secondary effort. God hath but the world's leavings: only that time and labor which thou canst spare from the world, or those few cold and careless thoughts which follow thy constant, earnest, and delightful thoughts of earthly things. Neither wouldst thou do any thing at all for heaven, if thou knewest how to keep the world. But lest thou shouldst be turned into hell when thou canst keep the world no longer, therefore thou wilt do something. For the same reason, thou thinkest the way of God too strict, and wilt not be persuaded to the constant labor of walking according to the gospel rule; and when it comes

to the trial, that thou must forsake Christ or **thy**
worldly happiness, then thou wilt venture heaven
rather than earth, and so wilfully deny thy obedience to God. And certainly, if God would but
give thee leave to live in health and wealth for
ever on earth, thou wouldst think it a better
state than the rest of heaven—let them seek for
heaven that would, thou wouldst think this thy
chief happiness. This is thy case, if thou art yet
an unregenerate person, and hast no title to the
saints' rest.

And as thou takest God for thy chief good, so
thou dost heartily *accept of Christ* for thy only
Saviour and Lord, to bring thee to this rest. The
former mark was the sum of the first and great
command of the law, " Thou shalt love the Lord
thy God with all thy heart." The second mark is
the sum of the command of the gospel, " Believe in
the Lord Jesus Christ and thou shalt be saved."
And the performance of these two is the whole of
godliness and Christianity. This mark is but the
definition of faith. Dost thou heartily consent that
Christ alone shall be thy Saviour, and no further
trust to thy duties and works than as means appointed in subordination to him; not looking at
them as in the least measure able to satisfy the
curse of the law, or as a legal righteousness or any
part of it; but consent to trust thy salvation on the
redemption made by Christ? Art thou also con-

tent to take him for thy only Lord and King, to govern and guide thee by his laws and Spirit, and to obey him even when he commandeth the hardest duties, and those which most cross the desires of the flesh ? Is it thy sorrow when thou breakest thy resolution herein, and thy joy when thou keepest closest in obedience to him? Wouldst thou not change thy Lord and Master for all the world? Thus is it with every true Christian. But if thou be a hypocrite, it is far otherwise. Thou mayest call Christ thy Lord and thy Saviour, but thou never foundest thyself so lost without him as to drive thee to seek him and trust him, and lay thy salvation on him alone; at least, thou didst never heartily consent that he should govern thee as thy Lord, nor resign thy soul and life to be ruled by him, nor take his word for the law of thy thoughts and actions. Doubtless thou art willing to be saved from hell by Christ when thou diest; but, in the meantime, he must command thee no further than will consist with thy credit or pleasure or other worldly ends. And if he would give thee leave, thou hadst far rather live after the world and the flesh than after the word and the Spirit. And though thou mayest now and then have a motion or purpose to the contrary, yet this that I have mentioned is the ordinary desire and choice of thy heart. Thou art therefore no true believer in Christ; for though thou confess him in words, yet in works thou dost deny him, " being abominable and disobedient, and unto every good work reprobate." This is the case with those that shall be shut out of the saints' rest.

Observe, it is *the consent of the heart*, or will, which I especially lay down to be inquired after. I do not ask whether thou be assured of salvation, nor whether thou canst believe that thy sins are pardoned, and that thou art beloved of God in Christ. These are no parts of justifying faith, but excellent fruits of it, and they that receive them are comforted by them; but perhaps thou mayest never receive them while thou livest, and mayest yet be a true heir of rest. Do not say then, "I cannot believe that my sins are pardoned, or that I am in God's favor; and therefore I am no true believer." This is a most mistaken conclusion. The question is, whether thou dost heartily accept of Christ, that thou mayest be pardoned, reconciled to God, and so saved. Dost thou consent that He shall be thy Lord who hath bought thee, and that he shall bring thee to heaven in his own way? This is justifying, saving faith, and the mark by which thou must try thyself. Yet still observe that all this consent must be hearty and real, not feigned or with reservations. It is not like that of the dissembling son, who said, "I go, sir; and went not." If any have more of the government of thee than Christ, thou art not his disciple. I am sure these two marks are such as every Christian hath, and none but sincere Christians. O that the Lord would now persuade thee to the close performance of this self-trial, that thou mayest not tremble with horror of soul when the Judge of the world shall try thee ; but be able so to prove thy title to rest, that the prospect and approach of death and judgment may raise thy spirits and fill thee with joy.

On the whole, if Christians would have comforts that will not deceive them, let them make it the great labor of their lives to grow in grace, to strengthen and advance the interest of Christ in their souls, and to weaken and subdue the interest of the flesh. Deceive not yourselves with a persuasion that Christ hath done all, and left you nothing to do. To overcome the world, the flesh, and the devil, and, in order to that, to stand always armed upon our watch, and valiantly and patiently to fight it out, is of great importance to our assurance and salvation. Indeed, it is so great a part of our baptismal obligations, that he who performeth it not is no more than a nominal Christian. Not to every one that presumptuously believeth, but "to him that overcometh, will Christ give to eat of the hidden manna ; and will give him a white stone, and in the stone a new name written, which no man knoweth, saving he that receiveth it : he shall eat of the tree of life which is in the midst of the paradise of God, and shall not be hurt of the second death. Christ will confess his name before his Father, and be ›re his angels, and make him a pillar in the temple of God, and he shall go no more out ; and will write upon him the name of his God, and the name of the city of his God, which is New Jerusalem, which cometh down out of heaven from his God, and will write upon him his new name." Yea, " He will grant to him to sit with him on his throne, even as he also overcame, and is set down with his Father on his throne. He that hath an ear, let him hear what the Spirit saith unto the churches."

CHAPTER IX

THE DUTY OF THE PEOPLE OF GOD TO EXCITE OTHERS TO SEEK THIS REST

The author laments that Christians do so little to help others
to obtain the saints' rest: I. Shows the nature of this
duty; particularly, 1. In having our hearts affected with
the misery of our brethren's souls; 2. In taking all opportunities to instruct them in the way of salvation; 3. In
promoting their profit by public ordinances. II. Assigns
various reasons why this duty is so much neglected, and
answers some objections against it. III. Urges to the
discharge of it, by several considerations: 1. Addressed
to such as have knowledge, learning, and utterance;
2. Those that are acquainted with sinners; 3. Physicians
that attend dying men; 4. Persons of wealth and power;
5. Ministers; 6. And those that are intrusted with the
care of children or servants. The chapter concludes with
an earnest request to Christian parents to be faithful to
their trust.

HATH God set before us such a glorious prize as
the saints' rest, and made us capable of such inconceivable happiness? Why, then, do not all the
children of this kingdom exert themselves more to
help others to the enjoyment of it? Alas, how
little are poor souls about us beholden to most of
us! We see the glory of the kingdom, and they do
not; we see the misery of those that are out of it,
and they do not; we see some wandering quite out
of the way, and know, if they hold on, they can

never come there, and they themselves discern it
not. And yet we will not seriously show them
their danger and error, and help to bring them into
the way, that they may live. Alas, how few
Christians are there to be found who set themselves
with all their might to save souls! No thanks to
us, if heaven be not empty, and if the souls of our
brethren perish not for ever. Considering how important this duty is to the glory of God and the
happiness of men, I will show—how it is to be
performed ; why it is so much neglected ; and then
offer some considerations to persuade to it.

First. THE DUTY *of exciting and helping others
to discern their title to the saints' rest.* This does
not mean that every man should turn a public
preacher, or that any should go beyond the bounds
of their particular calling ; much less does it consist in promoting a party spirit ; and, least of all,
in speaking against men's faults behind their backs,
and being silent before their faces. This duty is of
another nature, and consists of the following things:
in having our hearts affected with the misery of our
brethren's souls, in taking all opportunities to instruct them in the way of salvation, and in promoting their profit by public ordinances.

1. Our *hearts must be affected* with the misery of
our brethren's souls. We must be compassionate
towards them, and yearn after their recovery and
salvation. If we earnestly longed for their conver-

sion, and our hearts were solicitous to do them good, it would set us at work, and God would usually bless it.

2. We must take *every opportunity* that we possibly can to instruct them how to attain salvation. If the person be ignorant, labor to make him understand the chief happiness of man; how far he was once possessed of it; the covenant God then made with him; how he broke it, and what penalty he incurred; and into what misery he brought himself. Teach him his need of a Redeemer; how Christ mercifully interposed, and bore the penalty; what the new covenant is; how men are drawn to Christ; and what are the riches and privileges which believers have in him. If he is not moved by these things, then show him the excellency of the glory he neglects; the extremity and eternity of the torments of the damned; the justice of enduring them for wilfully refusing grace; the certainty, nearness, and terrors of death and judgment; the vanity of all things below; the sinfulness of sin; the preciousness of Christ; the necessity of regeneration, faith, and holiness, and their true nature. If, after all, you find him entertaining false hopes, then urge him to examine his state; show him the necessity of doing so; help him in it; nor leave him till you have convinced him of his misery and remedy. Show him how vain and destructive it is to join Christ and his duties to

compose his justifying righteousness. Yet be sure
to draw him to the use of all means; such as hearing and reading the word, calling upon God, and
associating with the godly; persuade him to forsake sin, avoid all temptations to sin, especially
evil companions, and to wait patiently on God in
the use of means, as the way in which God will be
found.

But, because the manner of performing this work
is of great moment, observe therefore these rules:
Enter upon it with *right intentions*. Aim at the
glory of God in the person's salvation. Do it not
to get a name or esteem to thyself, or to bring
men to depend upon thee, or to get thee followers;
but in obedience to Christ, in imitation of him, and
tender love to men's souls. Do not as those who
labor to reform their children or servants from such
things as are against their own profit or humor, but
never seek to save their souls in the way which God
has appointed. Do it speedily. As you would not
have them delay their return, do not you delay to
seek their return. While you are purposing to teach
and help him, the man goes deeper in debt; wrath
is heaping up; sin taking root; custom fastens
him; temptations to sin multiply; conscience grows
seared; the heart hardened; the devil rules;
Christ is shut out; the Spirit is resisted; God is
daily dishonored; his law violated; he is robbed of
that service which he should have; time runs on;

death and judgment are at the door; and what if the man die, and drop into hell while you are purposing to prevent it. If, in the case of his bodily distress, you "must not say to him, go and come again, and to-morrow I will give, when thou hast it by thee;" how much less may you delay the succor of his soul. That physician is no better than a murderer, who negligently delays till his patient be dead or past cure. Lay by excuses, then, and all lesser business, and "exhort one another daily, while it is called to-day, lest any be hardened through the deceitfulness of sin." Let your exhortation proceed from compassion and love. To jeer and scoff, to rail and vilify, is not a likely way to reform men, or convert them to God. Go to poor sinners with tears in your eyes, that they may see you believe them to be miserable, and that you unfeignedly pity their case. Deal with them with earnest, humble entreaties. Let them perceive it is the desire of your heart to do them good; that you have no other end but their everlasting happiness; and that it is your sense of their danger, and your love to their souls, that forces you to speak; even because you "know the terrors of the Lord," and for fear you should see them in eternal torments. Say to them, "Friend, you know I seek no advantage of my own; the method to please you, and keep your friendship, were to soothe you in your way, or let you alone; but love will not suffer me to see you perish, and be silent. I seek nothing at your hands but that which is necessary to your own happiness. It is yourself that will have the gain and comfort if you come to Christ." If we were thus to go to every ignorant and wicked neighbor, what blessed fruit should we quickly see.

Do it with all possible *plainness and faithfulness.* Do not make their sins less than they are, nor encourage them in a false hope. If you see the case dangerous, speak plainly : " Neighbor, I am afraid God has not yet renewed your soul; I fear you are not yet recovered 'from the power of Satan to God;' I fear you have not chosen Christ above all, nor unfeignedly taken him for your sovereign Lord. If you had, surely you durst not so easily disobey him, nor neglect his worship in your family and in public ; you could not so eagerly follow the world, and talk of nothing but the things of the world. If you were 'in Christ,' you would be 'a new creature ; old things' would be 'passed away, and all things' would 'become new.' You would have new thoughts, new conversation, new company, new endeavors, and a new life. Certainly without these you can never be saved ; you may think otherwise, and hope otherwise as long as you will, but your hopes will all deceive you, and perish with you." Thus must you deal faithfully with men, if ever you intend to do them good. It is not in curing men's souls, as in curing their bodies, where they must not know their danger, lest it hinder the cure. They are here agents in their own cure; and if they know not their misery, they will never bewail it, nor know their need of a Saviour.

Do it also *seriously, zealously, and effectually.* Labor to make men know that heaven and hell are not matters to be played with, or passed over with a few careless thoughts. "It is most certain that, one of these days, thou shalt be in everlasting joy or torment; and doth it not awaken thee? Are there so few that find the way of life, so many that go the way of death? Is it so hard to escape, so easy to miscarry; and yet you sit still and trifle? What do you mean? The world is passing away; its pleasures, honors, and profits are fading and leaving you; eternity is a little before you; God is just and jealous; his threatenings are true; the great day will be terrible; time runs on; your life is uncertain; you are far behindhand; your case is dangerous; if you die to-morrow, how unready are you. With what terror will your soul leave the body. And do you yet loiter? Consider, God is all this while waiting your leisure; his patience beareth; his long-suffering forbeareth; his mercy entreateth you; Christ offereth you his blood and merits; the Spirit is persuading; conscience is accusing; Satan waits to have you. This is your time; now or never. Had you rather burn in hell than repent on earth; have devils your tormentors

than Christ your governor? Will you renounce
your part in God and glory, rather than renounce
your sins? O friends, what do you think of these
things? God hath made you men; do not renounce
your reason where you should chiefly use it." Alas,
it is not a few dull words between jest and earnest,
between sleeping and waking, that will rouse a
dead-hearted sinner. If a house be on fire, you will
not make a cold oration on the nature and danger
of fire, but will run and cry, Fire, fire! To tell a
man of his sins as softly as Eli did his sons, or to
reprove him as gently as Jehoshaphat did Ahab,
"Let not the king say so," usually does as much
harm as good. Loathness to displease men makes
us undo them.

Yet, lest you run into extremes, I advise you to
do it with *prudence and discretion*. Choose the
fittest season. Deal not with men when they are
in a passion, or where they will take it for a disgrace. When the earth is soft the plough will
enter. Take a man when he is under affliction, or
newly impressed under a sermon. Christian faithfulness requires us not only to do good when it falls
in our way, but to watch for opportunities. Suit
yourself also to the quality and temper of the person. You must deal with the ingenious more by
argument than persuasion. There is need of both
to the ignorant. The affections of the convinced
should be chiefly excited. The obstinate must be

sharply reproved. The timorous must be dealt with
tenderly. Love and plainness and seriousness take
with all; but words of terror some can hardly bear.
Use also the aptest expressions. Unseemly language makes the hearers loathe the food they should
live by, especially if they be men of curious ears
and carnal hearts.

Let all your reproofs and exhortations be backed
with *the authority of God.* Let sinners be convinced that you speak not merely your own thoughts.
Turn them to the very chapter and verse where their
sin is condemned and their duty commanded. The
voice of man is contemptible, but the voice of God
is awful and terrible. They may reject your words
who dare not reject the words of the Almighty.

Be frequent with men in this duty of exhortation.
If we are "always to pray, and not to faint," because God will have us importunate with himself,
the same course, no doubt, will be most prevailing
with men. Therefore we are commanded "to
exhort one another daily," and "with all long-suffering." The fire is not always brought out of the
flint at one stroke; nor men's affections kindled at
the first exhortation; and if they were, yet if they
be not followed, they will soon grow cold again.
Follow sinners with your loving and earnest entreaties, and give them no rest in their sin. This is
true charity, the way to save men's souls, and will
afford you comfort upon review.

Strive to bring all your exhortations *to an issue.* If we speak the most convincing words, and all our care is over with our speech, we shall seldom prosper in our labors; but God usually blesses their labors whose very heart is set upon the conversion of their hearers, and who are therefore inquiring after the success of their work. If you reprove a sin, cease not till the sinner promises you to leave it and avoid the occasions of it. If you are exhorting to a duty, urge for a promise to enter upon it without delay. If you would draw men to Christ, leave them not till they are brought to confess the misery of their present unregenerate state, and the necessity of Christ and of a change, and have promised you to be faithful in the use of means. O that all Christians would take this course with all their neighbors that are enslaved to sin, and strangers to Christ.

Once more, be sure *your example* exhort as well as your words. Let them see you constant in all the duties to which you persuade them. Let them see in your life that superiority to the world which your lips recommend. Let them see, by your constant labors for heaven, that you indeed believe what you would have them believe. A holy and heavenly life is a continual sting to the consciences of sinners around you, and continually solicits them to change their course.

3. Besides the duty of private admonition, you

must endeavor to *help men to profit by public ordinances.* In order to that, endeavor to procure for
them faithful ministers where they are wanting.
"How shall they hear without a preacher?" Improve your interest and diligence to this end till
you prevail. Extend your purposes to the utmost.
How many souls may be saved by the ministry you
have procured. It is a higher and nobler charity
than relieving their bodies. What abundance of
good might great men do, if they would support, in
academical education, such youth as they have first
carefully chosen for their talents and piety, till they
should be fit for the ministry; and when a faithful
ministry is obtained, help poor souls to receive the
fruit of it—draw them constantly to attend it—
remind them often what they have heard, and, if
it be possible, let them hear it repeated in their
families or elsewhere—promote their frequent meeting together besides publicly in the congregation,
not as a separate church, but as a part of the church
more diligent than the rest in redeeming time and
helping the souls of each other heavenward. Labor
also to keep the ordinances and ministry in esteem:
no man will be much wrought on by that which
he despiseth. An apostle says, "We beseech you,
brethren, to know them who labor among you, and
are over you in the Lord, and admonish you; and
to esteem them very highly in love, for their works'
sake."

Secondly, let us inquire what may be the CAUSES
OF THE GROSS NEGLECT *of this duty; that the hinderances, being discovered, may the more easily be
overcome.*

One hinderance is men's *own sin and guilt.*
They have not themselves been ravished with
heavenly delights; how then should they draw
others so earnestly to seek them? They have not
felt their own lost condition, nor their need of
Christ, nor the renewing work of the Spirit; how
then can they discover these to others? They are
guilty of the sins they should reprove, and this
makes them ashamed to reprove.

Another is, *a secret infidelity* prevailing in men's
hearts. Did we verily believe that all the unregenerate and unholy shall be eternally tormented,
how could we refrain from speaking, or avoid burst-
ing into tears, when we look them in the face,
especially when they are our near and dear friends?
Thus doth secret unbelief consume the vigor of each
grace and duty. O Christian, if you did verily
believe that your ungodly neighbors, wife, husband,
or child, should certainly lie for ever in hell, except
they be thoroughly changed before death shall
snatch them away, would not this make you address them day and night till they were persuaded?
Were it not for this cursed unbelief, our own and
our neighbors' souls would gain more by us than
they do.

These attempts are also much hindered by our want of charity and *compassion for men's souls.* We look on miserable souls, and pass by, as the priest and Levite by the wounded man. What though the sinner, wounded by sin and captivated by Satan, do not desire thy help himself; yet his misery cries aloud. If God had not heard the cry of our miseries before he heard the cry of our prayers, and been móved by his own pity before he was moved by our importunity, we might long have continued the slaves of Satan. You will pray to God for them, to open their eyes and turn their hearts ; and why not endeavor their conversion, if you desire it ? And if you do not desire it, why do you ask it ? Why do you not pray them to consider and return, as well as pray to God to convert and turn them? If you should see your neighbor fallen into a pit, and should pray God to help him out. but neither put forth your hand to help him, nor once direct him to help himself, would not any man censure you for your cruelty and hypocrisy ? It is as true of the soul as of the body. If any man "seeth his brother have need, and shutteth up his bowels of compassion from him, how dwelleth the *love of God in him;*" or what love hath he to his brother's soul ?"

We are also hindered by a base *man-pleasing* disposition. We are so desirous to keep in credit and favor with men, that it makes us most unreasonably

neglect our own duty. He is a foolish and unfaith-
ful physician that will let a sick man die for fear
of troubling him. If our friends are deranged, we
please them in nothing that tends to their hurt.
And yet when they are beside themselves in point
of salvation, and in their madness posting on to
damnation, we will not stop them for fear of displeasing them. How can we be Christians, that
"love the praise of men more than the praise of
God?" For if we "seek to please men, we shall
not be the servants of Christ."

It is common to be hindered by sinful *bashfulness.*
When we should shame men out of their sins, we
are ourselves ashamed of our duties. May not
these sinners condemn us, when they blush not to
swear, be drunk, or neglect the worship of God;
and we blush to tell them of it, and persuade
them from it? Bashfulness is unseemly in cases
of necessity. It is not a work to be ashamed of, to
obey God in persuading men from their sins to
Christ. Reader, hath not thy conscience told thee
of thy duty many a time, and urged thee to speak
to poor sinners; and yet thou hast been ashamed
to open thy mouth, and so let them alone to sink or
swim? O read and tremble: "Whosoever shall be
ashamed of me, and of my words, in this adulterous and sinful generation, of him also shall the Son
of man be ashamed, when he cometh in the glory
of his Father, with the holy angels."

An *idle and impatient* spirit hindereth us. It is an ungrateful work, and sometimes makes men our enemies. Besides, it seldom succeeds at the first, except it be followed on. You must be long in teaching the ignorant, and persuading the obstinate. We consider not what patience God used towards us when we were in our sins. Woe to us, if God had been as impatient with us as we are with others.

Another hinderance is *self-seeking.* "All seek their own, not the things which are Jesus Christ's," and their brethren's. With many, *pride* is a great impediment. If it were to speak to a great man, and it would not displease him, they would do it; but to go among the poor, and take pairs with them in their cottages, where is the person that will do it? Many will rejoice in being instrumental to convert a gentleman, and they have good reason, but overlook the multitude, as if the souls of all were not alike to God. Alas, these men little consider how low Christ stooped to us! Few rich and noble and wise are called. It is the poor that receive the glad tidings of the gospel. And with some, their ignorance of the duty hindereth them from performing it; either they know it not to be a duty, or at least not to be their duty. If this be thy case, reader, I am in hope thou art now acquainted with thy duty, and wilt enter upon it.

Do not object to this duty, that you are *unable*

to manage an exhortation ; but either set those at
the work who are more able, or faithfully and
humbly use the small ability you have, and tell
them, as a weak man may do, what God says in
his word.   Decline not the duty because it is your
superior who needs advice and exhortation.   Order must be dispensed with in cases of necessity
Though it be a husband, a parent, a minister, you
must teach him in such a case.   If parents are in
want, children must relieve them.   If a husband
be sick, the wife must fill up his place in family
affairs.   If the rich are reduced to beggary, they
must receive charity.   If the physician be sick,
somebody must look to him.   Thus the meanest
servant must admonish his master, and the child
his parent, and the wife her husband, and the people their minister ; so that it be done when there is
real need, and with all possible humility, modesty,
and meekness.   Do not say, this will make us all
preachers ; for every good Christian is a teacher,
and has a charge of his neighbor's soul.   Every
man is a physician, when a regular physician cannot be had, and when the hurt is so small that any
man may relieve it ; and in the same cases every
man must be a teacher.   Do not despair of success
Cannot God give it ?   And must it not be by means ?
Do not plead, it will only be casting pearls before
swine.   When you are in danger to be torn in
pieces, Christ would have you forbear ; but what

is that to you who are in no such danger? As long
as they will hear, you will have encouragement to
speak, and may not cast them off as contemptible
swine. Say not, "It is a friend on whom I much
depend; and by telling him his sin and misery, I
may lose his love, and be undone." Is his love
more to be valued than his safety; or thy own
benefit by him, than the salvation of his soul; or
wilt thou connive at his damnation because he is
thy friend? Is that thy best requital of his friendship? Hadst thou rather he should burn in hell
for ever, than thou shouldst lose his favor, or the
maintenance thou hast from him?

Thirdly. But that all who fear God may be
excited to do their utmost to help others to this
blessed rest, *let me entreat you to consider the following* MOTIVES: As, for instance, not only *nature*,
but especially *grace*, disposes the soul to be com-
municative of good; therefore, to neglect this work
is a sin both against nature and grace. Would you
not think him unnatural who would suffer his children or neighbors to starve in the streets, while he
has provision at hand? And is not he more unnatural who will let them eternally perish, and not
open his mouth to save them? An unmerciful,
cruel man, is a monster to be abhorred of all. If
God had bid you give them all your estate, or lay
down your life to save them, you would surely have
refused, when you will not bestow a little breath

to save them. Is not the soul of a husband, or wife, or child, or neighbor worth a few words? Cruelty to men's bodies is a most damnable sin ; but to their souls much more, as the sou is of greater worth than the body, and eternity th ı time. Little know you what many a soul may n v be feeling in hell, who died in their sins for want of your faithful admonition.

Consider *what Christ did* towards the saving of souls. He thought them worth his blood ; and shall we not think them worth our breath ? Will you not do a little where Christ hath done so much ? Consider what fit objects of pity ungodly people are. They are dead in trespasses and sins, have not hearts to feel their miseries, nor to pity themselves. If others do not pity them, they will have no pity ; for it is the nature of their disease to make them pitiless to themselves, yea, their own most cruel destroyers. Consider, it was once thy own case. It was God's argument to the Israelites to be kind to strangers, because they themselves had been " strangers in the land of Egypt." So should you pity them that are strangers to Christ, and to the hopes and comforts of the saints, because you were once strangers to them yourselves. Consider your relation to them. It is thy neighbor, thy brother, whom thou art bound to love as thyself. He that loveth not his brother, whom he seeth daily, doth not love God whom he never saw. And doth he love his brother that will see him go to hell, and never hinder him?

Consider what *a load of guilt* this neglect lays upon thy own soul. Thou art guilty of the murder and damnation of all those souls whom thou dost thus neglect; and of every sin they now commit, and of all the dishonor done to God thereby; and of all these judgments which their sins bring upon the town or country where they live. Consider what it will be to look upon your poor friends in eternal flames, and to think that your neglect was a great cause of it. If you should there perish with them, it would be no small aggravation of your torment. If you be in heaven, it would surely be a sad thought, were it possible that any sorrow could dwell there, to hear a multitude of poor souls cry out, for ever, "O, if you would but have told me plainly of my sin and danger, and set it home, I might have escaped all this torment, and be now in rest!" What a sad voice will this be! Consider what a joy it will be in heaven, to meet those there whom you have been the means to bring thither; to see their faces, and join with them for ever in the praises of God, whom you were the happy instruments of bringing to the knowledge and obedience of Jesus Christ. Consider how many souls you may have drawn into the way of damnation, or hardened in it. We have had, in the days of our ignorance, our companions in sin, whom we

enticed or encouraged. And doth it not become us
to do as much to save men as we have done to
destroy them? Consider how diligent are all the
enemies of these poor souls to draw them to hell.
The devil is tempting them day and night; their
inward lusts are still working for their ruin; the
flesh is still pleading for its delights; their old
companions are increasing their dislike of holiness.
And if nobody be diligent in helping them to heav-
en, what is like to become of them?

Consider how deep the neglect of this duty will
wound *when conscience is awakened*. When a man
comes to die, conscience will ask him, "What good
hast thou done in thy lifetime? The saving of
souls is the greatest good work; what hast thou
done towards it? How many hast thou dealt faithfully with?" I have often observed that the consciences of dying men very much wounded them
for this omission. For my own part, when I have
been near death, my conscience hath accused me
more for this than for any sin; it would bring every
ignorant, profane neighbor to my remembrance, to
whom I never made known their danger; it would
tell me, "Thou shouldst have gone to them in private, and told them plainly of their desperate danger, though it had been when thou shouldst have
eaten or slept, if thou hadst no other time." Conscience would remind me how, at such or such a
time, I was in company with the ignorant, or riding

by the way with a wilful sinner, and had a fit opportunity to have dealt with him, but did not, or at least did it to little purpose. The Lord grant I may better obey conscience while I have time, that it may have less to accuse me of at death. Consider what a seasonable time you now have for this work. There are times in which it is not safe to speak; it may cost you your liberty or your life. Besides, your neighbors will shortly die, and so will you. Speak to them, therefore, while you may. Consider, though this is a work of the greatest charity, yet every one of you may perform it; the poorest as well as the rich : every one hath a tongue to speak to a sinner.

Once more, consider *the happy consequences* of this work where it is faithfully done. You may be instrumental in saving souls, for whom Christ came down and died, and in whom the angels of God rejoice. Such souls will bless you here and hereafter; God will have much glory by it; the church will be multiplied and edified by it; your own soul will enjoy more improvement and vigor in the divine life, more peace of conscience, more rejoicing in spirit. Of all the personal mercies that I ever received, next to the love of God in Christ to my own soul, I must most joyfully bless him for the plentiful success of my endeavors upon others. O what fruits, then, might I have seen, if I had been more faithful! I know we need to be

very jealous of our deceitful hearts on this point,
lest our rejoicing should come from our pride.
Naturally we would have the praise of every good
work ascribed to ourselves; yet to imitate our
Father in goodness and mercy, and to rejoice in
the degree of them we attain to, is the duty of
every child of God. I therefore tell you my own
experience, to persuade you that, if you did but
know what a joyful thing it is, you would follow
it, night and day, through the greatest discourage-
ments.

Up, then, every man that hath a tongue, and is
a servant of Christ, and do something of your Master's work. Why hath he given you a tongue, but
to speak in his service? And how can you serve
him more eminently than in laboring for the salvation of souls? He that will pronounce you blessed
at the last day, and invite you to "the kingdom
prepared for you," because you "fed him and
clothed him and visited him," in his poor members, will surely pronounce you blessed for so great
a work as bringing souls to his kingdom. He that
saith, "the poor you have always with you," hath
left the ungodly always with you, that you might
still have matter to exercise your charity upon
If you have the heart of a Christian or of a man,
let it yearn towards your ignorant, ungodly neighbors. Say, as the lepers of Samaria, "We do not
well; this day is a day of good tidings, and we hold

our peace." Háth God had so much mercy on you, and will you have no mercy on your poor neighbors? But as this duty belongs to all Christians, so especially to some, according as God hath called them to it, or qualified them for it ; to them, therefore, I will more particularly address the exhortation :

1. God especially expects this duty at your hands, to whom he has given more *learning and knowledge*, and endued with better utterance, than your neighbors. The strong are made to help the weak, and those that see must direct the blind. God looketh for this faithful improvement of your powers and gifts, which, if you neglect, it were better you had never received them ; for they will but aggravate your condemnation, and be as useless to your own salvation as they were to others.

2. All those who are *particularly acquainted* with some ungodly men, and who have peculiar interest in them, God looks for this duty at your hands. Christ himself did eat and drink with publicans and sinners; but it was only to be their physician, and not their companion. Who knows but God gave you interest in them to this end, that you might be the means of their recovery? They that will not regard the words of a stranger, may regard a brother, or sister, or husband, or wife, or near friend ; besides that, the bond of friendship engages you to special kindness and compassion.

3. *Physicians* that are much about dying **men** should, in a special manner, make conscience of this duty. It is their peculiar advantage that they are at hand—that they are with men in sickness and danger, when the ear is more open and the heart less stubborn than in time of health; and that men look upon their physician as a person in whose hands is their life, or, at least, who may do much to save them; and therefore they will the more regard his advice. You that are of this honorable profession, do not think this a work beside your calling, as if it belonged to none but ministers; except you think it beside your calling to be compassionate, or to be Christians. O help, therefore, to fit your patients for heaven; and whether you see they are for life or death, teach them both how to live and die, and point them to a remedy for their souls as you do for their bodies. Blessed be God that very many of the chief physicians of this age have, by their eminent piety, vindicated their profession from the common imputation of atheism and profaneness.

4. Men of *wealth and authority*, and that have many dependents, have excellent advantages for this duty. O what a world of good might gentlemen do, if they had but hearts to improve their influence over others! Have you not all your honor and riches from God? Doth not Christ say, "Unto whomsoever much is given, of him much shall be

required?" If you speak to your dependents for God and their souls, you may be regarded when even a minister would be despised. As you value the honor of God, your own comfort, and the salvation of souls, improve your influence over your tenants and neighbors; visit their houses; see whether they worship God in their families; and take all opportunities to press them to their duty. Despise them not. Remember, God is no respecter of persons. Let men see that you excel others in piety, compassion, and diligence in God's work, as you do in the riches and honors of the world. I confess you will, by this means, be singular, but then you will be singular in glory; for few of the "mighty and noble are called."

5. As for the *ministers of the gospel*, it is the very work of their calling to help others to heaven. Be sure to make it the main end of your studies and preaching. He is the able, skilful minister, that is best skilled in the art of instructing, convincing, persuading, and, consequently, of winning souls; and that is the best sermon that is best in these. When you seek not God, but yourselves, God will make you the most contemptible of men. It is true of your reputation, as Christ says of your life, "He that loveth it, shall lose it." Let the vigor of your persuasions show that you are sensible on how weighty a business you are sent. Preach with seriousness and fervor, as men who believe their

own doctrine, and know their hearers must be prevailed with, or be damned. Think not that all
your work is in your studies and pulpits. You are
shepherds, and must know every sheep, and what
is their disease, and mark their strayings, and help
to cure them, and fetch them home. Learn of
Paul, not only to teach your people "publicly," but
"from house to house." Inquire how they grow
in knowledge and holiness, and on what grounds
they build their hopes of salvation, and whether
they walk uprightly, and perform the duties of their
several relations. See whether they worship God
in their families, and teach them how to do it. Be
familiar with them, that you may maintain your
interest in them, and improve it all for God. Know
of them how they profit by public teaching. If any
too little "savor the things of the Spirit," let them
be pitied, but not neglected. If any walk disorderly,
recover them with diligence and patience. If they
be ignorant, it may be your fault as much as theirs.
Be not asleep while the wolf is waking. Deal not
slightly with any. Some will not tell their people
plainly of their sins, because they are great men ;
and some, because they are godly ; as if none but
the poor and the wicked should be dealt plainly
with. Yet labor to be skilful and discreet, that the
manner may answer to the excellency of the matter.
Every reasonable soul hath both judgment and affection ; and every rational, spiritual sermon must

have both. Study and pray, and pray and study, till you are become "workmen that need not be ashamed, rightly divining the word of truth," that your people may not be ashamed nor weary in hearing you. Let your conversation teach men as well as your doctrine. Be as forward in a holy and heavenly life as you are in pressing others to it. Let your discourse be edifying and spiritual. Suffer any thing, rather than the gospel and men's souls should suffer. Let men see that you use not the ministry only for a trade to live by, but that your hearts are set upon the welfare of souls. Whatsoever meekness, humility, condescension, or self-denial you teach them from the gospel, teach it them also by your undissembled example. Study and strive after unity and peace. If ever you would promote the kingdom of Christ and your people's salvation, do it in a way of peace and love. It is as hard a thing to maintain in your people a sound understanding, a tender conscience, a lively, gracious, heavenly frame of spirit, and an upright life amidst contention, as to keep your candle lighted in the greatest storms. "Blessed is that servant whom his Lord, when he cometh, shall find so doing."

6. All you whom God has intrusted with *the care of children and servants*, I would also persuade to this great work of helping others to the heavenly rest. Consider what plain and pressing commands

of God require this at your hands. " These words
thou shalt teach diligently unto thy children, and
shalt talk of them when thou sittest in thine house,
and when thou walkest by the way, and when thou
liest down, and when thou risest up. Train up a
child in the way he should go, and when he is old
he will not depart from it. Bring up your children
in the nurture and admonition of the Lord." Joshua
resolved that "he and his house would serve the
Lord." And God himself says of Abraham, "I know
him, that he will command his children and his
household after him, and they shall keep the way
of the Lord."

Consider, it is a duty you owe your children in
point of *justice*. From you they received the defilement and misery of their nature ; and therefore
you owe them all possible help for their recovery.
Consider how near your children are to you : they
are parts of yourselves. If they prosper when you
are dead, you view it as if you lived and prospered
in them ; and should you not be of the same mind
for their everlasting rest ? Otherwise, you will be
witnesses against your own souls. Your care and
pains and cost for their bodies will condemn you for
your neglect of their precious souls. Yea, all the
brute creation may condemn you. Which of them
is not tender of its young ?

Consider, God hath made your children *your
charge*, and your servants too. Every one will

confess they are the minister's charge. And have not you a greater charge of your own families than any minister can have of them? Doubtless at your hands God will require the blood of their souls. It is the greatest charge you ever were intrusted with, and woe to you, if you suffer them to be ignorant or wicked for want of your instruction or correction. Consider what work there is for you in their dispositions and lives. Theirs is not one sin, but thousands. They have hereditary diseases bred in their nature. The things you must teach them are contrary to the interests and desires of their flesh May the Lord make you sensible what a work and charge lie upon you.

Consider what sorrows you prepare for yourselves by the neglect of your children. If they prove thorns in your eyes, they are of your own planting. If you should repent and be saved, is it nothing to think of their damnation; and yourselves the occasion of it? But if you die in your sins, how will they cry out against you in hell, "All this was wrong of you; you should have taught us better, and did not; you should have restrained us from sin and corrected us, but did not." What an addition will such outcries be to your misery. On the other hand, think what a comfort you may have if you be faithful in this duty. If you should not succeed, you have freed your own souls, and may have peace in your own consciences. If you suc-

ceed, the comfort is inexpressible, in their love and
obedience, their supplying your wants, and delighting you in all your remaining path to glory. Yea,
all your family may fare the better for one pious
child or servant. But the greatest joy will be
when you shall say, "Lord, here am I, and the
children thou hast given me;" and shall joyfully
live with them for ever. Consider how much the
welfare of the church and the state depends on this
duty. Good laws will not reform us, if reformation
begin not at home. This is the cause of all our
miseries in the church and the state, even the want
of a holy education of children.

I also entreat parents to consider what excellent
advantages they have for promoting the salvation
of their children. They are with you while they
are tender and flexible; you have a twig to bend,
not an oak. None in the world have such an interest in their affections as you have; you have also
the greatest authority over them. Their whole
dependence is upon you for a maintenance. You
best know their temper and inclinations. And you
are ever with them, and can never want opportunities; especially you, mothers, remember this, who
are more with your children, while young, than their
fathers. What pains do you take for their bodies.
What do you suffer to bring them into the world
And will you not be at as much pains for the saving
of their souls? Your affections are tender, and will

it not move you to think of their perishing for ever? I beseech you, for the sake of the children of your own flesh, teach them, admonish them, watch over them, and give them no rest till you have brought them to Christ.

I shall conclude with this earnest request to all Christian parents that read these lines, that they would have compassion on the souls of their poor children, and be faithful to the great trust that God hath put on them. If you cannot do what you would for them, yet do what you can. Both the church and the state, the city and the country groan under the neglect of this weighty duty. Your children know not God nor his laws, but "take his name in vain," and slight his worship, and you neither instruct them nor correct them; and therefore God corrects both them and you. You are so tender of them that God is the less tender of both them and you. Wonder not if God makes you smart for your children's sins; for you are guilty of all they commit by your neglect of your duty to reform them. Will you resolve therefore to enter upon this duty, and neglect it no longer? Remember Eli. Your children are like Moses in the bulrushes, ready to perish if they have not help. If you would not be charged before God as murderers of their souls, nor have them cry out against you in everlasting fire, see that you teach them how to escape it, and bring them up in holiness and the fear of God. I charge every one of you, upon your allegiance to God, as you will very shortly answer the contrary at your peril, that you neither refuse nor neglect this most necessary duty. If you are not willing to do it, now you know it to be so great a duty, you are rebels, and no true subjects of Jesus Christ. If you are willing, but know not how, I will add a few words of direction to help you. Lead them, by your own example, to prayer, reading, and other religious duties; inform their understandings; store their memories; rectify their wills; quicken their affections; keep tender their consciences; restrain their tongues, and teach them gracious speech; reform and watch over their outward conversation. To these ends, get them Bibles and pious books, and see that they read them. Examine them often as to what they learn; especially spend the Lord's day in this work; and suffer them not to spend it in sports or idleness. Show them the meaning of what they read or learn. Instruct them out of the holy Scriptures. Keep them out of evil company, and acquaint them with the godly. Especially show them the necessity, excellency, and pleasure of serving God, and labor to fix all upon their hearts.

CHAPTER X

THE SAINTS' REST IS NOT TO BE EXPECTED ON EARTH

In order to show the sin and folly of expecting rest here,
I. The reasonableness of present afflictions is considered;
1. That they are the way to rest; 2. Keep us from mistaking our rest; 3. From losing our way to it; 4. Quicken our pace towards it; 5. Chiefly incommode our flesh; 6. Under them the sweetest foretastes of rest are often enjoyed.
II. How unreasonable to rest in present enjoyments;
1. That it is idolatry; 2. That it contradicts God's end in giving them; 3. Is the way to have them refused, withdrawn, or imbittered; 4. That to be suffered to take up our rest here is the greatest curse; 5. That it is seeking rest where it is not; 6. That the creatures, without God, would aggravate our misery; 7. And all this is confirmed by experience. III. The unreasonableness of our unwillingness to die, and possess the saints' rest, is largely considered.

WE are not yet come to our resting-place. Doth it remain? How great then is our sin and folly to seek and expect it here. Where shall we find the Christian that deserves not this reproof? We would all have continual prosperity, because it is easy and pleasing to the flesh; but we consider not the unreasonableness of such desires. And when we enjoy convenient houses, goods, lands, and revenues, or the necessary means God hath appointed for our spiritual good, we seek rest in these enjoyments. Whether we are in an afflicted or prosperous state, it is apparent we exceedingly make the creature our rest. Do we not desire earthly enjoyments more violently when we want them, than we desire God himself? Do we not delight more in the possession of them, than in the enjoyment of God? And if we lose them, doth it not trouble us more than our loss of God? Is it not enough that they are refreshing helps in our way to heaven, but they must also be made our heaven itself? Christian reader, I would as willingly make thee sensible of this sin as of any sin in the world, if I knew how to do it; for the Lord's great controversy with us is in this point. In order to this, I most earnestly beseech thee to consider the reasonableness of present afflictions, and the unreasonableness of resting in present enjoyments, as also of our unwillingness to die that we may possess eternal rest.

First, to show the *reasonableness of present afflictions*, consider, they are the way to rest; they keep us from mistaking our rest, and from losing the way to it; they quicken our pace towards it; they chiefly incommode our flesh; and under them God's people have often the sweetest foretastes of their rest.

1. Consider, that labor and trouble are *the common way* to rest, both in the course of nature and grace. Can there possibly be rest without weari-

ness? Do you not travail and toil first, and rest afterwards? The day for labor is first, and then follows the night for rest. Why should we desire the course of grace to be perverted, any more than the course of nature? It is an established decree, "that we must, though much tribulation, enter into the kingdom of God;" and that, "if we suffer, we shall also reign with Christ." And what are we, that God's statutes should be reversed for our pleasure?

2. Afflictions are exceedingly useful to us, to keep us from *mistaking* our rest. A Christian's motion towards heaven is voluntary, and not constrained. Those means therefore are most profitable which help his understanding and will. The most dangerous mistake of our souls is, to take the creature for God, and earth for heaven. What warm, affectionate, eager thoughts have we of the world, till afflictions cool and moderate them. Afflictions speak convincingly, and will be heard when preachers cannot. Many a poor Christian is sometimes bending his thoughts to wealth, or flesh-pleasing, or applause, and so loses his relish of Christ and the joy above, till God breaks in upon his riches, or children, or conscience, or health, and breaks down his mountain which he thought so strong. And then when he lieth in Manasseh's fetters, or is fastened to his bed with pining sickness, the world is nothing, and heaven is something. If our dear

Lord did not put these thorns under our head, we should sleep out our lives and lose our glory.

3. Afflictions are also God's most effectual means to keep us from *losing our way* to our rest. Without this hedge of thorns on the right hand and left, we should hardly keep the way to heaven. If there be but one gap open, how ready are we to find it, and turn out at it. When we grow wanton, or worldly, or proud, how much doth sickness or other affliction reduce us. Every Christian, as well as Luther, may call affliction one of the best schoolmasters; and, with David, may say, "Before I was afflicted I went astray; but now have I kept thy word." Many thousand recovered sinners may cry, "O healthful sickness! O comfortable sorrows! O gainful losses! O enriching poverty! O blessed day that ever I was afflicted!" Not only the "green pastures and still waters, but the rod and staff, they comfort us." Though the word and Spirit do the main work, yet suffering so unbolts the door of the heart, that the word hath easier entrance.

4. Afflictions likewise serve to *quicken our pace* in the way to our rest. It were well if mere love would prevail with us, and that we were rather drawn to heaven than driven. But, seeing our hearts are so bad that mercy will not do it, it is better to be urged onward with the sharpest scourge than loiter, like the foolish virgins, till the door is

shut. O what a difference is there between our prayers in health and in sickness—between our repentings in prosperity and adversity. Alas, if we did not sometimes feel the spur, what a slow pace would most of us hold towards heaven. Since our vile natures require it, why should we be unwilling that God should do us good by sharp means? Judge, Christian, whether thou dost not go more watchfully and speedily in the way to heaven in thy sufferings than in thy more pleasing and prosperous state.

5. Consider, further, *it is but the flesh* that is chiefly troubled and grieved by afflictions. In most of our sufferings the soul is free, unless we ourselves wilfully afflict it. "Why then, O my soul, dost thou side with this flesh, and complain as it complaineth? It should be thy work to keep it under, and bring it into subjection; and, if God do it for thee, shouldst thou be discontented? Hath not the pleasing of it been the cause of almost all thy spiritual sorrows? Why, then, may not the displeasing of it further thy joy? Must not Paul and Silas sing, because their feet are in the stocks. Their spirits were not imprisoned. Ah, unworthy soul, is this thy thanks to God for preferring thee so far before thy body? When it is rotting in the grave thou shalt be a companion of the perfected spirits of the just. In the meantime, hast thou not consolation which the flesh knows not of? Murmur not, then, at God's dealings with thy body: if it were

for want of love to thee, he would not have dealt so
by all his saints. Never expect thy flesh should
truly expound the meaning of the rod. It will
call love hatred, and say God is destroying when
he is saving. It is the suffering party, and therefore not fit to be the judge." Could we once believe God, and judge of his dealings by his word,
and by their usefulness to our souls and reference
to our rest, and could we stop our ears against all
the clamors of the flesh, then we should have a
truer judgment of our afflictions.

6. Once more, consider, God seldom gives his
people so sweet a *foretaste* of their future rest as in
their deep afflictions. He keeps his most precious
cordials for the time of our greatest faintings and
dangers. He gives them when he knows they are
needed and will be valued, and when he is sure to
be thanked for them, and that his people will be
rejoiced by them. Especially when our sufferings
are more directly for his cause, then he seldom fails
to sweeten the bitter cup. The martyrs have possessed the highest joys. When did Christ preach
such comfort to his disciples as when "their hearts
were sorrowful" at his departure? When did he
appear among them and say, "Peace be unto you,"
but when they were shut up for fear of the Jews?
When did Stephen see heaven opened, but when he
was giving up his life for the testimony of Jesus?
Is not that our best state wherein we have most of

God? Why else do we desire to come to heaven? If we look for a heaven of fleshly delights, we shall find ourselves mistaken. Conclude, then, that affliction is not so bad a state for a saint in his way to rest. Are we wiser than God? Doth he not know what is good for us as well as we, or is he not as careful of our good as we are of our own? Woe to us if he were not much more so, and if he did not love us better than we love either him or ourselves.

Say not, "I could bear any other affliction but this." If God had afflicted thee where thou canst bear it, thy idol would neither have been discovered nor removed. Neither say, "If God would ere long deliver me, I could be content to bear it." Is it nothing that he hath promised it "shall work for thy good?" Is it not enough that thou art sure to be delivered at death? Nor let it be said, "If my affliction did not disable me from my duty, I could bear it." It doth not disable thee for that duty which tendeth to thy own personal benefit, but is the greatest quickening help thou canst expect. As for thy duty to others, it is not thy duty when God disables thee. Perhaps thou wilt say, "The godly are my afflicters; if it were ungodly men, I could easily bear it." Whoever is the instrument, the affliction is from God, and the deserving cause thyself; and is it not better to look more to God than to thyself? Didst thou not know that the best men are still sinful in part? Do not plead, "If I had but that consolation which God reserveth for suffering times, I should suffer more contentedly; but I do not perceive any such thing." The more you suffer for righteousness' sake, the more of this blessing you may expect; and the more you suffer for your own evil-doing, the longer it will be before that sweetness comes. Are not the comforts you desire neglected or resisted? Have your afflictions wrought kindly with you, and fitted you for comfort? It is not suffering that prepares you for comfort, but the success and fruit of suffering upon your heart.

Secondly, to show *the unreasonableness of resting in present enjoyments*, consider, it is idolizing them; it contradicts God's end in giving them; it is the way to have them refused, withdrawn, or imbittered; to be suffered to take up our rest here is the greatest curse; it is seeking rest where it is not to be found; the creatures, without God, would aggravate our misery; and to confirm all this, we may consult our own and others' experience.

1. It is gross *idolatry* to make any creature or means our rest. To be the rest of the soul is God's own prerogative. As it is evident idolatry to place our rest in riches or honor, so it is but a more refined idolatry to take up our rest in excellent means of grace. How must we offend our dear Lord when we give him cause to complain, as he

did of our fellow-idolaters, "My people have been lost sheep; they have forgotten their resting-place. My people can find rest in any thing rather than in me. They can delight in one another, but not in me. They can rejoice in my creatures and ordinances, but not in me. Yea, in their very labors and duties they seek for rest, but not in me. They had rather be anywhere than be with me. Are these their gods? Have these redeemed them? Will these be better to them than I have been, or than I would be?" If you yourselves had a wife, a husband, a son, who had rather be anywhere than in your company, and was never so merry as when furthest from you, would you not take it ill? So our God must needs do.

2. You *contradict the end* of God in giving these enjoyments. He gave them to help thee to him, and dost thou take up with them in his stead? He gave them to be refreshments in thy journey, and wouldst thou dwell in thy inn and go no further? It may be said of all our comforts and ordinances, as is said of the Israelites, "The ark of the covenant of the Lord went before them, to search out a resting-place for them." So do all God's mercies here. They are not that rest—as John professed he was not the Christ—but they are "voices crying in this wilderness," to bid us prepare, "for the kingdom of God," our true rest, "is at hand." Therefore, to rest here were to turn

all mercies contrary to their own ends and to our own advantage, and to destroy ourselves with that which should help us.

3. It is the way to cause God either to deny the mercies we ask, or to take from us those we enjoy, or at least imbitter them to us. God is nowhere so jealous as here. If you had a servant whom your wife loved better than yourself, would you not take it ill of such a wife, and rid your house of such a servant? So, if the Lord see you begin to settle in the world, and say, "Here I will rest," no wonder if he soon, in his jealousy, unsettle you. If he love you, no wonder if he take that from you with which he sees you are destroying yourself. It hath long been my observation of many, that when they have attempted great works, and have just finished them; or have aimed at great things in the world, and have just obtained them; or have lived in much trouble, and have just overcome it, and begin to look on their condition with content and rest in it, they are then usually near to death or ruin. When a man is once at this language, "Soul, take thy ease," the next news usually is, "Thou fool, this night," or this month, or this year, "thy soul shall be required; and then whose shall these things be?" What house is there where this fool dwelleth not? Let you and I consider whether it be not our own case. Many a servant of God has been destroyed from the earth by being

overvalued and overloved. I am persuaded our discontents and murmurings are not so provoking to God, nor so destructive to the sinner, as our too sweet enjoying and resting in a pleasing state. If God hath crossed you in wife, children, goods, friends, either by taking them away, or the comfort of them, try whether this be not the cause; for wheresoever your desires stop, and you say, "Now I am well," that condition you make your god, and engage the jealousy of God against it. Whether you be a friend to God or an enemy, you can never expect that God should suffer you quietly to enjoy your idols.

4. Should God suffer you to take up your rest here, it is one of the greatest *curses* that could befall you. It were better never to have a day of ease in the world; for then weariness might make you seek after true rest. But if you are suffered to sit down and rest here, a restless wretch you will be through all eternity. To " have their portion in this life," is the lot of the most miserable, perishing sinners. Does it become Christians then to expect so much here? Our rest is our heaven; and where we take our rest, there we make our heaven. And wouldst thou have but such a heaven as this?

5. It is seeking rest where it *is not to be found.* Your labor will be lost; and if you proceed, your soul's eternal rest too. Our rest is only in the full

obtaining of our ultimate end. But that is not to be expected in this life; neither is rest, therefore, to be expected here. Is God to be enjoyed in the best church here as he is in heaven? How little of God the saints enjoy under the best means, let their own complainings testify. Poor comforters are the best ordinances without God. Should a traveller take up his rest in the way? No; because his home is his journey's end. When you have all that creatures and means can afford, have you that you believed, prayed, suffered for? I think you dare not say so. We are like little children strayed from home, and God is now bringing us home, and we are ready to turn into any house, stay and play with every thing in our way, and sit down on every green bank, and much ado there is to get us home. We are also in the midst of our labors and dangers; and is there any resting here? What painful duties lie upon our hands, to our brethren, to our own souls, and to God; and what an arduous work, in respect to each of these, doth lie before us. And can we rest in the midst of all our labors? Indeed, we may rest on earth, as the ark is said to have "rested in the midst of Jordan," a short and small rest; or as Abraham desired the "angels to turn in and rest themselves" in his tent, where they would have been loath to have taken up their dwelling. Should Israel have fixed their rest in the wilderness, among serpents and enemies, and weariness and famine? Should Noah have made the ark his home, and have been loath to come forth when the waters were assuaged? Should the mariner choose his dwelling on the sea, and settle his rest in the midst of rocks and sands and raging tempests? Should a soldier rest in the thickest of his enemies? And are not Christians such travellers, such mariners, such soldiers? Have you not fears within and troubles without? Are we not in continual dangers? We cannot eat, drink, sleep, labor, pray, hear, converse, but in the midst of snares; and shall we sit down and rest here?

O Christian, follow thy work, look to thy dangers, hold on to the end, win the field, and come off the ground before thou think of a settled rest. Whenever thou talkest of a rest on earth, it is like Peter on the mount, "thou knowest not what thou sayest." If, instead of telling the converted thief, "this day shalt thou be with me in paradise," Christ had said he should rest there upon the cross, would he not have taken it for derision? Methinks it would be ill resting in the midst of sickness and pain, persecutions and distresses. But if nothing else will convince us, yet sure the remains of sin, which so easily besets us, should quickly satisfy a believer that here is not his rest. I say, therefore, to every one that thinketh of rest on earth, "Arise ye, and depart, for this is not your rest, because it is polluted." These things cannot, in their nature,

be a true Christian's rest. They are too poor to
make us rich, too low to raise us to happiness, too
empty to fill our souls, and of too short a continuance to be our eternal content. If prosperity, and
whatsoever we here desire, be too base to make
gods of, they are too base to be our rest. The
soul's rest must be sufficient to afford it perpetual
satisfaction.   But the content which creatures
afford waxes old, and abates after a short enjoyment. If God should rain down angel's food, we
should soon loathe the manna. If novelty support
not, our delights on earth grow dull. All creatures are to us as flowers to the bee ; there is but
little honey on any one, and therefore there must
be but a superficial taste, and so to the next. The
more the world is known, the less it satisfieth.
Those only are taken with it who see no further
than its outward beauty, without discerning its
inward vanity. When we thoroughly know the
condition of other men, and have discovered the
evil as well as the good, and the defects as well as
the perfections, we then cease our admiration.

6. To have creatures and means without God, is
an aggravation of our misery. If God should say,
"Take my creatures, my word, my servants, my
ordinances, but not myself," would you take this for
happiness ? If you had the word of God, and not
"the Word," who is God ; or the bread of the Lord,
and not the Lord, who "is the true bread ;" or could

cry with the Jews, " The temple of the Lord," and had not the Lord of the temple, this were a poor happiness. Was Capernaum the more happy, or the more miserable, for seeing the mighty works which they had seen, and hearing the words of Christ which they did hear? Surely that which aggravates our sin and misery cannot be our rest.

7. To confirm all this, let us consult our own and others' *experience*. Millions have made the trial; but did any ever find a sufficient rest for his soul on earth? Delights I deny not but they have found, but rest and satisfaction they never found. And shall we think to find that which never man could find before us? Ahab's kingdom is nothing to him without Naboth's vineyard; and did that satisfy him when he obtained it? Were you, like Noah's dove, to look through the earth for a resting-place, you would return confessing that you could find none. Go ask honor, Is there rest here? You may as well rest on the top of tempestuous mountains, or in Ætna's flames. Ask riches, Is there rest here? Even such as is in a bed of thorns. If you inquire for the rest of worldly pleasure, it is such as the fish hath in swallowing the bait; when the pleasure is sweetest, death is nearest. Go to learning, and even to divine ordinances, and inquire whether there your soul may rest. You might indeed receive from these an olive-branch of hope, as they are means to your rest, and have relation to

eternity; but, in regard of any satisfaction in themselves, you would remain as restless as ever. How well might all these answer us, as Jacob did Rachel, "Am I in God's stead," that you come to me for soul-rest? Not all the states of men in the world; neither court nor country, towns nor cities, shops nor fields, treasuries, libraries, solitude, society, studies, nor pulpits can afford any such thing as this rest. If you could inquire of the dead of all generations, or of the living through all dominions, they would all tell you, "Here is no rest." Or, if other men's experience move you not, take a view of your own. Can you remember the state that did fully satisfy you; or, if you could, will it prove lasting? I believe we may all say of our earthly rest, as Paul of our hope, "If it were in this life only, we are of all men the most miserable."

If, then, either scripture or reason, or the experience of ourselves and all the world, will convince us, we may see there is no resting here. And yet how guilty are the generality of us of this sin. How many halts and stops do we make before we will make the Lord our rest. How must God even drive us, and fire us out of every condition, lest we should sit down and rest there. If he gives us prosperity, riches, or honor, we do in our hearts dance before them, as the Israelites before their calf, and say, "These are thy gods;" and conclude "it is good to be here." If he imbitter all these to us, how restless are we till our condition be sweetened, that we may sit down again and rest where we were. If he proceed in the cure, and take the creature quite away, then we labor and cry and pray that God would restore it, that we may make it our rest again. And while we are deprived of our former idol, yet, rather than come to God, we delight ourselves in the hope of recovering it, and make that very hope our rest, or search about from creature to creature to find out something to supply the room; yea, if we can find no supply, yet we will rather settle in this misery, and make a rest of a wretched being, than leave all and come to God.

O the cursed aversion of our souls from God. If any place in hell were tolerable, the soul would rather take up its rest there than come to God. Yea, when he is bringing us over to him, and hath convinced us of the worth of his ways and service, the last deceit of all is here; we will rather settle upon those ways that lead to him, and those ordinances that speak of him, and those gifts which flow from him, than come entirely over to himself. Christian, marvel not that I speak so much of resting in these; beware, lest it prove thy own case. I suppose thou art so far convinced of the vanity of riches, honor, and pleasure, that thou canst more easily disclaim these; and it is well if it be so; but the means of grace thou lookest on with less suspicion, and thinkest thou canst not delight in them too much, especially seeing most of the world despise them, or delight in them too little. I know they must be loved and valued; and he that delighteth in any worldly thing more than in them, is not a Christian. But when we are content with ordinances without God, and had rather be at public worship than in heaven, and a member of the church here than of the perfect church above, this is a sad mistake. So far let thy soul take comfort in ordinances as God doth accompany them; remembering, this is not heaven, but the first-fruits. "While we are present in the body, we are absent from the Lord;" and while we are absent from him, we are absent from our rest. If God were as willing to be absent from us as we from him, and as loath to be our rest as we to rest in him, we should be left to an eternal restless separation. In a word, as you are sensible of the sinfulness of your earthly discontents, so be you also of your irregular satisfaction, and pray God to pardon them much more. And, above all the plagues on this side hell, see that you watch and pray against settling anywhere short of heaven, or reposing your soul on any thing below God.

Thirdly, the next thing to be considered is our *unreasonable unwillingness to die, that we may possess the saints' rest.* We linger, like Lot in Sodom, till "the Lord being merciful unto us," doth pluck us away against our will. I confess that death, of itself, is not desirable; but the soul's rest with God is, to which death is the common passage. Because we are apt to make light of this sin, let me set before you its nature and remedy, in a variety of considerations.

It has in it much *infidelity*. If we did verily believe that the promise of this glory is the word of God, and that God truly means as he speaks, and is fully resolved to make it good; if we did verily believe that there is indeed such blessedness prepared for believers, surely we should be as impatient of living as we are now fearful of dying, and should think every day a year till our last day should come. Is it possible that we can truly believe that death will remove us from misery to such glory, and yet be loath to die? If the doubts of our own interest in that glory make us fear, yet a true belief of the certainty and excellency of this rest would make us restless till our title to it be cleared. Though there is much faith and Christianity in our mouths, yet there is much infidelity and paganism in our hearts, which is the chief cause that we are so loath to die.

It is also much owing to the *coldness of our love*. If we love our friend, we love his company; his presence is comfortable, his absence is painful: when he comes to us, we entertain him with gladness; when he dies, we mourn, and usually overmourn. To be separated from a faithful friend is like the rending of a member from our body. And would not our desires after God be such, if we really loved him? Nay, should it not be much more than such, as he is, above all friends, most lovely? May the Lord teach us to look closely to our hearts, and take heed of self-deceit in this point. Whatever we pretend, if we love either father, mother, husband, wife, child, friend, wealth, or life itself, more than Christ, we are yet "none of his" sincere "disciples." When it comes to the trial, the question will not be, who hath preached most, or heard most, or talked most; but, who hath loved most. Christ will not take sermons, prayers, fastings, no, nor the "giving our goods," nor the "burning our bodies," instead of love. And do we love him, and yet care not how long we are from him? Was it such a joy to Jacob to see the face of Joseph in Egypt; and shall we be contented without the sight of Christ in glory, and yet say we love him? I dare not conclude that we have no love at all, when we are so loath to die; but I dare say, were our love more, we should die more willingly. If this holy flame were thoroughly kindled in our breasts, we should cry out with David, "As the hart panteth after the water-brooks, so panteth my soul after thee, O God. My soul thirsteth for God, for the living God; when shall I come and appear before God?"

By our unwillingness to die, it appears we are *little weary of sin*. Did we feel sin to be the greatest evil, we should not be willing to have its company so long. "O foolish, sinful heart, hast thou been so long a cage of all unclean lusts, a fountain incessantly pouring forth the bitter waters of transgression, and art thou not yet weary? Wretched soul, hast thou been so long wounded in all thy faculties, so grievously languishing in all thy performances, so fruitful a soil of all iniquities, and art thou not yet more weary? Wouldst thou still lie under thy imperfections? Hath thy sin proved so profitable a commodity, so necessary a companion, such a delightful employment, that thou dost so much dread the parting day? May not God justly grant thee thy wishes, and seal thee a lease of thy desired distance from him, and nail thy ears to these doors of misery, and exclude thee eternally from his glory?"

It shows that we are *insensible of the vanity* of earth, when we are so loath to hear or think of a removal. "Ah, foolish, wretched soul, doth every prisoner groan for freedom, and every slave desire his jubilee, and every sick man long for health, and every hungry man for food, and dost thou alone abhor deliverance? Doth the sailor wish to see land? Doth the husbandman desire the harvest, and the laborer to receive his pay? Doth the traveller long to be at home, and the racer to win the prize, and the soldier to win the field; and art thou loath to see thy labors finished, and to receive

the end of thy faith and sufferings? Have thy
griefs been only dreams? If they were, yet methinks thou shouldst not be afraid of waking. Or
is it not rather the world's delights that are all
mere dreams and shadows? Or is the world become of late more kind? We may at our peril
reconcile ourselves to the world, but it will never
reconcile itself to us. O unworthy soul, who hadst
rather dwell in this land of darkness, and wander
in this barren wilderness, than be at rest with
Jesus Christ; who hadst rather stay among the
wolves, and daily suffer the scorpion's stings, than
praise the Lord with the host of heaven."

This unwillingness to die doth actually impeach
us of high treason against the Lord. Is it not
choosing earth before him, and taking present
things for our happiness, and consequently making
them our very god? If we did indeed make God
our end, our rest, our portion, our treasure, how is
it possible but we should desire to enjoy him? It
moreover discovers some dissimulation. Would
you have any man believe you when you call the
Lord your only hope, and speak of Christ as all in
all, and of the joy that is in his presence, and yet
would endure the hardest life, rather than die and
enter into his presence? What self-contradiction
is this, to talk so hardly of the world and the flesh,
to groan and complain of sin and suffering, and yet
fear no day more than that we expect should bring

our final freedom. What hypocrisy is this to profess to strive and fight for heaven, which we are loath to come to ; and spend one hour after another in prayer for that which we would not have. Hereby we wrong the Lord and his promises, and disgrace his ways in the eyes of the world ; as if we would persuade them to question whether God be true to his word or not—whether there be any such glory as the Scripture mentions. When they see those so loath to leave their hold of present things, who have professed to live by faith, and have boasted of their hopes in another world, and spoken disgracefully of all things below, in comparison with things above, how doth this confirm the world in their unbelief and sensuality. " Surely," say they, " if these professors did expect so much glory, and make so light of the world as they seem, they would not themselves be so loath to change." O, how are we ever able to repair the wrong which we do to God and souls by this scandal ? And what an honor to God, what a strengthening to believers, what a conviction to unbelievers would it be, if Christians in this did answer their profession, and cheerfully welcome the news of rest.

It also evidently shows that we have spent much time *to little purpose*. Have we not had all our lifetime to prepare to die ; so many years to make ready for one hour ; and are we so unready and

unwilling yet? What have we done? Why have
we lived? Had we any greater matters to mind?
Would we have wished for more frequent warnings?
How oft hath death entered the habitations of our
neighbors. How often hath it knocked at our own
door. How many diseases have vexed our bodies,
that we have been forced to receive the sentence
of death. And are we unready and unwilling after
all this? O careless, dead-hearted sinners; unworthy
neglecters of God's warnings; faithless betrayers of
our own souls!

Consider, *not to die is never to be happy.* To
escape death is to miss of blessedness, except God
should translate us, as Enoch and Elijah, which he
never did before or since. " If in this life only we
have hope in Christ, we are of all men most miserable." If you would not die and go to heaven, what
would you have more than an epicure or a beast?
Why do we pray and fast and mourn ; why do we
suffer the contempt of the world ; why are we
Christians, and not pagans and infidels, if we do
not desire a life to come? Wouldst thou lose thy
faith and labor, Christian—all thy duties and sufferings, all the end of thy life, and all the blood of
Christ, and be contented with the portion of a worldling or a brute? Rather say, as one did on his
death-bed, when he was asked whether he was
willing to die or not, " Let him be loath to die, who
is loath to be with Christ." Is God willing by death

to glorify us, and are we unwilling to die, that we may be glorified? Methinks, if a prince were willing to make you his heir, you would scarce be unwilling to accept it; the refusing such a kindness would discover ingratitude and unworthiness. As God hath resolved against them who make excuses when they should come to Christ, "None of those men who were bidden shall taste of my supper;" so it is just with him to resolve against us, who frame excuses when we should come to glory.

The Lord Jesus Christ was willing to come from heaven to earth for us, and shall we be unwilling to remove from earth to heaven for ourselves and him? He might have said, "What is it to me if these sinners suffer? If they value their flesh above their spirits, and their lusts above my Father's love; if they will sell their souls for naught, who is it fit should be the loser? Should I, whom they have wronged? Must they wilfully transgress my law, and I undergo their deserved pain? Must I come down from heaven to earth, and clothe myself with human flesh, be spit upon and scorned by man, and fast, and weep, and sweat, and suffer, and bleed, and die a cursed death; and all this for wretched worms who would rather hazard their souls than forbear one forbidden morsel? Do they cast away themselves so slightly, and must I redeem them so dearly?" Thus we see Christ had reason enough to have made him unwilling; and yet did he volun-

tarily condescend. But we have no reason against
our coming to him, except we will reason against
our hopes, and plead for a perpetuity of our own
calamities. Christ came down to raise us up; and
would we have him lose his blood and labor and go
again without us? Hath he bought our rest at so
dear a rate? Is our inheritance "purchased with
his blood?" And are we, after all this, loath to
enter? Ah, sirs, it was Christ, and not we, that
had cause to be loath. May the Lord forgive and
heal this foolish ingratitude.

Do we not *combine with our most cruel foes* in
their most malicious designs, while we are loath to
die and go to heaven? What is the devil's daily
business? Is it not to keep our souls from God?
And shall we be content with this? Is it not the
one half of hell which we wish to ourselves, while
we desire to be absent from heaven? What sport
is this to Satan, that his desires and thine, Christian,
should so concur; that, when he sees he cannot get
thee to hell, he can so long keep thee out of heaven,
and make thee the earnest petitioner for it thyself.
O gratify not the devil so much to thy own injury.
Do not our daily fears of death make our lives a continual torment? Those lives, which might be full
of joy in the daily contemplation of the life to come,
and the sweet, delightful thoughts of bliss, how do
we fill them up with causeless terrors. Thus we
consume our own comforts, and prey upon our truest

pleasures. When we might lie down, and rise up, and walk abroad with our hearts full of the joys of God, we continually fill them with perplexing fears ; for he that fears dying must be always fearing, because he hath always reason to expect it. And how can that man's life be comfortable who lives in continual fear of losing his comforts? Are not these fears of death self-created sufferings, as if God had not inflicted enough upon us, but we must inflict more upon ourselves? Is not death bitter enough to the flesh of itself, but we must double and treble its bitterness? The sufferings laid upon us by God do all lead to happy issues ; the progress is from tribulation to patience, from thence to experience, and so to hope, and at last to glory. But the sufferings we make for ourselves are circular and endless, from sin to suffering, from suffering to sin, and so to suffering again ; and not only so, but they multiply in their course ; every sin is greater than the former, and so every suffering also : so that, except we think God hath made us to be our own tormentors, we have small reason to nourish our fears of death.

And are they not useless, unprofitable fears? As all our care "cannot make one hair white or black, nor add one cubit to our stature," so neither can our fear prevent our sufferings, nor delay our death one hour : willing or unwilling, we must away. Many a man's fears have hastened his end, but no man's did ever avert it. It is true, a cautious fear concerning the danger after death hath profited many, and is very useful to the preventing of that danger; but for a member of Christ and an heir of heaven to be afraid of entering his own inheritance, is a sinful, useless fear. And do not our fears of dying ensnare our souls, and add strength to many temptations? What made Peter deny his Lord? What makes apostates in suffering times forsake the truth? Why does the green blade of unrooted faith wither before the heat of persecution? Fear of imprisonment and poverty may do much, but fear of death will do much more. So much fear as we have of death, so much cowardice we usually have in the cause of God; besides the multitude of unbelieving contrivances, and discontents at the wise disposal of God, and hard thoughts of most of his providences, of which this sin makes us guilty.

Let us further consider what *sufficient time* most of us have had. Why should not a man, that would die at all, be as willing at thirty or forty, if God see fit, as at seventy or eighty? Length of time does not conquer corruption; it never withers nor decays through age. Except we receive an addition of grace as well as time, we naturally grow worse. "O my soul, depart in peace. As thou wouldst not desire an unlimited state in wealth and honor, so desire it not in point of time. If thou

wast sensible how little thou deservest an hour of
that patience which thou hast enjoyed, thou wouldst
think thou hadst had a large part. Is it not divine
wisdom that sets the bounds? God will honor himself by various persons and ages, and not by one
person or age. Seeing thou hast acted thy own
part, and finished thy appointed course, come down
contentedly, that others may succeed, who must
have their turns as well as thyself. Much time
hath much duty; beg therefore for grace to improve it better; but be content with thy share of
time.

"Thou hast also had a competency of *the comforts of life.* God might have made thy life a burden, till thou hadst been as weary of possessing it
as thou art now afraid of losing it. He might have
suffered thee to have consumed thy days in ignorance, without the true knowledge of Christ; but
he hath opened thy eyes in the morning of thy days,
and acquainted thee betimes with the business of
thy life. Hath thy heavenly Father caused thy lot
to fall in Europe, not in Asia or Africa; in England, not in Spain or Italy? Hath he filled up all
thy life with mercies, and dost thou now think thy
share too small? What a multitude of hours of
consolation, of delightful Sabbaths, of pleasant
studies, of precious companions, of wonderful deliverances, of excellent opportunities, of fruitful
labors, of joyful tidings, of sweet experiences, of

astonishing providences, hath thy life partaken of. Hath thy life been so sweet that thou art loath to leave it? Is this thy thanks to Him who is thus drawing thee to his own sweetness? O foolish soul, would thou wast as covetous after eternity as thou art for a fading, perishing life; and after the presence of God in glory as thou art for continuance on earth. Then thou wouldst cry, 'Why is his chariot so long in coming? Why tarry the wheels of his chariot?' How long, Lord, how long? What if God should let thee live many years, but deny thee the mercies which thou hast hitherto enjoyed? Might he not give thee life, as he gave the murmuring Israelites quails? He might give thee life till thou art weary of living, and as glad to be rid of it as Judas or Ahithophel; and make thee like many miserable creatures in the world, who can hardly forbear laying violent hands on themselves. Be not therefore so importunate for life, which may prove a judgment instead of a blessing. How many of the precious servants of God, of all ages and places, have gone before thee. Thou art not to enter an untrodden path, nor appointed first to break the ice. Except Enoch and Elijah, which of the saints have escaped death? And art thou better than they? There are many millions of saints dead, more than now remain on earth. What a number of thine own bosom friends and companions in duty are now gone; and why shouldst thou be so loath to follow? Nay, hath not Jesus Christ himself gone this way? Hath he not sanctified the grave to us, and perfumed the dust with his own body; and art thou loath to follow him too? Rather say as Thomas, 'Let us also go, that we may die with him.'"

If what has been said will not persuade, scripture and reason have little force. And I have said the more on this subject, finding it so needful to myself and others—finding, among so many Christians who could do and suffer much for Christ, so few that can willingly die; and of many who have somewhat subdued other corruptions, so few that have gotten the conquest of this. I persuade not the ungodly from fearing death; it is a wonder that they fear it no more, and spend not their days in continual horror.

CHAPTER XI

THE IMPORTANCE OF LEADING A HEAVENLY LIFE UPON EARTH

The reasonableness of delighting in the thoughts of the saints' rest. Christians exhorted to it, by considering, 1. It will evidence their sincere piety; 2. It is the highest excellence of the Christian temper; 3. It leads to the most comfortable life; 4. It will be the best preservative from temptations to sin; 5. It will invigorate their graces and duties; 6. It will be their best cordial in afflictions; 7. It will render them most profitable to others; 8. It will honor God; 9. Without it we disobey the commands, and lose the most gracious and delightful discoveries of the word of God; 10. It is the more reasonable to have our hearts with God, as his is much on us; and, 11. In heaven, where we have so much interest and relation; 12. Besides, there is nothing but heaven worth setting our hearts upon.

Is there such a rest remaining for us? Why then are not our thoughts more upon it? Why are not our hearts continually there? Why dwell we not there in constant contemplation? What is the cause of this neglect? Are we reasonable in this, or are we not? Hath the eternal God provided us such a glory, and promised to take us up to dwell with himself; and is not this worth thinking on? Should not the strongest desires of our hearts be after it? Do we believe this, and yet forget and neglect it? If God will not give us leave to approach this light, what mean all his earnest invitations? Why doth he so condemn our earthly-mindedness, and command us to set our affections on things above? Ah, vile hearts! Were God against it, we were likelier to be for it; but when he commands our hearts to heaven, then they will not stir one inch: like our predecessors the sinful Israelites, when God would have them march for Canaan, then they mutiny, and will not stir; but when God bids them not go, then will they be presently marching. If God say, "Love not the world, nor the things of the world," we dote upon it. How freely, how frequently can we think of our pleasures, our friends, our labors, our flesh and its lusts, yea, our wrongs and miseries, our fears and sufferings. But where is the Christian whose heart is on his rest? What is the matter? Are we so full of joy that we need no more? Or is there nothing in heaven for our joyous thoughts? Or rather, are not our hearts carnal and stupid? Let us humble these sensual hearts, that have in them no more of Christ and glory. If this world was the only subject of our discourse, all would call us ungodly; why then may we not call our hearts ungodly, that have so little delight in Christ and heaven?

But I am speaking only to those whose portion is in heaven, whose hopes are there, and who have forsaken all to enjoy this glory; and shall I be dis-

couraged from persuading such to be heavenly-
minded? Fellow-Christians, if you will not hear
and obey, who will? Well may we be discouraged
to exhort the blind ungodly world, and may say, as
Moses did, "Behold, the children of Israel have not
hearkened unto me ; how then shall Pharaoh hear
me?" I require thee, reader, as ever thou hopest
for a part in this glory, that thou presently take thy
heart to task, chide it for its wilful strangeness to
God, turn thy thoughts from the pursuit of vanity,
bend thy soul to study eternity, busy it about the
life to come, habituate thyself to such contemplations, and let not those thoughts be seldom and
cursory, but bathe thy soul in heaven's delights ;
and if thy backward soul begin to flag and thy
thoughts to scatter, call them back, hold them to
their work, bear not with their laziness, nor connive at one neglect. And when thou hast, in obedience to God, tried this work, got acquainted with
it, and kept a guard on thy thoughts till they are
accustomed to obey, thou wilt then find thyself in
the suburbs of heaven, and that there is indeed a
sweetness in the work and way of God, and that
the life of Christianity is a life of joy. Thou wilt
meet with those abundant consolations which thou
hast prayed, panted, and groaned after, and which
so few Christians do ever here obtain, because they
know not this way to them, or else make not conscience of walking in it.

Say not, "We are unable to set our own hearts on heaven; this must be the work of God only." Though God be the chief disposer of your hearts, yet, next under him, you have the greatest command of them yourselves. Though without Christ you can do nothing, yet under him you may do much; and must, or else it will be undone, and yourselves undone through your neglect. Christians, if your souls were healthful and vigorous, they would perceive incomparably more delight and sweetness in the believing, joyful thoughts of your future blessedness, than the soundest stomach finds in its food, or the strongest senses in the enjoyment of their objects, so little painful would this work be to you. But because I know, while we have flesh about us and any remains of that "carnal mind which is enmity against God" and this noble work, that all motives are little enough, I will here lay down some considerations, which, if you will deliberately weigh with an impartial judgment, I doubt not will prove effectual with your hearts, and make you resolve on this excellent duty. More particularly consider, it will evidence your sincere piety; it is the highest excellence of the Christian temper; it is the way to live most comfortably; it will be the best preservative from temptations to sin; it will enliven your graces and duties; it will be your best cordial in all afflictions; it will render you most profitable to others; it will honor God; without it you will disobey the commands and lose the most gracious and delightful discoveries of the word of God : it is also the more reasonable to have your hearts with God, as his is so much on you, and in heaven, where you have so much interest and relation; besides, there is nothing but heaven worth setting your hearts upon.

1. Consider, that a heart set upon heaven will be *one of the most unquestionable evidences of your sincerity*, and a clear discovery of a true work of saving grace upon your souls. You are often asking, "How shall we know that we are truly sanctified?" Here you have a sign infallible from the mouth of Jesus Christ himself: "Where your treasure is, there will your hearts be also." God is the saints' treasure and happiness; heaven is the place where they must fully enjoy him. A heart therefore set upon heaven, is a heart set upon God ; and surely a heart set upon God, through Christ, is the truest evidence of saving grace. When learning will be no proof of grace ; when knowledge, duties, gifts will fail ; when arguments from thy tongue or hand may be confuted, yet then will this, from the bent of thy heart, prove thee sincere. Take a poor Christian, of a weak understanding, a feeble memory, a stammering tongue ; yet his heart is set on God, he hath chosen him for his portion, his thoughts are on eternity, his desires are there ; he cries out, "O that I were there !" He takes that

day for a time of imprisonment, in which he hath not had one refreshing view of eternity. I had rather die in this man's condition, than in the case of him who hath the most eminent gifts, and is most admired for his performances, while his heart is not thus taken up with God. The man that Christ will find out at the last day, and condemn for want of a "wedding garment," will be one that wants this frame of heart. The question will not then be, How much have you known, or professed, or talked; but, How much have you loved, and where was your heart? Christians, as you would have a proof of your title to glory, labor to get your hearts above. If sin and Satan keep not your affections from thence, they will never be able to keep away your persons.

2. A heart in heaven is *the highest excellence of Christian temper*. As there is a common excellence by which Christians differ from the world, so there is this peculiar dignity of spirit by which the more excellent differ from the rest. As the noblest of creatures, so the noblest of Christians are they whose faces are set most direct for heaven. Such a heavenly saint, who hath been rapt up to God in his contemplations, and is newly come down from the views of Christ, what discoveries will he make of those superior regions; how high and sacred is his discourse: enough to convince an understanding hearer that he hath seen the Lord, and that no

man could speak such words, except he had been with God. This, this is the noble Christian. The most famous mountains and trees are those that reach nearest to heaven, and he is the choicest Christian whose heart is most frequently and most delightfully there. If a man have lived near the king, or hath seen the sultan of Persia or the grand Turk, he will be thought a step higher than his neighbors. What then shall we judge of him that daily travels as far as heaven, and there hath seen the King of kings, hath frequent admittance into the divine presence, and feasteth his soul upon the tree of life? For my part, I value this man before the noblest, the richest, the most learned in the world.

3. A heavenly mind is *the nearest and truest way to a life of comfort*. The countries far north are cold and frozen, because they are distant from the sun. What makes such frozen, uncomfortable Christians, but their living so far from heaven? And what makes others so warm in comforts, but their living higher, and having nearer access to God? When the sun in the spring draws nearer to our part of the earth, how do all things congratulate its approach. The earth looks green, the trees shoot forth, the plants revive, the birds sing, and all things smile upon us. If we would but try this life with God, and keep these hearts above, what a spring of joy would be within us; how should we

forget our winter sorrows; how early should we rise to sing the praise of our great Creator. O Christian, get above. Those that have been there have found it warmer; and I doubt not but thou hast sometimes tried it thyself. When hast thou largest comforts? Is it not when thou hast conversed with God, and talked with the inhabitants of the higher world, and viewed their mansions, and filled thy soul with the forethoughts of glory? If thou knowest by experience what this practice is, I dare say thou knowest what spiritual joy is. If, as David professes, "the light of God's countenance more gladdens the heart than corn and wine," then surely they that draw nearest, and most behold it, must be fullest of these joys. Whom should we blame, then, that we are so void of consolation, but our own negligent hearts? God hath provided us a crown of glory, and promised to set it shortly on our heads, and we will not so much as think of it. He bids us behold and rejoice, and we will not so much as look at it; and yet we complain for want of comfort. It is by believing that we are "filled with joy and peace," and no longer than we continue believing. It is in hope the saints rejoice, and no longer than they continue hoping. God's Spirit worketh our comforts by setting our own spirits at work upon the promises, and raising our thoughts to the place of our comforts. As you would delight a covetous man by showing him gold, so God delights his people by leading them, as it were, into heaven, and showing them himself and their rest with him. He does not kindle our joys while we are idle, or taken up with other things. He gives the fruits of the earth while we plough and sow and weed and water and dress, and with patience expect his blessing; so doth he give the joys of the soul. I entreat thee, reader, in the name of the Lord, and as thou valuest the life of constant joy, and that good conscience which is a continual feast, to enter upon this work seriously, and learn the art of heavenly-mindedness, and thou shalt find the increase a hundred-fold, and the benefit abundantly exceed thy labor. But this is the misery of man's nature : though every man naturally hates sorrow and loves the most merry and joyful life, yet few love the way to joy, or will endure the pains by which it is obtained ; they will take the first that comes to hand, and content themselves with earthly pleasures, rather than ascend to heaven to seek it ; and yet, when all is done, they must have it there, or be without it.

4. A heart in heaven will be a most excellent *preservative against temptations to sin.* It will keep the heart well employed. When we are idle, we tempt the devil to tempt us ; as careless persons make thieves. A heart in heaven can reply to the tempter, as Nehemiah did, "I am doing a great work, so that I cannot come." It hath no leisure

to be lustful or wanton, ambitious or worldly. If you were but busy in your lawful callings, you would not be so ready to hearken to temptations ; much less, if you were also busy above with God. Would a judge be persuaded to rise from the bench, when he is sitting upon a case of life and death, to go and play with children in the streets ? No more will a Christian, when he is taking a survey of his eternal rest, give ear to the alluring charms of Satan. The children of that kingdom should never have time for trifles, especially when they are employed in the affairs of the kingdom ; and this employment is one of the saints' chief preservatives from temptations.

A heavenly mind is the freest from sin, because it has truer and livelier apprehensions of spiritual things. He hath so deep an insight into the evil of sin, the vanity of the creature, the brutishness of fleshly, sensual delights, that temptations have little power over him. " In vain the net is spread," says Solomon, "in the sight of any bird ;" and usually in vain doth Satan lay his snares to entrap the soul that plainly sees them. Earth is the place for his temptations, and the ordinary bait ; and how shall these ensnare the Christian who hath left the earth and walks with God ? Is converse with wise and learned men the way to make one wise ? Much more is converse with God. If travellers return home with wisdom and experience, how much more

he that travels to heaven.   If our bodies are suited
to the air and climate we most live in, his understanding must be fuller of light who lives with the
Father of lights.   The men of the world that dwell
below, and know no other conversation but earthly,
no wonder if their "understanding be darkened,"
and Satan "take them captive at his will."   How
can worms and moles see, whose dwelling is always
in the earth ?   While this dust is in their eyes, no
wonder they mistake gain for godliness, sin for
grace, the world for God, their own wills for the
law of Christ, and, in the issue, hell for heaven.
But when a Christian withdraws himself from his
worldly thoughts, and begins to converse with God
in heaven, methinks he is, as Nebuchadnezzar, taken
from the beasts of the field to the throne, and "his
reason returneth unto him."   When he has had a
glimpse of eternity, and looks down on the world
again, how doth he charge with folly his neglects of
Christ, his fleshly pleasures, his earthly cares.   How
doth he say of his laughter, It is mad ; and of his
vain mirth, What doeth it ?   How doth he verily
think there is no man in Bedlam so truly mad as
wilful sinners, and unworthy slighters of Christ and
glory.   This makes a dying man usually wiser than
others, because he looks on eternity as near, and
hath more heart-piercing thoughts of it than he
ever had in health and prosperity.   Then many of
the most bitter enemies of the saints have their

eyes opened, and like Balaam, cry out, "O that I might die the death of the righteous, and that my last end might be like his." Yet let the same men recover, and lose their apprehensions of the life to come, and how quickly do they lose their understanding with it. Tell a dying sinner of the riches, honors, or pleasures of the world, and would he not answer, "What is all this to me, who must presently appear before God, and give an account of all my life?" Christian, if the apprehended nearness of eternity will work such strange effects upon the ungodly, and make them so much wiser than before, O what rare effects would it produce in thee, couldst thou always dwell in the views of God, and in lively thoughts of thy everlasting state. Surely a believer, if he improve his faith, may ordinarily have more quickening apprehensions of the life to come, in the time of his health, than an unbeliever hath at the hour of his death.

A heavenly mind is also fortified against temptations, because the affections are thoroughly prepossessed with the high delights of another world. He that loves most, and not he that only knows most, will most easily resist the motions of sin. The will doth as sweetly relish goodness as the understanding doth truth; and here lies much of a Christian's strength. When thou hast had a fresh, delightful taste of heaven, thou wilt not be so easily persuaded from it. You cannot persuade a child to part with his sweetmeats while the taste is in his mouth. O that you would be much in feeding on the hidden manna, and frequently tasting the delights of heaven. How would this confirm thy resolutions, and make thee despise the fooleries of the world, and scorn to be cheated with such childish toys. If the devil had set upon Peter in the mount of transfiguration, when he saw Moses and Elias talking with Christ, would he so easily have been drawn to deny his Lord? What, with all that glory in his eye? No. So if he should set upon a believing soul when he is taken up into the mount with Christ, what should such a soul say? "Get thee behind me, Satan; wouldst thou persuade me hence with trifling pleasures, and steal my heart from this my rest? Wouldst thou have me sell these joys for nothing? Is any honor or delight like this; or can that be profit, for which I must lose this?" But Satan stays till we are come down, and the taste of heaven is out of our mouths, and the glory we saw is even forgotten, and then he easily deceives our hearts. Though the Israelites below eat and drink, and rise up to play before their idol, Moses in the mount will not do so. O, if we could keep the taste of our souls continually delighted with the sweetness above, with what disdain should we spit out the baits of sin.

Besides, while the heart is set on heaven, a man is under God's protection. If Satan then assault

us, God is more engaged for our defence, and will
doubtless stand by us and say, "My grace is sufficient for thee." When a man is in the way of
God's blessing, he is in the less danger of sin's en-
ticing. Amidst thy temptations, Christian reader,
use much this powerful remedy; keep close with
God by a heavenly mind; follow your business
above with Christ, and you will find this a surer
help than any other. "The way of life is above
to the wise, that he may depart from hell beneath."
Remember, that "Noah was a just man, and perfect
in his generation," for he "walked with God;"
and that God said to Abraham, "Walk before me,
and be thou perfect."

5. The diligent keeping your hearts in heaven
*will maintain the vigor of all your graces, and put
life into all your duties.* The heavenly Christian
is the lively Christian. It is our strangeness to
heaven that makes us so dull. How will the soldier hazard his life, and the mariner pass through
storms and waves, and no difficulty keep them
back, when they think of an uncertain, perishing
treasure. What life, then, would it put into a
Christian's endeavors, if he would frequently think
of his everlasting treasure. We run so slowly, and
strive so lazily, because we so little mind the prize.
Observe but the man who is much in heaven, and
you shall see he is not like other Christians; something of what he hath seen above appeareth in all

his duty and conversation. If a preacher, how
heavenly are his sermons. If a private Christian,
what heavenly converse, prayers, and deportment.
Set yourself upon this employment, and others will
see the face of your conversation shine, and say,
Surely he hath been "with God on the mount."
But if you lie complaining of deadness and dulness—that you cannot love Christ, nor rejoice in
his love—that you have no life in prayer or any
other duty, and yet neglect this quickening employment, you are the cause of your own complaints. Is not thy life "hid with Christ in God?"
Where must thou go but to Christ for it? And
where is that but to heaven, "where Christ is?"
"Thou wilt not come to Christ, that thou mayest
have life." If thou wouldst have light and heat,
why art thou no more in the sunshine? For want
of this recourse to heaven, thy soul is as a lamp
not lighted, and thy duties as a sacrifice without
fire. Fetch one coal daily from this altar, and see
if thy offering will not burn. Light thy lamp at
this flame, and feed it daily with oil from hence,
and see if it will not gloriously shine. Keep close
to this reviving fire, and see if thy affections will
not be warm. In thy want of love to God, lift up
thy eye of faith to heaven, behold his beauty, contemplate his excellencies, and see whether his
amiableness and perfect goodness will not ravish
thy heart. As exercise gives appetite, strength,

and vigor to the body, so these heavenly exercises will quickly cause the increase of grace and spiritual life.

Besides, it is not false or strange fire which you fetch from heaven for your sacrifices: the zeal which is kindled by your meditations on heaven, is most likely to be a heavenly zeal. Some men's fervency is only drawn from their books, some from the sharpness of affliction, some from the mouth of a moving minister, and some from the attention of an auditory; but he that knows this way to heaven, and derives it daily from the true fountain, shall have his soul revived with the water of life, and enjoy that quickening which is peculiar to the saints. By this faith thou mayest offer Abel's sacrifice, more excellent than that of common men, and "by it obtain witness that thou art righteous, God testifying of thy gifts" that they are sincere. When others are ready, like Baal's priests, to "cut themselves," because their sacrifice will not burn, thou mayest breathe the spirit of Elijah, and in the chariot of contemplation soar aloft, till thy soul and sacrifice gloriously flame, though the flesh and the world should cast upon them all the water of their opposing enmity. Say not, How can mortals ascend to heaven? Faith hath wings, and meditation is its chariot. Faith is as a burning glass to thy sacrifice, and meditation sets it to the face of the sun; only take it not away too soon, but hold

it there a while, and thy soul will feel the happy
effect.   Reader, art thou not thinking, when thou
seest a lively Christian, and hearest his fervent
prayers and edifying discourse, "O how happy a
man is this.   O that my soul were in this blessed
condition."   Why, I here advise thee, from God,
set thy soul conscientiously to this work, wash thee
frequently in this Jordan, and thy leprous, dead soul
will revive, "and thou shalt know that there is a
God in Israel," and that thou mayest live a vigorous and joyful life if thou dost not wilfully neglect
thy own mercies.

6. *Frequent believing views of glory are the most
precious cordials in all afflictions.*   These cordials,
by cheering our spirits, render our sufferings far
more easy, enable us to bear them with patience
and joy, and so strengthen our resolutions that we
forsake not Christ for fear of trouble.   If the way
be ever so rough, can it be tedious if it lead to
heaven?   O sweet sickness, reproaches, imprison-
ments, or death, accompanied with these tastes of
our future rest!   This keeps the suffering from the
soul, so that it can only touch the flesh.   Had it
not been for that little—alas, too little—taste
which I had of rest, my sufferings would have
been grievous, and death more terrible.   I may
say, "I had fainted, unless I had believed to see
the goodness of the Lord in the land of the living."
Unless this promised rest "had been my delight, I

should then have perished in mine affliction. One thing have I desired of the Lord, that will I seek after : that I may dwell in the house of the Lord all the days of my life, to behold the beauty of the Lord, and to inquire in his temple. For in the time of trouble he shall hide me in his pavilion ; in the secret of his tabernacle shall he hide me ; he shall set me upon a rock. And now shall my head be lifted up above mine enemies round about me. Therefore will I offer in his tabernacle sacrifices of joy ; I will sing, yea, I will sing praises unto the Lord." All sufferings are nothing to us, so far as we have these supporting joys. When persecution and fear have shut the doors, Christ can come in and stand in the midst, and say to his disciples, " Peace be unto you." Paul and Silas can be in heaven, even when they are thrust into the inner prison, their bodies scourged with "many stripes and their feet fast in the stocks." The martyrs find more rest in their flames than their persecutors in their pomp and tyranny, because they foresee the flames they escape, and the rest to which their fiery chariot is conveying them. If the Son of God will walk with us, we are safe in the midst of those flames which shall devour them that cast us in. Abraham went out of his country, "not knowing whither he went," because "he looked for a city which hath foundations, whose builder and maker is God." Moses "esteemed the reproach of Christ greater riches than the treasures in Egypt, because he had respect unto the recompense of reward. He forsook Egypt, not fearing the wrath of the king, because he endured as seeing Him who is invisible. Others were tortured, not accepting deliverance, that they might obtain a better resurrection." Even Jesus, "the author and finisher of our faith, for the joy that was set before him, endured the cross, despising the shame, and is set down at the right hand of the throne of God."

This is the noble advantage of faith : it can look on the means and end together. The great reason of our impatience and censuring of God is, that we gaze on the evil itself, but fix not our thoughts on what is beyond it. They that saw Christ only on the cross or in the grave, shook their heads, and thought him lost ; but God saw him dying, buried, rising, glorified ; and all this at one view. Faith will, in this, imitate God, so far as it hath the glass of a promise to help it. We see God burying us under ground, but we foresee not the spring, when we shall all revive. Could we but clearly see heaven as the end of all God's dealings with us, surely none of his dealings could be grievous. If God would once raise us to this life, we should find that though heaven and sin are at a great distance, yet, heaven and a prison or banishment, heaven and the belly of a whale or a den of lions, heaven and consuming sickness or invading death,

are at no such distance. But as "Abraham saw
Christ's day and rejoiced," so we, in our most forlorn state, might see that day when Christ shall
give us rest, and therein rejoice. I beseech thee,
Christian, for the honor of the gospel, and for thy
soul's comfort, leave not this heavenly art to be
learned when, in thy greatest extremity, thou
hast most need to use it. He that, with Stephen,
"sees the glory of God, and Jesus standing on the
right hand of God," will comfortably bear the
shower of stones. "The joy of the Lord is our
strength," and that joy must be drawn from the
place of our joy; and if we walk without our
strength, how long are we likely to endure?

7. *He whose conversation is in heaven, is the
profitable Christian to all about him.* When a
man is in a strange country, how glad is he of the
company of one of his own nation; how delightful
is it to talk of their own country, their acquaintance, and affairs at home. With what pleasure
did Joseph talk with his brethren, and inquire after
his father and his brother Benjamin. Is it not so
to a Christian, to talk with his brethren that have
been above, and inquire after his Father, and Christ
his Lord? When a worldly man will talk of nothing
but the world, and a politician of state affairs, and
a mere scholar of human learning, and a common
professor of his duties, the heavenly man will be
speaking of heaven, and the strange glory his faith

hath seen, and our speedy and blessed meeting
there. O how refreshing and useful are his expressions. How his words pierce and melt the
heart, and transform the hearers into other men.
How doth his "doctrine drop as the rain, and his
speech distil as the dew, as the small rain upon
the tender herb, and as the showers upon the
grass," while his lips publish the name of the
Lord, and ascribe greatness unto his God. His
sweet discourse of heaven is like the "box of precious ointment," which, being "poured upon the
head of Christ, filled the house with the odor"
All that are near may be refreshed by it.

Happy the people that have a heavenly minister.
Happy the children and servants that have a heavenly father or master. Happy the man that hath
a heavenly companion, who will watch over thy
ways, strengthen thee when thou art weak, cheer
thee when thou art drooping, and "comfort thee
with the comfort wherewith he himself" hath been
so often comforted of God. This is he that will
always be blowing at the spark of thy spiritual
life, and drawing thy soul to God, and will say to
thee, as the Samaritan woman, "Come and see
one that hath told me all that ever I did;" one
that hath loved our souls to the death. "Is not
this the Christ?" Is not the knowledge of God
in Christ eternal life? Is it not the glory of the
saints to see his glory? Come to this man's house

and sit at his table, and he will feast thy soul with the dainties of heaven; travel with him by the way, and he will direct and quicken thee in thy journey to heaven; trade with him in the world, and he will counsel thee to buy "the pearl of great price." If thou wrong him, he can pardon thee, remembering that Christ hath pardoned his greater offences. If thou be angry, he is meek, considering the meekness of his heavenly Pattern; or, if he fall out with you, he is soon reconciled, when he recollects that in heaven you must be everlasting friends. This is the Christian of the right stamp, and all about him are better for him. How unprofitable is the society of all other sorts of Christians, in comparison with this. If a man should come from heaven, how would men long to hear what reports he would make of the other world, and what he had seen, and what the blessed there enjoy. Would they not think this man the best companion, and his discourses the most profitable? Why, then, do you value the company of saints no more, and inquire no more of them, and relish their discourse no better? For every saint shall go to heaven in person, and is frequently there in spirit, and hath often viewed it in the glass of the gospel. For my part, I had rather have the company of a heavenly-minded Christian, than that of the most learned disputants or princely commanders.

8. No man so highly *honoreth God*, as he whose

conversation is in heaven.　Is not a parent dishonored when his children feed on husks, are clothed
in rags, and keep company with none but rogues
and beggars?　And is not our heavenly Father,
when we, who call ourselves his children, feed on
earth, and the garb of our souls is like that of the
world and our hearts familiarly converse with and
" cleave to the dust," rather than stand continually
in our Father's presence?　Surely we live below
the children of the King, not according to the
height of our hopes, nor the provision of our Father's house, and the great preparations made for his
saints.　It is well we have a Father of tender compassion, who will own his children in rags.　If he
did not first challenge his interest in us, neither ourselves nor others could know us to be his people.
But when a Christian can live above, and rejoice
his soul with the things that are unseen, how is
God honored by such a one.　The Lord will testify
for him, This man believes me, and takes me at
my word ; he rejoices in my promise before he has
possession ; he can be thankful for what his bodily
eyes never saw ; his rejoicing is not in the flesh ;
his heart is with me ; he loves my presence, and
he shall surely enjoy it in my kingdom for ever.
" Blessed are they that have not seen, and yet have
believed.　Them that honor me, I will honor."
How did God esteem himself honored by Caleb
and Joshua, when they went into the promised

land and brought back to their brethren a taste of
the fruits, and spoke well of the good land, and
encouraged the people.   What a promise and recompense did they receive.

9. A soul that does not set its affections on things
above, *disobeys the commands, and loses the most
gracious and delightful discoveries of the word of
God*.   The same God that hath commanded thee
to believe, and to be a Christian, hath commanded
to " seek those things which are above, where Christ
sitteth on the right hand of God ; and to set our
affections on things above, not on things on the
earth."   The same God that has forbidden thee to
murder, steal, or commit adultery, has forbidden
thee the neglect of this great duty ; and darest thou
wilfully disobey him ?   Why not make conscience
of one as well as the other ?   He hath made it thy
duty, as well as the means of thy comfort, that a
double bond may engage thee not to forsake thy own
mercies.   Besides, what are all the most glorious
descriptions of heaven, all those discoveries of our
future blessedness and precious promises of our rest,
but lost to thee ?   Are not these the stars in the
firmament of Scripture, and the golden lines in that
book of God ?   Methinks thou shouldst not part
with one of these promises, no, not for a world.
As heaven is the perfection of all our mercies, so
the promises of it in the gospel are the very soul
of the gospel.   Is a comfortable word from the

mouth of God of such worth, that all the comforts
in the world are nothing to it? And dost thou
neglect and overlook so many of them? Why
should God reveal so much of his counsel, and tell
us beforehand of the joys we shall possess, but to
make us know it for our joy? If it had not been
to fill us with the delights of our foreknown blessedness, he might have kept his purpose to himself.
and never have let us know it till we came to en
joy it. Yea, when we had got possession of our
rest, he might still have concealed its eternity from
us, and then the fears of losing it would have di-
minished the sweetness of our joys. But it hath
pleased our Father to open his counsel, and let us
know the very intent of his heart, that our joy
might be full, and that we might live as the heirs
of such a kingdom. And shall we now overlook
all? Shall we live in earthly cares and sorrows,
and rejoice no more in these discoveries than if the
Lord had never written them? If thy prince had
but sealed thee a patent of some lordship, how oft
wouldst thou cast thy eyes upon it, and make it
thy delightful study, till thou shouldst come to
possess the dignity itself. And hath God sealed
thee a patent of heaven, and dost thou let it lie by
thee as if thou hadst forgotten it? O that our
hearts were as high as our hopes, and our hopes as
high as these infallible promises!

10. It is but equal that our hearts should be on

God, *when the heart of God is so much on us.* If the Lord of glory can stoop so low as to set his heart on sinful dust, methinks we should easily be persuaded to set our hearts on Christ and glory, and ascend to him in our daily affections, who so much condescends to us. Christian, dost thou not perceive that the heart of God is set upon thee, and that he is still minding thee with tender love, even when thou forgettest both thyself and him? Is he not following thee with daily mercies, moving upon thy soul, providing for thy body, preserving both? Doth he not bear thee continually in the arms of love, and promise that "all shall work together for thy good," and suit all his dealings to thy greatest advantage, and "give his angels charge over thee?" And canst thou be taken up with the joys below, and forget thy Lord, who forgets not thee? Unkind ingratitude! When he speaks of his own kindness for us, hear what he says: "Zion said, The Lord hath forsaken me, and my Lord hath forgotten me. Can a woman forget her sucking child, that she should not have compassion on the son of her womb? Yea, they may forget, yet will I not forget thee. Behold, I have graven thee upon the palms of my hands; thy walls are continually before me." But when he speaks of our regards to him, the case is otherwise. "Can a maid forget her ornaments, or a bride her attire? Yet my people have forgotten me, days without number."

As if he should say, "You will not rise one morning, but you will remember to cover your nakedness, nor forget your vanity of dress ; and are these
of more worth than your God—of more importance
than your eternal life ? And yet you can forget
these, day after day." Give not God cause thus
to expostulate with us. Rather let our souls get
up to God, and visit him every morning, and our
hearts be towards him every moment.

11. *Our interest in heaven, and our relation to
it*, should continually keep our hearts upon it.
There our Father keeps his court. We call him
"Our Father, who art in heaven." Unworthy
children, that can be so taken up in their play as to
be mindless of such a Father. There also is Christ,
our head, our husband, our life ; and shall we not
look towards him, and send to him as oft as we can,
till we come to see him face to face ? Since "the
heavens must receive him until the times of the
restitution of all things," let them also receive our
hearts with him. There also is the "New Jerusalem, which is the mother of us all." And there
are multitudes of our elder brethren. There are
our friends and old acquaintance, whose society in
the flesh we so much delighted in, and whose
departure hence we so much lamented ; and is this
not attractive to thy thoughts ? If they were
within thy reach on earth, thou wouldst go and
visit them ; and why not oftener visit them in

spirit, and rejoice beforehand to think of meeting them there? "Socrates rejoiced that he should die, because he believed he should see Homer, Hesiod, and other eminent persons. How much more do I rejoice," said a pious old minister, "who am sure to see Christ my Saviour, the eternal Son of God, in his assumed flesh; besides so many wise, holy, and renowned patriarchs, prophets, and apostles." A believer should look to heaven, and contemplate the blessed state of the saints, and think with himself, "Though I am not yet so happy as to be with you, yet this is my daily comfort—you are my brethren and fellow-members in Christ, and therefore your joys are my joys, and your glory, by this near relation, is my glory; especially while I believe in the same Christ, and hold fast the same faith and obedience by which you were thus dignified, and rejoice in spirit with you, and congratulate your happiness in my daily meditations."

Moreover, our house and home is above, "For we know that if our earthly house of this tabernacle were dissolved, we have a building of God, a house not made with hands, eternal in the heavens." Why do we then look no oftener towards it, and "groan, earnestly desiring to be clothed upon with our house which is from heaven?" If our home were far meaner, surely we should remember it, because it is our home. If you were but banished into a strange land, how frequently would your

thoughts be at home. And why is it not thus with
us in respect to heaven? Is not that more truly
and properly our home, where we must take up our
everlasting abode, than this, which we are every
hour expecting to be separated from, and to see no
more? We are strangers, and that is our country.
We are heirs, and that is our inheritance, even
"an inheritance incorruptible, undefiled, and that
fadeth not away, reserved in heaven for us." We
are here in continual distress and want, and there
lies our substance, even "a better and an enduring
substance." Yea, the very hope of our souls is
there; all our hope of relief from our distresses;
all our hope of happiness, when here we are miserable: all this "hope is laid up for us in heaven."
Why, beloved Christians, have we so much interest, and so few thoughts there; so near relation,
and so little affection? Doth it become us to be
delighted in the company of strangers, so as to forget our Father and our Lord; or to be so well
pleased with those that hate and grieve us, as to
forget our best and dearest friends; or to be so fond
of borrowed trifles, as to forget our own possession
and treasure; or to be so much impressed with
fears and wants as to forget our eternal joy and
rest? God usually pleads his property in us;
and thence concludes he will do us good, even
because we are his own people, whom he hath
chosen out of all the world. Why then do we not

plead our interest in him, and so raise our hearts above, even because he is our own God, and because the place is our own possession? Men commonly overlove and overvalue their own things, and mind them too much. O that we could mind our own inheritance, and value it half as much as it deserves.

12. Once more consider, *there is nothing but heaven worth setting our hearts upon.* If God have them not, who shall? If thou mind not thy rest, what wilt thou mind? Hast thou found out some other god; or something that will serve thee instead of rest? Hast thou found on earth an eternal happiness? Where is it? What is it made of? Who was the man that found it out? Who was he that last enjoyed it? Where dwelt he? What was his name? Or art thou the first that ever discovered heaven on earth? Ah, wretch, trust not to thy discoveries; boast not of thy gain till experience bid thee boast. Disquiet not thyself in looking for that which is not on earth, lest thou learn thy experience with the loss of thy soul, which thou mightest have learned on easier terms, even by the warnings of God in his word and the loss of thousands of souls before thee. If Satan should take thee up to the mountain of temptation, and "show thee all the kingdoms of the world, and the glory of them," he could show thee nothing that is worthy thy thoughts, much less to be preferred before

thy rest. Indeed, so far as duty and necessity require it, we must be content to mind the things below; but who is he that contains himself within the compass of those limits? and yet, if we ever so diligently contract our cares and thoughts, we shall find the least to be bitter and burdensome. Christian, see the emptiness of all these things, and the preciousness of the things above. If thy thoughts should, like the laborious bee, go over the world from flower to flower, from creature to creature, they would bring no honey or sweetness home, save what they gathered from their relations to eternity. Though every truth of God is precious, and ought to be defended, yet even all our study of truth should be still in reference to our rest; for the observation is too true, that "the lovers of controversies in religion have never been warmed with one spark of the love of God." And as for minding the "affairs of the church and the state," so far as they illustrate the providence of God, and tend to the settling of the gospel and the government of Christ, and consequently to the saving of our own souls and those of our posterity, they are well worth our diligent observation; but these are only their relations to eternity. Even all our dealings in the world, our buying and selling, our eating and drinking, our building and marrying, our peace and war, so far as they relate not to the life to come, but tend only to the pleasing of the flesh, are not worthy the frequent thoughts of a Christian. And now, doth not thy conscience say that there is nothing but heaven, and the way to it, that is worth thy minding?

Now, reader, are these considerations weighty or not? Have I proved it to be thy duty to keep thy heart on things above, or have I not? If thou say, Not, I am confident thou contradictest thy own conscience. If thou acknowledge thyself convinced of the duty, that very tongue of thine shall condemn thee, and that confession be pleaded against thee, if thou wilfully neglect such a confessed duty. Be thoroughly willing, and the work is more than half done. I have now a few plain directions to give you for your help in this great work; but, alas, it is in vain to mention them, except you be willing to put them into practice. However, I will propose them to thee, and may the Lord persuade thy heart to the work.

CHAPTER XII

DIRECTIONS HOW TO LEAD A HEAVENLY LIFE UPON EARTH

I. The hinderances to a heavenly life: 1. Living in any known sin; 2. An earthly mind; 3. Ungodly companions; 4. A notional religion; 5. A haughty spirit; 6. A slothful spirit; 7. Resting in preparatives for a heavenly life, without the thing itself. II. The duties which will promote a heavenly life: 1. Be convinced that heaven is the only treasure and happiness; 2. Labor to know your interest in it; 3. And how near it is; 4. Frequently and seriously talk of it; 5. Endeavor, in every duty, to raise your affections nearer to it; 6. To the same purpose improve every object and event; 7. Be much in the angelical work of praise; 8. Possess your souls with believing thoughts of the infinite love of God; 9. Carefully observe and cherish the motions of the Spirit of God; 10. Nor even neglect the due care of your bodily health.

As thou valuest the comforts of a heavenly conversation, I must here charge thee, from God, to avoid carefully some dangerous *hinderances;* and then faithfully and diligently to practise such *duties* as will especially assist thee in attaining to a heavenly life.

First, let us consider those HINDERANCES which are to be avoided with all possible care.

1. *Living in any known sin* is a grand impediment to a heavenly life. What havoc will this

make in thy soul. O the joys that this hath destroyed; the ruin it hath made among men's graces; the soul-strengthening duties it hath hindered. Christian reader, art thou one that hast used violence with thy conscience? Art thou a wilful neglecter of known duty, either public, private, or secret? Art thou a slave to thine appetite, or to any other commanding sense? Art thou a proud seeker of thine own esteem? Art thou a peevish and passionate person, ready to take fire at every word, or look, or supposed slight? Art thou a deceiver of others in thy dealings, or one that will be rich, right or wrong? If this be thy case, I dare say heaven and thy soul are very great strangers. These "beams in thine eye" will not suffer thee to look to heaven; they will be "a cloud between thee and thy God." When thou dost but attempt to study eternity and gather refreshment from the life to come, thy sin will presently look thee in the face, and say, "These things belong not to thee. How shouldst thou take comfort from heaven, who takest so much pleasure in the lusts of the flesh? How will this damp thy joys, and make the thoughts of that day and state become thy trouble and not thy delight. Every wilful sin will be to thy joys as water to the fire; when thou thinkest to quicken them, this will quench them. It will utterly indispose and disable thee, that thou canst no more ascend in divine meditation than a bird can fly

when its wings are clipped. Sin cuts the **very**
sinews of this heavenly life. O man, what a life
dost thou lose. What daily delights dost thou sell
for vile lusts. If heaven and hell can meet together,
and God become a lover of sin, then mayest thou live
in thy sin, and in the foretastes of glory ; and have
a conversation in heaven, though thou cherish thy
corruption. And take heed, lest it banish thee from
heaven, as it does thy heart. And though thou be
not guilty, and knowest no reigning sin in thy soul,
think what a sad thing it would be, if ever this
should prove thy case. Watch, therefore ; especially
resolve to keep from the occasions of sin, and out
of the way of temptations. What need have we
daily to pray, " Lead us not into temptation, but
deliver us from evil."

2. An *earthly mind* is another hinderance carefully to be avoided. God and mammon, earth and
heaven cannot both have the delight of thy heart.
When the heavenly believer is blessing himself in
his God, and rejoicing in hope of the glory to come,
perhaps thou art blessing thyself in thy worldly
prosperity, and rejoicing in hope of thy thriving
here. When he is comforting his soul in the views
of Christ, of angels and saints, whom he shall live
with for ever, then thou art comforting thyself with
thy wealth, in looking over thy bills and bonds, thy
goods, thy cattle, or thy buildings ; and in thinking
of the favor of the great, of the pleasure of a plen-

tiful estate, of larger provisions for thy children after thee, of the advancement of thy family, or the increase of thy dependents. If Christ pronounced him a fool that said, "Soul, take thy ease; thou hast much goods laid up for many years;" how much more so art thou, who knowingly speakest in thy heart the same words? Tell me, What difference between this fool's expressions and thy affections? Remember, thou hast to do with the Searcher of hearts. Certainly, so much as thou delightest and takest up thy rest on earth, so much of thy delight in God is abated. Thine earthly mind may consist with thy outward profession and common duties, but it cannot consist with this heavenly duty. Thou thyself knowest how seldom and cold, how cursory and reserved thy thoughts have been of the joys above, ever since thou didst trade so eagerly for the world.

O the cursed madness of many that seem to be religious! They thrust themselves into a multitude of employments, till they are so loaded with labors and clogged with cares, that their souls are as unfit to converse with God, as a man to walk with a mountain on his back; and as unapt to soar in meditation, as their bodies to leap above the sun. And when they have lost that heaven upon earth which they might have had, they take up with a few rotten arguments to prove it lawful; though indeed they cannot. I advise thee, Christian, who hast

tasted the pleasures of a heavenly life, if ever thou
wouldst taste them more, avoid this devouring gulf
of an earthly mind. If once thou come to this, that
thou "wilt be rich," thou fallest into temptation
and a snare, and into many foolish and hurtful
lusts. Keep these things loose about thee like thy
upper garments, that thou mayest lay them by
whenever there is need ; but let God and glory be
next thy heart. Ever remember, that "the friendship of the world is enmity with God. Whosoever,
therefore, will be a friend of the world, is the enemy
of God." "Love not the world, neither the things
that are in the world. If any man love the world,
the love of the Father is not in him." This is plain
dealing, and happy he that faithfully receives it.

3. *Beware of the company of the ungodly.* Not
that I would dissuade thee from necessary converse,
or from doing the many office of love ; especially,
not from endeavoring the good of their souls as long
as thou hast any opportunity or hope ; nor would I
have thee to conclude them to be dogs and swine,
in order to evade the duty of reproof; nor even to
judge them such at all, as long as there is any hope
for the better ; much less can I approve of their
practice who conclude men to be dogs or swine
before ever they faithfully and lovingly admonish
them, or perhaps before they have known them, or
spoken with them. But it is the unnecessary society of ungodly men, and too much familiarity with

unprofitable companions, from which I would dissuade you. Not only the profane, the swearer, the
drunkard, and the enemies of godliness will prove
hurtful companions to us—though these indeed are
chiefly to be avoided—but too frequent society with
persons merely civil and moral, whose conversation
is empty and unedifying, may much divert our
thoughts from heaven. Our backwardness is such,
that we need the most constant and powerful helps.
A stone or a clod is as fit to rise and fly in the air,
as our hearts are naturally to move towards heaven.
You need not hinder the rocks from flying up to the
sky, it is sufficient that you do not help them; and
surely, if our spirits have not great assistance, they
may easily be kept from soaring upwards, though
they should never meet with the least impediment.
O think of this in the choice of your company.
When your spirits are so disposed for heaven that
you need no help to lift them up, but, as flames,
you are always mounting, and carrying with you
all that is in your way, then indeed you may be
less careful of your company; but till then, as you
love the delights of a heavenly life, be careful
herein. What will it advantage thee in a divine
life, to hear how the market goes, or what the
weather is or is likely to be, or what news is stir-
ring? This is the discourse of earthly men. What
will it conduce to the raising of thy heart to God,
to hear that this is an able minister, or that an emi-

nent Christian, or this an excellent sermon, or that an excellent book; or to hear some difficult but unimportant controversy? Yet this, for the most part, is the sweetest discourse thou art like to have from a formal, speculative, dead-hearted professor. Nay, if thou hadst been newly warming thy heart in the contemplation of the blessed joys above, would not this discourse benumb thy affections and quickly freeze thy heart again? I appeal to the judgment of any man that hath tried it, and maketh observations on the frame of his spirit. Men cannot well talk of one thing and mind another, especially things of such different natures. You, young men, who are most liable to this temptation, think seriously of what I say: can you have your hearts in heaven while among your roaring companions in an alehouse or tavern; or when you work in your shops with those whose common language is oaths, "filthiness, or foolish talking or jesting?" Nay, let me tell you, if you choose such company when you might have better, and find most delight in such, you are so far from a heavenly conversation, that as yet you have no title to heaven at all, and in that state shall never come there. If your treasure was there, your heart could not be on things so distant. In a word, our company will be a part of our happiness in heaven, and it is a singular part of our furtherance to it, or hinderance from it.

4. *Avoid frequent disputes about lesser truths, and a religion that lies only in opinions.* They are usually least aquainted with a heavenly life, who are violent disputers about the circumstantials of religion. He whose religion is all in his opinions, will be most frequently and zealously speaking his opinions ; and he whose religion lies in the knowledge and love of God and Christ, will be most delightfully speaking of that happy time when he shall enjoy them. He is a rare and precious Christian who is skilful to improve well-known truths. Therefore let me advise you who aspire after a heavenly life, not to spend too much of your thoughts, your time, your zeal, or your speech, upon disputes that less concern your souls ; but when hypocrites are feeding on husks or shells, do you feed on the joys above. I wish you were able to defend every truth of God, and to this end would read and study ; but still I would have the chief truths to be chiefly studied, and none to cast out your thoughts of eternity. The least controverted points are usually most weighty, and of most necessary, frequent use to our souls. Therefore study well such scripture precepts as these : "Him that is weak in the faith receive ye, but not to doubtful disputations. Foolish and unlearned questions avoid, knowing that they do gender strifes. And the servant of the Lord must not strive." "Avoid foolish questions and genealogies, and contentions

and strivings about the law ; for they are unprofitable and vain." "If any man teach otherwise, and
consent not to wholesome words, even the words of
our Lord Jesus Christ, and to the doctrine which is
according to godliness, he is proud, knowing nothing, but doting about questions and strifes of words,
whereof cometh envy, strife, railings, evil surmis-
ings, perverse disputings of men of corrupt minds
and destitute of the truth, supposing that gain is
godliness ; from such withdraw thyself."

5. *Take heed of a proud and lofty spirit.* There
is such an antipathy between this sin and God, that
thou wilt never get thy heart near him, nor get him
near thy heart, as long as this prevaileth in it.   If
it cast the angels out of heaven, it must needs keep
thy heart from heaven.   If it cast our first parents
out of paradise, and separated between the Lord
and us, and brought his curse on all the creatures
here below, it will certainly keep our hearts from
paradise, and increase the cursed separation from
our God.   Intercourse with God will keep men
lowly, and that lowliness will promote their intercourse.   When a man is used to be much with
God, and taken up in the study of his glorious attributes, he abhors himself in dust and ashes ; and
that self-abhorrence is his best preparative to obtain admittance to God again.   Therefore, after a
soul-humbling day, or in times of trouble when the
soul is lowest, it useth to have freest access to God,

and savor most of the life above. The delight of
God is in "him that is poor, and of a contrite
spirit, and trembleth at his word;" and the delight
of such a soul is in God; and where there is mutual delight, there will be the freest admittance,
heartiest welcome, and most frequent converse.
But God is so far from dwelling in the soul that is
proud, that he will not admit it to any near access. "The proud he knoweth afar off;" "God
resisteth the proud, and giveth grace to the humble." A proud mind is high in conceit, self-esteem,
and carnal aspiring; a humble mind is high indeed
in God's esteem, and in holy aspiring. These two
sorts of high-mindedness are most of all opposite to
each other, as we see most wars are between
princes and princes, and not between a prince and
a ploughman.

Well, then, art thou a man of worth in thy
own eyes? Art thou delighted when thou hearest
of thy esteem with men, and much dejected when
thou hearest that they slight thee? Dost thou
love those best that honor thee, and think meanly
of them that do not, though they be otherwise
men of godliness and honesty? Must thou have
thy humors fulfilled, and thy judgment be a rule
and thy word a law to all about thee? Are thy
passions kindled if thy word or will be crossed?
Art thou ready to judge humility to be sordid base-
ness, and knowest not how to submit to humble

confession, when thou hast sinned against God or injured thy brother? Art thou one that lookest strange at the godly poor, and art almost ashamed to be their companion? Canst thou not serve God in a low place as well as a high? Are thy boastings restrained more by prudence or artifice than humility? Dost thou desire to have all men's eyes upon thee, and to hear them say, "This is he?" Art thou unacquainted with the deceitfulness and wickedness of thy heart? Art thou more ready to defend thy innocence, than accuse thyself or confess thy fault? Canst thou hardly bear a close reproof, or digest plain dealing? If these symptoms be undeniably in thy heart, thou art a proud person. There is too much of hell abiding in thee to have any acquaintance with heaven; thy soul is too like the devil to have any familiarity with God. A proud man makes himself his god, and sets up himself as his idol; how, then, can his affections be set on God—how can he possibly have his heart in heaven? Invention and memory may possibly furnish his tongue with humble and heavenly expressions, but in his spirit there is no more heaven than there is humility. I speak the more of it, because it is the most common and dangerous sin in morality, and most promotes the great sin of infidelity.

O Christian, if thou wouldst live continually in the presence of thy Lord, lie in the dust, and he

will thence take thee up. "Learn of him to be
meek and lowly, and thou shalt find rest unto thy
soul." Otherwise thy soul will be "like the troubled
sea, when it cannot rest, whose waters cast up mire
and dirt;" and instead of these sweet delights in
God, thy pride will fill thee with perpetual disquiet.
As he that humbleth himself as a little child shall
hereafter be greatest in the kingdom of heaven, so
shall he now be greatest in the foretastes of that
kingdom. God "dwells with a contrite and humble spirit, to revive the spirit of the humble, and
to revive the heart of the contrite ones." Therefore, "humble yourselves in the sight of the Lord,
and he shall lift you up." And when "others are
cast down, then thou shalt say, there is lifting up;
and he shall save the humble person."

6. *A slothful spirit is another impediment to this
heavenly life.* And I verily think there is nothing
hinders it more than this in men of a good understanding. If it were only the exercise of the body,
the moving of the lips, the bending of the knee,
men would as commonly step to heaven as they go
to visit a friend. But to separate our thoughts and
affections from the world, to draw forth all our
graces, and increase each in its proper object, and
hold them to it till the work prospers in our hands,
this, this is the difficulty. Reader, heaven is above
thee, and dost thou think to travel this steep ascent
without labor and resolution? Canst thou get

that earthly heart to heaven, and bring that backward mind to God, while thou liest still and takest thine ease? If lying down at the foot of the hill, and looking towards the top and wishing we were there, would serve the turn, then we should have daily travellers for heaven. But "the kingdom of heaven suffereth violence, and the violent take it by force." There must be violence used to get these first-fruits, as well as to get the full possession. Dost thou not feel it so, though I should not tell thee? Will thy heart get upward, except thou drive it? Thou knowest that heaven is all thy hope, that nothing below can yield thee rest, that a heart seldom thinking of heaven can draw but little comfort thence; and yet dost thou not lose thy opportunities and lie below, when thou shouldst walk above and live with God? Dost thou not commend the sweetness of a heavenly life, and judge those the best Christians that use it, and yet never try it thyself? As the sluggard that stretches himself on his bed and cries, O that this were working! so dost thou talk and trifle and live at thy ease, and say, O that I could get my heart to heaven! How many read books and hear sermons, expecting to hear of some easier way, or to meet with a shorter course to comfort than they are ever like to find in Scripture. Or they ask for directions for a heavenly life, and if the hearing them will serve, they will be heavenly Christians; but if we show them their work, and tell them they cannot have these delights on easier terms, then they leave us, as the young man left Christ, sorrowful.

If thou art convinced, reader, that this work is necessary to thy comfort, set upon it resolutely : if thy heart draw back, force it on with the command of reason ; if thy reason begin to dispute, produce the command of God, and urge thy own necessity with the other considerations suggested in the former chapter. Let not such an incomparable treasure lie before thee with thy hand in thy bosom, nor thy life be a continual vexation when it might be a continual feast, only because thou wilt not exert thyself. Sit not still with a disconsolate spirit while comforts grow before thine eyes, like a man in the midst of a garden of flowers, that will not rise to get them and partake of their sweetness. This I know, Christ is the fountain ; but the well is deep, and thou must get forth this water before thou canst be refreshed with it. I know, so far as you are spiritual, you need not all this striving and violence ; but in part you are carnal, and as long as it is so there is need of labor. It was the custom of the Parthians not to give their children any meat in the morning before they saw the sweat on their faces with some labor. And you shall find this to be God's usual course, not to give his children the tastes of his delights till they begin to sweat in seeking after them. Judge, therefore,

whether a heavenly life or thy carnal ease be bet‧
ter, and, as a wise man, make thy choice accordingly. Yet, let me add for thy encouragement,
thou needest not employ thy thoughts more than
thou now dost; it is only to fix them upon better
and more pleasant objects. Employ but as many
serious thoughts every day upon the excellent glory
of the life to come, as thou now dost upon worldly
affairs, yea, on vanities and impertinences, and thy
heart will soon be in heaven. On the whole, it is
"the field of the slothful that is all grown over
with thorns and nettles; and the desire of the
slothful killeth his joy, for his hands refuse to
labor; and it is the slothful man that saith, There
is a lion in the way—a lion is in the streets. As
the door turneth upon its hinges, so doth the slothful man upon his bed. The slothful hideth his
hand in his bosom; it grieveth him to bring it
again to his mouth," though it be to feed himself
with the food of life. What is this but throwing
away our consolations, and consequently the pre
cious blood that bought them? For "he that is
slothful in his work, is brother to him that is a
great waster." Apply this to thy spiritual work,
and study well the meaning of it.

7. *Contentment with the mere preparatives to
this heavenly life, while we are utter strangers to
the life itself,* is also a dangerous and secret hinderance; when we take up with the mere study of

heavenly things, and the notions of them, or the talking with one another about them; as if this were enough to make us heavenly. None are in more danger of the snare than those that are employed in leading the devotions of others, especially preachers of the gospel. O how easily may such be deceived; while they do nothing so much as read and study of heaven, preach and pray and talk of heaven: is not this the heavenly life? Alas, all this is but mere preparation; this is but collecting the materials, not erecting the building itself; it is but gathering the manna for others, and not eating and digesting it ourselves. As he that sits at home may draw exact maps of countries, and yet never see them nor travel towards them, so may you describe to others the joys of heaven, and yet never come near it in your own hearts. A blind man, by learning, may dispute of light and colors; so may you set forth to others that heavenly light which never enlightened your own souls, and bring that fire from the hearts of your people which never warmed your own hearts. What heavenly passages had Balaam in his prophecies, yet how little of it in his spirit. Nay, we are under a more subtle temptation than any other men to draw us from this heavenly life. Studying and preaching of heaven more resembles a heavenly life than thinking and talking of the world does; and the resemblance is apt to deceive us.

This is to die the most miserable death, even to famish ourselves because we have bread on our tables, and to die for thirst while we draw water for others ; thinking it enough that we have daily to do with it, though we never drink for the refreshment of our own souls.

Secondly, having thus shown what hinderances will resist the work, I expect that thou resolve against them, consider them seriously, and avoid them faithfully, or else thy labor will be vain. I must also tell thee that I here expect thy promise, as thou valuest the delights of these foretastes of heaven, to make conscience of performing the following DUTIES ; particularly,

1. Be convinced that *heaven is the only treasure and happiness,* and labor to know what a treasure and happiness it is. If thou do not believe it to be the chief good, thou wilt never set thy heart upon it ; and this conviction must sink into thy affections ; for if it be only a notion, it will have little efficacy. If Eve once supposes she sees more worth in the forbidden fruit than in the love and enjoyment of God, no wonder if it have more of her heart than God. If your judgment once prefer the delights of the flesh before the delights of the presence of God, it is impossible your heart should be in heaven. As it is ignorance of the emptiness of things below that makes men so overvalue them, so it is ignorance of the high delights above which

is the cause that men so little mind them. If you see a purse of gold, and believe it to be but counters, it will not entice your affections to it. It is not the real excellence of a thing itself, but its known excellence, that excites desire. If an ignorant man see a book containing the secrets of arts and sciences, he values it no more than a common scroll, because he knows not what is in it ; but he that knows it, highly values it, and can even forbear his meat, drink, and sleep to read it. As the Jews killed the Messiah while they waited for him, because they did not know him, so the world cries out for rest, and busily seeks for delight and happiness, because they know it not; for did they thoroughly know what it is, they could not so slight the everlasting treasure.

2. Labor also to know that heaven is *thy own happiness*. We may confess heaven to be the best condition, though we despair of enjoying it ; and we may desire and seek it, if we see the attainment but probable ; but we can never delightfully rejoice in it till we are in some measure persuaded of our title to it. What comfort is it to a man that is naked to see the rich attire of others ? What delight is it for a man that hath not a house to put his head in to see the sumptuous buildings of others ? Would not all this rather increase his anguish, and make him more sensible of his own misery ? So, for a man to know the excellencies of heaven, and

not know whether he shall ever enjoy them, may raise desire and urge pursuit, but he will have little joy. Who will set his heart on another man's possessions? If your houses, your goods, your cattle, your children were not your own, you would less mind them, and less delight in them. O, Christian, rest not till you can call this rest your own: bring thy heart to the bar of trial; set the qualifications of the saints on one side, and of thy soul on the other, and then judge how nearly they resemble. Thou hast the same word to judge thyself by now, as thou must be judged by at the great day. Mistake not the Scriptures' description of a saint, that thou neither acquit nor condemn thyself upon mistakes. For as groundless hopes tend to confusion, and are the greatest cause of most men's damnation, so groundless doubts tend to, and are the great cause of the saints' perplexity and distress. Therefore, lay thy foundation for trial safely, and proceed in the work deliberately and resolutely, nor give over till thou canst say either thou hast or hast not yet a title to this rest. O if men did truly know that God is their own Father, and Christ their only Redeemer and Head, and that those are their own everlasting habitations, and that there they must abide and be happy for ever, how could they but be transported with the forethought thereof. If a Christian could but look upon sun, moon, and stars, and reckon all his own in Christ, and say, "These are the blessings that my Lord hath procured me, and things incomparably greater than these," what holy raptures would his spirit feel.

The more do they sin against their own comforts, as well as against the grace of the gospel, who plead for their unbelief, and cherish distrustful thoughts of God, and injurious thoughts of their Redeemer; who represent the covenant as if it were of works, and not of grace; and Christ as an enemy rather than a saviour; as if he were willing they should die in their unbelief, when he hath invited them so often and so affectionately, and suffered the agonies that they should suffer. Wretches that we are, to be keeping up jealousies of our Lord when we should be rejoicing in his love. As if any man could choose Christ before Christ hath chosen him; or any man were more willing to be happy than Christ is to make him happy. Away with these injurious, if not blasphemous, thoughts. If ever thou hast harbored such thoughts in thy breast, cast them from thee, and take heed how thou ever entertainest them more. God hath written the names of his people in heaven, as you use to write your names or marks on your goods; and shall we be attempting to raze them out, and to write our names on the doors of hell? But blessed be "God, whose foundation standeth sure," and who "keepeth us by his power, through faith, unto salvation."

3. Labor to apprehend *how near thy rest is.* What we think near at hand we are more sensible of, than that which we behold at a distance. When judgments or mercies are afar off, we talk of them with little concern; but when they draw close to us, we tremble at or rejoice in them. This makes men think on heaven so insensibly, because they conceive it at too great a distance; they look on it as twenty, thirty, or forty years off. How much better were it to receive "the sentence of death in ourselves," and to look on eternity as near at hand. While I am thinking and writing of it, it hasteneth near, and I am even entering into it before I am aware. While thou art reading this, whoever thou art, time posteth on, and thy life will be gone, "as a tale that is told." If you verily believed you should die to-morrow, how seriously would you think of heaven to-night. When Samuel had told Saul, "To-morrow shalt thou be with me," this struck him to the heart. And if Christ should say to a believing soul, "To-morrow shalt thou be with me," this would bring him in spirit to heaven beforehand. Do but suppose that you are still entering into heaven, and it will greatly help you more seriously to mind it.

4. Let thy eternal rest be *the subject of thy frequent serious discourse*, especially with those that can speak from their hearts, and are seasoned themselves with a heavenly nature. It is pity

Christians should ever meet together without some talk of their meeting in heaven, or of the way to it, before they part. It is pity so much time is spent in vain conversation and useless disputes, and not a serious word of heaven among them. Methinks we should meet together on purpose to warm our spirits with discoursing of our rest. To hear a Christian set forth that blessed, glorious state with life and power from the promises of the gospel, methinks should make us say, "Did not our hearts burn within us while he opened to us the Scriptures?" If a Felix will tremble when he hears his judgment powerfully represented, why should not the believer be revived when he hears his eternal rest described? Wicked men can be delighted in talking together of their wickedness; and should not Christians then be delighted in talking of Christ, and the heirs of heaven in talking of their inheritance? This may make our hearts revive, as did Jacob's to hear the message that called him to Goshen, and to see the chariots that should bring him to Joseph. O that we were furnished with skill and resolution to turn the stream of men's common discourse to these more sublime and precious things; and when men begin to talk of things unprofitable, that we could tell how to put in a word for heaven, and say, as Peter of his bodily food, "Not so, for I have never eaten any thing that is common or unclean." O the

good that we might both do and receive by this
course. Had it not been to deter us from unprofitable conversation, Christ would not have talked of
our "giving an account of every idle word in the
day of judgment." Say, then, as the psalmist,
when you are in company, "Let my tongue cleave
to the roof of my mouth, if I prefer not Jerusalem
above my chief joy." Then you shall find it true,
that a "wholesome tongue is a tree of life."

5. Endeavor, in every duty, *to raise thy affections nearer to heaven.* God's end in the institu-
tion of his ordinances was, that they should be as
so many steps to advance us to our rest, and by
which, in subordination to Christ, we might daily
ascend in our affections. Let this be thy end in
using them, and doubtless they will not be unsuc-
cessful. How have you been rejoiced by a few
lines from a friend, when you could not see him
face to face. And may we not have intercourse
with God in his ordinances, though our persons be
yet so far remote? May not our spirits rejoice in
reading those lines which contain our legacy and
charter for heaven? With what gladness and triumph may we read the expressions of divine love,
and hear of our celestial country, though we have
not yet the happiness to behold it. Men that are
separated by sea and land can by letters carry on
great and gainful trades; and may not a Christian,
in the wise improvement of duties, drive on this

happy trade for rest? Come, then, renounce formality, custom, and applause, and kneel down in
secret or public prayer, with hope to get thy heart
nearer to God before thou risest up. When thou
openest thy Bible, or other book, hope to meet with
some passage of divine truth, and such a blessing
of the Spirit with it, as will give thee a fuller taste
of heaven. When thou art going to the house of
God, say, "I hope to meet with somewhat from
God to raise my affections before I return; I hope
the Spirit will give me his presence and sweeten
my heart with those celestial delights; I hope
Christ will 'appear to me in that way, and shine
about me with light from heaven;' let me hear his
instructing and reviving voice, and cause the scales
to fall from my eyes, that I may see more of that
glory than I ever yet saw. I hope, before I return,
my Lord will bring my heart within the view of
rest, and set it before his Father's presence, that I
may return as 'the shepherds' from the heavenly
vision, 'glorifying and praising God for all the
things I have heard and seen.'" When the In-
dians first saw that the English could converse
together by letters, they thought there was some
spirit enclosed in them. So would by-standers ad-
mire, when Christians have communion with God
in duties, what there is in those scriptures, in that
sermon, in this prayer, that fills their hearts so full
of joy, and so transports them above themselves.

Certainly God would not fail us in our duties, if we did not fail ourselves. Remember, therefore, always to pray for your minister, that God would put some divine message into his mouth which may leave a heavenly relish upon your spirit.

6. *Improve every object and every event* to remind thy soul of its approaching rest. As all providences and creatures are means to our rest, so they point us to that as their end. God's sweetest dealings with us at present would not be half so sweet as they are, if they did not intimate some further sweetness. Thou takest but the bare earnest, and overlookest the main sum, when thou receivest thy mercies and forgettest thy crown. O that Christians were skilful in this art! You can open your Bible; learn to open the volumes of creation and providence, to read there also of God and glory. Thus we might have a fuller taste of Christ and heaven in every common meal than most men have in a sacrament. If thou prosper in the world, let it make thee more sensible of thine eternal prosperity. If thou art weary with labor, let it make the thoughts of thy eternal rest more sweet. If things go cross, let thy desires be more earnest to have sorrows and sufferings for ever cease. Is thy body refreshed with food or sleep? remember the inconceivable refreshment with Christ. Dost thou hear any good news? remember what glad tidings it will be to hear the trump of God and the applaud-

ing sentence of Christ. Art thou delighted with
the society of the saints? remember what the
perfect society in heaven will be. Is God communicating himself to thy spirit? remember the time
of thy highest advancement, when both thy communion and joy shall be full. Dost thou hear the
raging noise of the wicked and the confusions of
the world? think of the blessed harmony in heav-
en. Dost thou hear the tempest of war? remember
the day when thou shalt be in perfect peace, under
the wings of the Prince of peace for ever. Thus,
every condition and creature affords us advantages
for a heavenly life, if we had but hearts to improve
them.

7. *Be much in the angelic work of praise.* The
more heavenly the employment, the more it will
make the spirit heavenly. Praising God is the work
of angels and saints in heaven, and will be our own
everlasting work ; and if we were more in it now,
we should be more like what we shall be then. As
desire, faith, and hope are of shorter continuance
than love and joy, so also preaching, prayer, and
ordinances, and all means for expressing and confirming our faith and hope, shall cease when our
triumphant expressions of love and joy shall abide
for ever. The liveliest emblem of heaven that I
know upon earth is, when the people of God, in the
deep sense of his excellency and bounty, from hearts
abounding with love and joy, join together, both in

heart and voice, in the cheerful and melodious singing of his praises. These delights, like the testimony of the Spirit, witness themselves to be of God, and bring the evidences of their heavenly parentage along with them.

Little do we know how we wrong ourselves by shutting out of our prayers the praises of God, or allowing them so narrow a room as we usually do, while we are copious enough in our confessions and petitions. Reader, I entreat thee, remember this : let praises have a larger room in thy duties ; keep matter ready at hand to feed thy praise, as well as matter for confession and petition. To this end, study the excellencies and goodness of the Lord as frequently as thy own wants and unworthiness ; the mercies thou hast received, and those which are promised, as often as the sins thou hast committed. "Praise is comely for the upright. Whoso offereth praise, glorifieth God. Praise ye the Lord, for the Lord is good ; sing praises unto his name, for it is pleasant. Let us offer the sacrifice of praise to God continually, that is, the fruit of our lips, giving thanks to his name." Had not David a most heavenly spirit, who was so much in this heavenly work ? Doth it not sometimes raise our hearts when we only read the song of Moses and the psalms of David ? How much more would it raise and refresh us to be skilful and frequent in the work ourselves. O the madness of youth, that lay

out that vigor of body and mind upon vain delights
and fleshly lusts, which is so fit for the noblest
work of man.   And O the sinful folly of many ot
the saints, who drench their spirits in continual
sadness, and waste their days in complaints and
groans, and so make themselves, both in body and
mind, unfit for this sweet and heavenly work.   Instead of joining with the people of God in his praises,
they are questioning their worthiness and studying
their miseries; and so rob God of his glory and
themselves of their consolation.   But the greatest
destroyer of our comfort in this duty, is our taking
up with the tune and melody, and suffering the
heart to be idle, which ought to perform the principal part of the work, and use the melody to revive and exhilarate itself.

8. *Ever keep thy soul possessed with believing
thoughts of the infinite love of God.*   Love is the
attractive of love.   Few so vile but will love those
that love them.   No doubt it is the death of our
heavenly life to have hard thoughts of God, to conceive of him as one that would rather damn than
save us.   This is to put the blessed God into the
similitude of Satan.   When our ignorance and unbelief have drawn the most deformed picture of God
in our imaginations, then we complain that we
cannot love him, nor delight in him.   This is the
case of many thousand Christians.   Alas, that
we should thus blaspheme God and blast our own

joys. Scripture assures us that "God is love; that fury is not in him; that he hath no pleasure in the death of the wicked, but that the wicked turn from his way and live." Much more hath he testified his love to his chosen, and his full resolution to save them. O that we could always think of God as we do of a friend; as of one that unfeignedly loves us, even more than we do ourselves; whose very heart is set upon us to do us good, and hath therefore provided for us an everlasting dwelling with himself: it would not then be so hard to have our hearts ever with him. Where we love most heartily, we shall think most sweetly and most freely. I fear, most Christians think higher of the love of a hearty friend than of the love of God; and what wonder, then, if they love their friends better than God, and trust them more confidently than God, and had rather live with them than with God?

9. Carefully *observe and cherish the motions of the Spirit of God.* If ever thy soul get above this earth, and get acquainted with this heavenly life, the Spirit of God must be to thee as the chariot to Elijah, yea, the very living principle by which thou must move and ascend. O then grieve not thy guide, quench not thy life, knock not off thy chariot wheel. You little think how much the life of all your graces and the happiness of your souls depend upon your ready and cordial obedience to the Spirit.

When the Spirit urges thee to secret prayer, or forbids thee thy transgressions, or points to thee the way in which thou shouldst go, and thou wilt not regard, no wonder if heaven and thy soul be strange. If thou wilt not follow the Spirit while he would draw thee to Christ and thy duty, how should he lead thee to heaven, and bring thy heart into the presence of God? What supernatural help, what bold access shall the soul find in its approaches to the Almighty, that constantly obeys the Spirit And how backward, how dull, how ashamed will he be in these addresses, who hath often broke away from the Spirit that would have guided him. Christian reader, dost thou not feel sometimes a strong impression to retire from the world and draw near to God? Do not disobey, but take the offer, and hoist up thy sails while this blessed gale may be had. The more of the Spirit we resist, the deeper will it wound; and the more we obey, the speedier will be our pace.

10. I advise thee, as a further help to this heavenly life, *neglect not the due care of thy bodily health*. Thy body is a useful servant if thou give it its due, and no more than its due; but it is a most devouring tyrant, if thou suffer it to have what it unreasonably desires; and it is as a blunted knife, if thou unjustly deny what is necessary to its support. When we consider how frequently men offend on both extremes, and how few use their bodies

aright, we cannot wonder if they be much hindered in their converse with heaven. Most men are slaves to their appetite, and can scarcely deny any thing to their flesh, and are therefore willingly carried by it to their sports, or profits, or vain companions, when they should raise their minds to God and heaven. As you love your souls, "make not provision for the flesh, to fulfil the lust thereof;" but remember, "to be carnally minded is death; because the carnal mind is enmity against God; for it is not subject to the law of God, neither indeed can be. So, then, they that are in the flesh cannot please God. Therefore, brethren, we are debtors not to the flesh, to live after the flesh. For if ye live after the flesh, ye shall die; but if ye through the Spirit do mortify the deeds of the body, ye shall live." There are a few who much hinder their heavenly joy by denying the body its necessaries, and so making it unable to serve them: if such wronged their flesh only, it would be no great matter; but they wrong their souls also; as he that spoils the house injures the inhabitants. When the body is sick and the spirits languish, how heavily do we move in the thoughts and joys of heaven.

CHAPTER XIII

THE NATURE OF HEAVENLY CONTEMPLATION; WITH THE TIME, PLACE, AND TEMPER FITTEST FOR IT

The duty of heavenly contemplation is recommended and defined. The definition is illustrated. I. The times fittest for it are represented as, 1. Stated; 2. Frequent; 3. Seasonable—every day, particularly every Lord's day; but more especially when our hearts are warmed with a sense of divine things, or when we are afflicted or tempted, or when we are near death. II. The fittest place for it. III. The fittest temper for it, 1. When our minds are most clear of the world, 2. And most solemn and serious.

Once more I entreat thee, reader, as thou makest conscience of a revealed duty, and darest not wilfully resist the Spirit—as thou valuest the high delights of a saint, and the soul-ravishing exercise of heavenly contemplation, that thou diligently study, and speedily and faithfully practice the following directions. If, by this means, thou dost not find an increase of all thy graces, and dost not grow beyond the stature of a common Christian, and art not made more serviceable in thy place, and more precious in the eyes of all discerning persons—if thy soul enjoy not more communion with God, and thy life be not fuller of comfort, and thou hast not more support in a dying hour, then cast away these directions, and exclaim against me for ever as a deceiver.

The duty which I press upon thee so earnestly, and in the practice of which I am now to direct thee, is, "The set and solemn acting of all the powers of thy soul in meditation upon thy everlasting rest." More fully to explain the nature of this duty, I will here illustrate a little the description itself; and then point out the fittest time, place, and temper of mind for it.

It is not improper to illustrate a little the manner in which we have described this duty of meditation, or the considering and contemplating of spiritual things. It is *confessed to be a duty* by all, but practically denied by most. Many that make conscience of other duties, easily neglect this. They are troubled if they omit a sermon, a fast, or a prayer, in public or private, yet were never troubled that they have omitted meditation perhaps all their life time to this very day; though it be that duty by which all other duties are improved, and by which the soul digests truth for its nourishment and comfort. It was God's command to Joshua, "This book of the law shall not depart out of thy mouth, but thou shalt meditate therein day and night, that thou mayest observe to do according to all that is written therein." As digestion turns food into chyle and blood for vigorous health, so meditation turns the truths received and remembered into warm affection, firm resolution, and holy conversation.

This meditation is the acting of *all the powers of the soul*. It is the work of the living, and not of the dead. It is a work the most spiritual and sublime, and therefore not to be well performed by a heart that is merely carnal and earthly. Men must necessarily have some relation to heaven before they can familiarly converse there. I suppose them to be such as have a title to rest, when I persuade them to rejoice in the meditations of rest. And supposing thee to be a Christian, I am now exhorting thee to be an active Christian. And it is the work of the soul I am setting thee to, for bodily exercise here profiteth little. And it must have all the powers of the soul to distinguish it from the common meditation of students; for the understanding is not the whole soul, and therefore cannot do the whole work. As, in the body, the stomach must turn the food into chyle and prepare for the liver, the liver and spleen turn it into blood and prepare for the heart and brain; so, in the soul, the understanding must take in truths, and prepare them for the will, and that for the affections. Christ and heaven have various excellencies, and therefore God hath formed the soul with different powers for apprehending these excellencies. What the better had we been for odoriferous flowers, if we had no smell; or what good would language or music have done us, if we could not hear; or what pleasure should we have found in meats and drinks

without the sense of taste? So what good could all
the glory of heaven have done us, or what pleasure
should we have had in the perfection of God himself, if we had been without the affections of love
and joy? And what strength or sweetness canst
thou possibly receive by thy meditations on eternity, while thou dost not exercise those affections of
the soul by which thou must be sensible of this
sweetness and strength? It is the mistake of
Christians to think that meditation is only the
work of the understanding and memory, when
every schoolboy can do this, or persons that hate
the things which they think on. So that you see
there is more to be done than barely to remember
and think of heaven. As some labors not only stir
a hand or a foot, but exercise the whole body, so doth
meditation the whole soul. As the affections of
sinners are set on the world, are turned to idols and
fallen from God as well as their understanding, so
must their affections be reduced to God as well as
the understanding; and as their whole soul was
filled with sin before, so the whole must be filled
with God now. See David's description of the
blessed man: "His delight is in the law of the Lord,
and in his law doth he meditate day and night."

This meditation is *set and solemn.* As there is
solemn prayer when we set ourselves wholly to
that duty, and ejaculatory prayer when, in the
midst of other business, we send up some short

request to God; so also there is solemn meditation when we apply ourselves wholly to that work, and transient meditation when, in the midst of other business, we have some good thoughts of God in our minds. And as solemn prayer is either set in a constant course of duty, or occasional, at an extraordinary season, so also is meditation. Now, though I would persuade you to that meditation which is mixed with your common labors, and also that to which special occasions direct you, yet I would have you likewise make it a constant standing duty, as you do hearing, praying, and reading the Scriptures; and no more intermix other matters with it, than you would with prayer, or other stated solemnities.

This meditation is *upon thy everlasting rest.* I would not have you cast off your other meditations; but surely, as heaven hath the preëminence in perfection, it should have it also in our meditation. That which will make us most happy when we possess it, will make us most joyful when we meditate upon it. Other meditations are as numerous as there are lines in the Scripture, or creatures in the universe, or particular providences in the government of the world. But this is a walk to mount Zion: from the kingdoms of this world to the kingdom of saints; from earth to heaven; from time to eternity: it is walking upon sun, moon, and stars, in the garden and paradise of God. It may

seem far off, but spirits are quick; whether in the
body or out of the body, their motion is swift. You
need not fear, like the men of the world, lest these
thoughts should make you mad. It is in heaven,
and not hell, that I persuade you to walk. It is
joy, and not sorrow, that I persuade you to exercise.
I urge you to look on no deformed objects, but only
upon the ravishing glory of saints, and the unspeakable excellencies of the God of glory, and the beams
that stream from the face of his Son. Will it dis
tract a man to think of his only happiness? Will
it distract the miserable to think of mercy, or the
prisoner to foresee deliverance, or the poor to think
of approaching riches and honor? Methinks it
should rather make a man mad to think of living
in a world of woe, and abiding in poverty and sickness, among the rage of wicked men, than to think
of living with Christ in bliss. "But wisdom is
justified of all her children." Knowledge hath no
enemy but the ignorant. This heavenly course
was never spoken against by any but those that
never knew it, or never used it. I fear more the
neglect of men that approve it, than the opposition
or arguments of any against it.

First, as to THE FITTEST TIME for this heavenly
contemplation, let me only advise that it be stated,
frequent, and seasonable.

1. Give it a *stated* time. If thou suit thy time
to the advantage of the work, without placing any

religion in the time itself, thou hast no need to fear superstition. Stated time is a hedge to duty, and defends it against many temptations to omission. Some have not their time at command, and therefore cannot set their hours ; and many are so poor, that the necessities of their families deny them this freedom : such persons should be watchful to redeem time as much as they can, and take their vacant opportunities as they fall, and especially join meditation and prayer as much as they can with the labors of their calling. Yet those who have more time to spare from their worldly necessities, and are masters of their time, I still advise to keep this duty to a stated time. And indeed, if every work of the day had its appointed time, we should be better skilled both in redeeming time and performing duty.

2. Let it be *frequent* as well as stated. How oft it should be I cannot determine, because men's circumstances differ ; but in general, Scripture requires it to be frequent, when it mentions meditating day and night. For those, therefore, who can conveniently omit other business, I advise that it be once a day at least.

Frequency in heavenly contemplation is particularly important to prevent a shyness between God and thy soul. Frequent society breeds familiarity, and familiarity increases love and delight, and makes us bold in our addresses. The chief end of this duty is, to have acquaintance and fellowship with God; and therefore, if thou come but seldom to it, thou wilt still keep thyself a stranger. When a man feels his need of God, and must seek his help in a time of necessity, then it is great encouragement to go to a God we know and are acquainted with. "O," saith the heavenly Christian, "I know both whither I go, and to whom. I have gone this way many a time before now. It is the same God that I daily converse with, and the way has been my daily walk. God knows me well enough, and I have some knowledge of him." On the other hand, what a horror and discouragement will it be to the soul, when it is forced to fly to God in straits, to think, "Alas, I know not whither to go. I never went the way before. I have no acquaintance at the court of heaven. My soul knows not that God that I must speak to, and I fear he will not know my soul." But especially when we come to die, and must immediately appear before this God, and expect to enter into his eternal rest, then the difference will plainly appear: then what a joy will it be to think, "I am going to the place that I daily conversed in; to the place from whence I tasted such frequent delights; to that God whom I have met in my meditation so often. My heart hath been in heaven before now, and hath often tasted its reviving sweetness; and if my eyes were so enlightened and my spirits so refreshed when I had but a taste, what will it be when I shall feed on it freely?" On the contrary, what a terror will it be to think, "I must die and go I know not whither; from a place where I am acquainted, to a place where I have no familiarity or knowledge." It is an inexpressible horror to a dying man to have strange thoughts of God and heaven. I am persuaded that it is the neglect of this duty which so commonly makes death, even to godly men, unwelcome and uncomfortable. Therefore I persuade to frequency in this duty.

And as it will prevent shyness between thee and God, so also it will prevent unskilfulness in the duty itself. How awkwardly do men set their hands to a work in which they are seldom employed. Whereas frequency will habituate thy heart to the work, and make it more easy and delightful. The hill which made thee pant and blow at first going up, thou mayest easily run up when thou art once accustomed to it.

Thou wilt also prevent the loss of the heat and life thou hast obtained. If thou eat but once in two or three days, thou wilt lose thy strength as fast as it comes. If in holy meditation thou get near to Christ and warm thy heart with the fire of love, and then come but seldom, thy former coldness will soon return, especially as the work is so spiritual and against the bent of depraved nature. It is true, the intermixing of other duties, especially secret prayer, may do much to the keeping of thy heart above; but meditation is the life of most other duties, and the view of heaven is the life of meditation.

3. Choose also the most *seasonable* time. All things are beautiful and excellent in their season. Unseasonableness may lose the fruit of thy labor, may raise difficulties in the work, and may turn a duty to a sin. The same hour may be seasonable to one and unseasonable to another. Servants and laborers must take that season which their business can best afford, either while at work, or in travelling, or when they lie awake in the night. Such as can choose what time of the day they will, should observe when they find their spirits most active and fit for contemplation, and fix upon that as the stated time. I have always found that the fittest time for myself is the evening, from sun-setting to the twilight. I the rather mention this, because it was the experience of a better and wiser man; for it is expressly said, "Isaac went out to meditate in the field at the even-tide."

The Lord's day is exceeding seasonable for this exercise. When should we more seasonably contemplate our rest than on that day of rest which typifies it to us? It being a day appropriated to spiritual duties, methinks we should never exclude this duty, which is so eminently spiritual. I verily think this is the chief work of a Christian Sabbath,

and most agreeable to the design of its positive insti-
tution.   What fitter time to converse with our Lord
than on the Lord's day?   What fitter day to ascend
to heaven than that on which he arose from earth,
and fully triumphed over death and hell?   The
fittest temper for a true Christian is, like John, to
" be in the Spirit on the Lord's day."   And what
can bring us to this joy in the Spirit, but the spiritual beholding of our approaching glory?   Take
notice of this, you that spend the Lord's day only
in public worship; your allowing no time to private
duty, and therefore neglecting this spiritual duty of
meditation, is very hurtful to your souls.   You also
that have time on the Lord's day for idleness and
vain discourse, were you but acquainted with this
duty of contemplation, you would need no other
pastime; you would think the longest day short
enough, and be sorry that the night had shortened
your pleasure.   Christians, let heaven have more
share in your Sabbaths, where you must shortly
keep your everlasting Sabbaths.   Use your Sabbaths as steps to glory, till you have passed them
all, and are there arrived.   Especially you that are
poor, and cannot take time in the week as you
desire, see that you well improve this day; as your
bodies rest from their labors, let your spirits seek
after rest from God.

Besides the constant seasonableness of every day,
and particularly every Lord's day, there are also

more peculiar seasons for heavenly contemplation.
As for instance,

When God hath more abundantly warmed thy
spirit with fire from above, then thou mayest soar
with greater freedom. A little labor will set thy
heart a going at such a time as this; whereas at
another time thou mayest take pains to little purpose. Observe the gales of the Spirit, and how the
Spirit of Christ doth move thy spirit. "Without
Christ we can do nothing;" and therefore let us
be doing while he is doing; and be sure not to be
out of the way, nor asleep, when he comes. When
the Spirit finds thy heart, like Peter, in prison and
in irons, and smites thee, and says, "Arise up
quickly, and follow me," be sure thou then arise
and follow; and thou shalt find thy chains fall off,
and all doors will open, and thou wilt be at heav-
en before thou art aware.

Another peculiar season for this duty is when
thou art in a *suffering*, distressed, or tempted state.
When should we take our cordials, but in time of
fainting? When is it more seasonable to walk to
heaven than when we know not in what corner of
earth to live with comfort? Or when should our
thoughts converse more above than when we have
nothing but grief below? Where should Noah's
dove be but in the ark, when the waters cover all
the earth, and she cannot find rest for the sole of
her foot? What should we think on but our Fa-

ther's house, when we have not even the husks of
the world to feed upon? Surely God sends thy
afflictions for this very purpose. Happy art thou,
poor man, if thou make this use of thy poverty;
and thou that art sick, if thou so improve thy sickness. It is seasonable to go to the promised land,
when our burdens are increased in Egypt and our
straits in the wilderness. Reader, if thou knewest what a cordial to thy griefs the serious views
of glory are, thou wouldst less fear these harmless
troubles, and more use that preserving, reviving
remedy. "In the multitude of my" troubled
"thoughts within me," saith David, "thy comforts
delight my soul." "I reckon," saith Paul, "that
the sufferings of this present time are not worthy
to be compared with the glory which shall be revealed in us." "For which cause we faint not;
but though our outward man perish, yet the inward
man is renewed day by day. For our light affliction, which is but for a moment, worketh for us a far
more exceeding and eternal weight of glory, while
we look not at the things which are seen, but at
the things which are not seen; for the things which
are seen are temporal, but the things which are not
seen are eternal."

And another season peculiarly fit for this heavenly duty is, when the messengers of God summon
us *to die*. When should we more frequently sweeten
our souls with the believing thoughts of another

life, than when we find that this is almost ended? No men have greater need of supporting joys than dying men; and these joys must be drawn from our eternal joy. As heavenly delights are sweetest when nothing earthly is joined with them, so the delights of dying Christians are oftentimes the sweetest they ever had. What a prophetic blessing had dying Isaac and Jacob for their sons. With what a heavenly song and divine benediction did Moses conclude his life. What heavenly advice and prayer had the disciples from their Lord, when he was about to leave them. When Paul was "ready to be offered," what heavenly exhortation and advice did he give the Philippians, Timothy, and the elders of Ephesus. How near to heaven was John in Patmos, but a little before his translation thither. It is the general temper of the saints to be then most heavenly, when they are nearest heaven. If it be thy case, reader, to perceive thy dying time draw on, O where should thy heart now be but with Christ? Methinks thou shouldst even behold him standing by thee, and shouldst bespeak him as thy father, thy husband, thy physician, thy friend. Methinks thou shouldst, as it were, see the angels about thee, waiting to perform their last office to thy soul; even those angels which disdained not to carry into Abraham's bosom the soul of Lazarus, nor will think much to conduct thee thither. Look upon thy pain and sickness as Jacob did on Joseph's chariots, and let thy spirit revive within thee, and say, "It is enough. Christ is yet alive; because he liveth, I shall live also." Dost thou need the choicest cordials? Here are choicer than the world can afford; here are all the joys of heaven, even the vision of God and Christ, and whatsoever the blessed here possess. These dainties are offered thee by the hand of Christ; he hath written the receipt in the promises of the gospel; he hath prepared the ingredients in heaven: only put forth the hand of faith and feed upon them, and rejoice and live. The Lord saith to thee, as to Elijah, "Arise and eat, because the journey is too great for thee." Though it be not long, yet the way is miry; therefore obey his voice, arise and eat, "and in the strength of that meat thou mayest go to the mount of God;" and, like Moses, "die in the mount whither thou goest up;" and say, as Simeon, "Lord, now lettest thou thy servant depart in peace, for mine eye" of faith "hath seen thy salvation."

Secondly, concerning the FITTEST PLACE for heavenly contemplation, it is sufficient to say that the most convenient is *some private retirement*. Our spirits need every help, and to be freed from every hinderance in the work. If, in private prayer, Christ directs us to "enter into our closet and shut the door, that our Father may see us in secret," so should we do this in meditation. How often did

Christ himself retire to some mountain or wilderness, or other solitary place. I give not this advice for occasional meditation, but for that which is set and solemn. Therefore withdraw thyself from all society, even that of godly men, that thou mayest a while enjoy the society of thy Lord. If a student cannot study in a crowd, who exerciseth only his invention and memory, much less shouldst thou be in a crowd, who art to exercise all the powers of thy soul, and upon an object so far above nature. We are fled so far from superstitious solitude, that we have even cast off the solitude of contemplative devotion. We seldom read of God's appearing, by himself or by his angels, to any of his prophets or saints in a crowd; but frequently when they were alone.

But observe for thyself what place best agrees with thy spirit, within doors or without. Isaac's example, in "going out to meditate in the field," will, I am persuaded, best suit with most. Our Lord so much used a solitary garden, that even Judas, when he came to betray him, knew where to find him: and though he took his disciples thither with him, yet he "was withdrawn from them" for more secret devotions; and though his meditation be not directly named, but only his praying, yet it is very clearly implied; for his soul is first made sorrowful with bitter meditations on his sufferings and death, and then he poureth it out in prayer. So that Christ had his accustomed place, and consequently accustomed duty; and so must we : he hath a place that is solitary, whither he retireth, even from his own disciples ; and so must we : his meditations go further than his thoughts ; they affect and pierce his heart and soul ; and so must ours. Only there is a wide difference in the object : Christ meditates on the sufferings that our sins had deserved, so that the wrath of his Father passed through all his soul ; but we are to meditate on the glory he hath purchased, that the love of the Father and the joy of the Spirit may enter our thoughts and revive our affections and overflow our souls.

Thirdly, I am next to advise thee concerning the PREPARATION OF THY HEART for this heavenly contemplation. The success of the work much depends on the frame of thy heart. When man's heart had nothing in it to grieve the Spirit, it was then the delightful habitation of his Maker. God did not quit his residence there till man expelled him by unworthy provocations. There was no shyness or reserve till the heart grew sinful, and too loathsome a dungeon for God to delight in. And were this soul reduced to its former innocency, God would quickly return to his former habitation ; yea, so far as it is renewed and repaired by the Spirit, and purged from its lusts, and beautified with his image, the Lord will yet acknowledge it as his own : Christ will manifest himself unto it, and the Spirit will take it for his temple and residence. So far as the heart is qualified for conversing with God, so far it usually enjoys him. Therefore, "with all diligence keep thy heart, for out of it are the issues of life." More particularly,

1. Get thy heart as *clear from the world* as thou canst. Wholly lay by the thoughts of thy business, troubles, enjoyments, and every thing that may take up any room in thy soul. Get it as empty as thou possibly canst, that it may be the more capable of being filled with God. If thou couldst perform some outward duty with a part of thy heart while the remainder is absent, yet this duty, above all, I am sure thou canst not. When thou shalt go into the mount of contemplation, thou wilt be like the covetous man at the heap of gold, who, when he might take as much as he could, lamented that he was able to carry no more : thou wilt find as much of God and glory as thy narrow heart is able to contain, and almost nothing to hinder thy full possession but the incapacity of thy own spirit. Then thou wilt think, "O that this understanding and these affections could contain more. It is more my unfitness than any thing else that even this place is not my heaven. 'God is in this place, and I know it not.' This 'mount is full of chariots of fire ;' but mine eyes are shut, and I cannot see them. O the words of love Christ hath

to speak, and wonders of love he hath to show, but I cannot bear them yet. Heaven is ready for me, but my heart is unready for heaven." Therefore, reader, seeing thy enjoyment of God in this contemplation much depends on the capacity and disposition of thy heart, seek him here, if ever, with all thy soul. Thrust not Christ into the stable and the manger, as if thou hadst better guests for the chief rooms. Say to all thy worldly business and thoughts, as Christ to his disciples, "Sit ye here, while I go and pray yonder;" or as Abraham to his servants, when he went to offer Isaac, "Abide ye here, and I will go yonder and worship, and come again to you." Even as "the priests thrust king Uzziah out of the temple," where he presumed to burn incense, when they saw the leprosy upon him; so do thou thrust those thoughts from the temple of thy heart, which have the badge of God's prohibition upon them.

2. Be sure to enter upon this work with the *greatest solemnity of heart and mind*. There is no trifling in holy things. "God will be sanctified in them that come nigh him." These spiritual, excellent, soul-raising duties are, if well used, most profitable; but, when used unfaithfully, most dangerous. Labor, therefore, to have the deepest apprehensions of the presence of God and his incomprehensible greatness. If queen Esther must not draw near "till the king hold out the sceptre,"

think, then, with what reverence thou shouldst approach Him who made the worlds with the word of his mouth, who upholds the earth as in the palm of his hand, who keeps the sun, moon, and stars in their courses, and who sets bounds to the raging sea! Thou art going to converse with Him before whom the earth will quake, and devils do tremble, and at whose bar thou and all the world must shortly stand and be finally judged. O think, "I shall then have lively apprehensions of his majesty. My drowsy spirits will then be awakened, and my irreverence be laid aside and why should I not now be roused with the sense of his greatness, and the dread of his name possess my soul?" Labor also to apprehend the greatness of the work which thou attemptest, and to be deeply sensible both of its importance and excellency. If thou wast pleading for thy life at the bar of an earthly judge, thou wouldst be serious, and yet that would be a trifle to this. If thou wast engaged in such a work as David against Goliath, on which the welfare of a kingdom depended, in itself considered, it were nothing to this. Suppose thou wast going to such a wrestling as Jacob's, or to see the sight which the three disciples saw in the mount, how seriously, how reverently wouldst thou both approach and behold. If but an angel from heaven should appoint to meet thee at the same time and place of thy contemplations, with what dread wouldst thou be filled.

Consider, then, with what a spirit thou shouldst meet the Lord, and with what seriousness and awe thou shouldst daily converse with him. Consider also the blessed issue of the work, if it succeed: it will be thy admission into the presence of God, and the beginning of thy eternal glory on earth; a means to make thee live above the rate of other men, and fix thee in the next room to the angels themselves, that thou mayest both live and die joyfully. The prize being so great, thy preparations should be answerable. None on earth live such a life of joy and blessedness as those who are acquainted with this heavenly conversation. The joys of all other men are but like a child's plaything, a fool's laughter, or a sick man's dream of health. He that trades for heaven is the only gainer, and he that neglects it is the only loser. How seriously, therefore, should this work be done.

CHAPTER XIV

WHAT USE HEAVENLY CONTEMPLATION MAKES OF
CONSIDERATION, THE AFFECTIONS, SOLILOQUY,
AND PRAYER.

I. The use of consideration, and its great influence over the
heart. II. Contemplation is promoted by the affections;
particularly, 1. By love; 2. Desire; 3. Hope; 4. Courage,
or boldness; 5. Joy. III. The usefulness of soliloquy and
prayer in heavenly contemplation.

HAVING set thy heart in tune, we now come to
the music itself. Having got an appetite, now approach to the feast, and delight thy soul as with
marrow and fatness. Come, for all things are now
ready. Heaven and Christ and the exceeding
weight of glory are before you. Do not make light
of this invitation, nor begin to make excuses; whosoever thou art, rich or poor, though in an alms-
house or hospital, though in the highways or
hedges, my commission is, if possible, to compel
you to come in; and blessed is he that shall eat
bread in the kingdom of God. The manna lieth
about your tents; walk out, gather it up, take it
home, and feed upon it. In order to this, I am
only to direct you how to use your consideration and
affections, your soliloquy and prayer.

First, CONSIDERATION is the great instrument by
which this heavenly work is carried on. This

must be voluntary, and not forced. Some men consider unwillingly; so God will make the wicked consider their sins, when he shall "set them in order before their eyes;" so shall the damned consider the excellency of Christ, whom they once despised, and the eternal joys which they have foolishly lost. Great is the power which consideration hath for moving the affections and impressing things on the heart; as will appear by the following particulars :

1. Consideration, as it were, opens the door between *the head and the heart.* The understanding having received truths, lays them up in the memory, and consideration conveys them from thence to the affections. What excellency would there be in much learning and knowledge, if the obstructions between the head and the heart were but opened, and the affections did but correspond to the understanding. He is usually the best scholar whose apprehension is quick, clear, and tenacious; but he is usually the best Christian whose apprehension is the deepest and most affectionate, and who has the readiest passages not so much from the ear to the brain, as from that to the heart. And though the Spirit be the principal cause, yet, on our part, this passage must be opened by consideration.

2. Consideration presents to the affections those things which are *most important.* The most delightful object does not entertain where it is not

seen, nor the most joyful news affect him who does not hear it; but consideration presents to our view those things which were as absent, and brings them to the eye and ear of the soul. Are not Christ and glory affecting objects? Would they not work wonders upon the soul, if they were but clearly discovered, and our apprehensions of them in some measure corresponded to their worth? It is consideration that presents them to us: this is the Christian's perspective by which he can see from earth to heaven.

3. Consideration also presents the most important things in *the most affecting way*. It reasons the case with a man's own heart. When a believer would reason his heart to heavenly contemplation, how many arguments offer themselves from God and Christ, from each of the divine perfections, from our former and present state, from promises, from present sufferings and enjoyments, from hell and heaven! Every thing offers itself to promote our joy, and consideration is the hand to draw them all out; it adds one reason to another, till the scales turn: this it does when persuading to joy, till it has silenced all our distrusts and sorrows, and our cause for rejoicing lies plain before us. If another's reasoning is powerful with us, though we are not certain whether he intends to inform or deceive us, how much more should our own reasoning prevail with us, when we are so well acquainted with

our own intentions. Nay, how much more should God's reasoning prevail with us, which we are sure cannot deceive, or be deceived. Now, consideration is but the reading over and repeating God's reasons to our hearts. As the prodigal had many and strong reasons to plead with himself why he should return to his father's house, so have we to plead with our affections, to persuade them to our Father's everlasting mansions.

4. Consideration *exalts reason to its just authority* It helps to deliver it from its captivity to the senses, and sets it again on the throne of the soul. When reason is silent, it is usually subject; for when it is asleep the senses domineer. But consideration awakens our reason, till, like Samson, it rouses up itself, and breaks the bonds of sensuality, and bears down the delusions of the flesh. What strength can the lion exert while asleep? What is a king, when dethroned, more than another man? Spiritual reason, excited by meditation, and not fancy or fleshly sense, must judge of heavenly joys. Consideration exalts the objects of faith, and comparatively disgraces the objects of sense. The most inconsiderate men are most sensual. It is too easy and common to sin against knowledge; but against sober, strong, persevering consideration men seldom offend.

5. Consideration makes reason *strong and active*. Before, it was a standing water, but now as a stream

which violently bears down all before it.   Before,
it was as the stones in the brook, but now like that
out of David's sling, which smites the Goliath of our
unbelief in the forehead.   As wicked men continue
wicked because they bring not reason into action
and exercise ; so godly men are uncomfortable because they let their reason and faith lie asleep, and
do not stir them up to action by this work of meditation.   What fears, sorrows, and joys will our very
dreams excite.   How much more, then, would serious meditation affect us.

6. Consideration can *continue* and persevere in
this rational employment.   Meditation holds reason
and faith to their work, and blows the fire till it
thoroughly burns.   To run a few steps will not get
a man heat, but walking an hour may ; and though
a sudden occasional thought of heaven will not raise
our affections to any spiritual heat, yet meditation
can continue our thoughts till our hearts grow warm.
Thus you see the powerful tendency of consideration to produce this great elevation of the soul in
heavenly contemplation.

Secondly, let us next see how this heavenly work
is promoted by the particular exercise of THE AF-
FECTIONS.   It is by consideration that we first have
recourse to the memory, and from thence take those
heavenly doctrines which we intend to make the
subject of our meditation ; such as promises of
eternal life, descriptions of the saints' glory, the

resurrection, etc. We then present them to our judgment, that it may deliberately view them and take an exact survey, and determine uprightly concerning the perfection of our celestial happiness, against all the dictates of flesh and sense, and so as to magnify the Lord in our hearts, till we are filled with a holy admiration. But the principal thing is to exercise not merely our judgment, but our faith in the truth of our everlasting rest; by which I mean both the truth of the promises, and of our own personal interest in them and title to them. If we did really and firmly believe that there is such a glory, and that within a few days our eyes shall behold it, O what passion would it raise within us; what astonishing apprehensions of that life would it produce; what love, what longing would it excite within us! O how it would actuate every affection—how it would transport us with joy, upon the least assurance of our title. Never expect to have love and joy move when faith stands still, which must lead the way. Therefore daily exercise faith, and set before it the freeness of the promise, God's urging all to accept it, Christ's gracious disposition, all the evidences of the love of Christ, his faithfulness to his engagement, and the evidences of his love in ourselves; lay all these together, and think whether they do not testify the good will of the Lord concerning our salvation, and may not properly be pleaded against our unbelief. Thus, when the judgment has determined, and faith has apprehended the truth of our happiness, then may our meditation proceed to raise our affections; and particularly love, desire, hope, courage or boldness, and joy.

1. *Love* is the first affection to be excited in heavenly contemplation; the object of it is goodness. Here, Christian, is the soul-reviving part of thy work. Go to thy memory, thy judgment, and thy faith, and from them produce the excellencies of thy rest; present these to thy affection of love, and thou wilt find thyself, as it were, in another world. Speak out, and love can hear. Do but reveal these things, and love can see. It is the brutish love of the world that is blind; divine love is exceedingly quick-sighted. Let thy faith take hold of thy heart, and show it the sumptuous buildings of thy eternal habitation, and the glorious ornaments of thy Father's house, even the mansions Christ is preparing, and the honors of his kingdom; let thy faith lead thy heart into the presence of God, and as near as thou possibly canst, and say to it, " Behold the Ancient of days, the Lord Jehovah, whose name is I AM: this is he who made all the worlds with his word, who upholds the earth, who rules the nations, who disposes of all events, who subdues his foes, who controls the swelling waves of the sea, who governs the winds, and causes the sun to run its race, and the stars to know their

courses. This is he who loved thee from everlasting, formed thee in the womb, gave thee this soul, brought thee forth, showed thee the light, and ranked thee with the chief of his earthly creatures; who endued thee with thy understanding, and beautified thee with his gifts; who maintains thy life and all its comforts, and distinguishes thee from the most miserable and vilest of men. O here is an object worthy of thy love! Here shouldst thou even pour out thy soul in love. Here it is impossible for thee to love too much. This is the Lord who hath blessed thee with his benefits, ' spread thy table in the sight of thine enemies, and made thy cup overflow.' This is he whom angels and saints praise, and the heavenly host for ever magnify." Thus do thou expatiate on the praises of God, and open his excellencies to thy heart, till the holy fire of love begins to kindle in thy breast.

If thou dost not yet feel thy love burn, lead thy heart further, and show it the Son of the living God, whose name is "Wonderful, Counsellor, the mighty God, the everlasting Father, the Prince of peace:" show it the King of saints on the throne of his glory, "the First and the Last; who is, and was, and is to come: who liveth and was dead, and behold, he liveth for evermore; who hath made thy peace by the blood of his cross," and hath prepared thee with himself a habitation of peace: his office is that of the great peace-maker; his kingdom is the kingdom of peace, his gospel is the tidings of peace, his voice to thee now is the voice of peace. Draw near and behold him. Dost thou not hear his voice? He that bade Thomas come near and see the print of the nails, and put his finger into his wounds—he it is that calls to thee, "Come near, and view the Lord thy Saviour, and be not faithless, but believing; peace be unto thee, fear not, it is I." Look well upon him. Dost thou not know him? It is he that brought thee up from the pit of hell, reversed the sentence of thy damnation, bore the curse which thou shouldst have borne, restored thee to the blessing thou hadst forfeited, and purchased the advancement which thou must inherit for ever. And dost thou not yet know him? His hands were pierced, his head, his side, his heart were pierced, that by these marks thou mightest always know him. Dost thou not remember when he "found thee lying in thy blood, and took pity on thee and dressed thy wounds, and brought thee home, and said unto thee, Live?" Hast thou forgotten, since he wounded himself to cure thy wounds, and let out his own blood to stop thy bleeding? If thou knowest him not by the face, the voice, the hands, thou mayest know him by that heart: that soul-pitying heart is his; it can be none but his; love and compassion are its certain signatures: this is he who chose thy life before his own; who pleads his blood before his Father, and makes continual intercession for thee. If he had not suffered, what hadst thou suffered! There was but a step between thee and hell when he interposed and bore the stroke. And is not here fuel enough for thy love to feed on? Doth not thy throbbing heart stop here to ease itself, and, like Joseph, "seek for a place to weep in?" or do not the tears of thy love bedew these lines? Go on, then, for the field of love is large; it will be thy eternal work to behold and love; nor needest thou want work for thy present meditation.

How often hath thy Lord found thee, like Hagar, sitting and weeping, and giving up thy soul for lost, and he opened to thee a well of consolation, and also opened thine eyes to see it. How often, in the posture of Elijah, desiring to die out of thy misery, hath he spread thee a table of unexpected relief, and sent thee on his work refreshed and encouraged. How often, in the case of the prophet's servant, crying out, "Alas, what shall we do, for a host doth encompass us," hath he "opened thine eyes to see more for thee than against thee." How often, like Jonah, peevish and weary of thy life, hath he mildly said, "Doest thou well to be angry" with me, or murmur against me? How often hath he set thee on "watching and praying," repenting and believing, "and, when he hath returned, hath found thee asleep;" and yet he hath covered thy neglect with a mantle of love, and gently pleaded for thee, that "the spirit is willing, but the flesh is weak." Can thy heart be cold when thou thinkest of this? Can it contain when thou rememberest these boundless compassions? Thus, reader, hold forth the goodness of Christ to thy heart; plead thus with thy frozen soul, till, with David, thou canst say, "My heart was hot within me; while I was musing, the fire burned." If this will not rouse up thy love, thou hast all Christ's personal excellencies to add, all his particular mercies to thyself, all his sweet and near relations to thee, and the happiness of thy everlasting abode with him. Only follow them close to thy heart. Deal with it as Christ did with Peter, when he thrice asked him, "Lovest thou me?" till he was grieved, and answered, "Lord, thou knowest that I love thee." So grieve and shame thy heart out of its stupidity, till thou canst truly say, " I know, and my Lord knows, that I love him."

2. The next affection to be excited in heavenly contemplation, is *desire*. The object of it is goodness, considered as absent, or not yet attained. If love be warm, desire will not be cold. Think with thyself, "What have I seen! O the incomprehensible glory; O the transcendent beauty; O blessed souls that now enjoy it, who see a thousand times more clearly what I have seen at a distance, and through dark, interposing clouds. What a difference between my state and theirs. I am

sighing, and they are singing; I am offending, and they are pleasing God. I am a spectacle of pity, like a Job or Lazarus; but they are perfect, and without blemish. I am here entangled in the love of the world, while they are swallowed up in the love of God. They have none of my cares and fears; they weep not in secret; they languish not in sorrows; these 'tears are wiped away from their eyes.' O happy, a thousand times happy souls ! Alas, that I must dwell in sinful flesh, when my brethren and companions dwell with God. How far out of sight and reach of their high enjoyment do I here live. What poor, feeble thoughts have I of God ; what cold affections towards him. How little have I of that life, that love, that joy in which they continually live. How soon doth that little depart, and leave me in thicker darkness. Now and then a spark falls upon my heart, and, while I gaze upon it, it dies, or rather, my cold heart quenches it. But they have their 'light in his light,' and drink continually at the spring of joy. Here we are vexing each other with quarrels, when they are of one heart and voice, and daily sound forth the hallelujahs of heaven with perfect harmony. O what a feast hath my faith beheld, and what a famine is yet in my spirit. O blessed souls, I may not, I dare not envy your happiness ; I rather rejoice in my brethren's prosperity, and am glad to think of the day when I shall be admitted into your

fellowship. I wish not to displace you, but to be
so happy as to be with you. Why must I stay and
weep and wait? My Lord is gone; he hath left
this earth, and is entered into his glory: my brethren are gone; my friends are there; my house, my
hope, my all is there. When I am so far distant
from my God, wonder not what aileth me, if I now
complain: an ignorant Micah will do so for his
idol, and shall not my soul do so for the living
God? Had I no hope of enjoyment, I would go
and hide myself in the deserts, and lie and howl in
some obscure wilderness, and spend my days in
fruitless wishes; but since it is the land of my
promised rest, and the state I must myself be advanced to, and my soul draws near, and is almost
there, I will love and long, I will look and desire,
I will be breathing, 'How long, Lord, how long
wilt thou suffer this soul to pant and groan, and
not open to him who waits and longs to be with
thee?'" Thus, Christian reader, let thy thoughts
aspire, till thy soul longs, as David, "O that one
would give me to drink of the wells of salvation;"
and till thou canst say, as he did, "I have longed
for thy salvation, O Lord." And as the mother
and brethren of Christ, when they could not come
at him because of the multitude, sent to him, saying, "Thy mother and brethren stand without, desiring to see thee," so let thy message to him be,
and he will own thee; for he hath said, "They that

hear my word, and do it, are my mother and my brethren."

3. Another affection to be exercised in heavenly contemplation, is *hope*. This helps to support the soul under sufferings, animates it in the greatest difficulties, gives it firmness in the severest trials, enlivens it in duties, and is the very spring that sets all the wheels in motion. Who would believe or strive for heaven, if it were not for the hope he hath of obtaining it? Who would pray, but for the hope of prevailing with God? If your hope dies, your duties die, your endeavors die, your joys die, and your soul dies. And if your hope be not in exercise, but asleep, it is next to dead. Therefore, Christian reader, when thou art raising thy affections to heaven, forget not to give one lift to thy hope. Think thus, and reason thus with thy own heart:

"Why should I not confidently and comfortably hope, when my soul is in the hands of so compassionate a Saviour, and when the kingdom is at the disposal of so bountiful a God? Did he ever discover the least backwardness to my good, or inclination to my ruin? Hath he not sworn that 'he delights not in the death of him that dieth, but rather that he should repent and live?' Have not all his dealings witnessed the same? Did he not warn me of my danger when I never feared it, because he would have me escape it? Did he not tell me of my happiness when I had no thoughts of it, because he would have me enjoy it? How often hath he drawn me to himself and his Christ, when I have drawn backward. How hath his Spirit incessantly solicited my heart. And would he have done all this, if he had been willing that I should perish? Should I not hope, if an honest man had promised me something in his power? And shall I not hope, when I have the covenant and oath of God? It is true, the glory is out of sight; we have not beheld the mansions of the saints; but is not the promise of God more certain than our sight? We must not be saved by sight, but 'by hope; and hope that is seen, is not hope; for what a man seeth, why doth he yet hope for? But if we hope for that we see not, then do we with patience wait for it.' I have been ashamed of my hope in an arm of flesh, but hope in the promise of God 'maketh not ashamed.' In my greatest sufferings I will say, 'The Lord is my portion; therefore will I hope in him. The Lord is good unto them that wait for him, to the soul that seeketh him. It is good that a man should both hope and quietly wait for the salvation of the Lord; for the Lord will not cast off for ever; but though he cause grief, yet will he have compassion, according to the multitude of his mercies.' Though I languish and die, yet will I hope; for 'the righteous hath hope in his death.' Though I must lie down in dust and

darkness, yet there 'my flesh shall rest in hope.'
And when my flesh hath nothing to rejoice in, yet
will I 'hold fast the rejoicing of the hope firm unto
the end;' for 'the hope of the righteous shall be
gladness.' Indeed, if I must myself satisfy divine
justice, then there had been no hope; but Christ
hath 'brought in a better hope, by the which we
draw nigh unto God.' Or, if I had to do with a
feeble creature, there were small hope; for how
could he raise this body from the dust and lift me
above the sun? But what is this to the almighty
power which made the heavens and the earth out
of nothing? Cannot that power which raised
Christ from the dead raise me, and that which
hath glorified the Head glorify also the members?
'Doubtless, by the blood of his covenant, God will
send forth his prisoners out of the pit wherein is no
water;' therefore will I 'turn to the strong hold, as
a prisoner of hope.'"

4. *Courage*, or boldness, is another affection to
be exercised in heavenly contemplation; it leads
to resolution, and concludes in action. When you
have raised your love, desire, and hope, go on, and
think thus with yourself: "Will God indeed dwell
with men? And is there such a glory within the
reach of hope? Why then do I not lay hold upon
it? Where is the cheerful vigor of my spirit?
Why do I not 'gird up the loins of my mind?'
Why do I not set upon my enemies on every side,

and valiantly break through all resistance? What should stop me or intimidate me? Is God with me or against me in the work? Will Christ stand by me, or will he not? 'If God and Christ be for me, who can be against me?' In the work of sin, almost all things are ready to help us, and only God and his servants are against us; yet how ill does that work prosper in our hands. But, in my course to heaven, almost all things are against me, but God is for me; and therefore how happily does the work succeed. Do I enter upon this work in my own strength, or rather in the strength of Christ my Lord? And 'cannot I do all things, through him that strengthens me?' Was he ever foiled by an enemy? He has indeed been assaulted, but was he ever conquered? Why, then, does my flesh urge me with the difficulties of the work? Is any thing too hard for Omnipotence? May not Peter boldly walk on the sea, if Christ give the word of command? If he begin to sink, is it from the weakness of Christ, or from the smallness of his faith? Do I not well deserve to be turned into hell, if mortal threats can drive me thither? Do I not well deserve to be shut out of heaven, if I will be frightened from thence with the reproach of tongues? What if it were father, or mother, or husband, or wife, or the nearest friend I have in the world, if they may be called friends who would draw me to damnation, should I not forsake all that would keep me from Christ? Will their friendship countervail the enmity of God, or be any comfort to my condemned soul? Shall I be yielding to the desires of men, and only harden myself against the Lord? Let them beseech me upon their knees, I will scorn to stop my course to behold them, I will shut my ears to their cries : let them flatter or frown, let them draw out tongues and swords against me; I am resolved, in the strength of Christ, to break through and look upon them as dust. If they would entice me with preferment, even with the kingdoms of the world, I will no more regard them than the dung of the earth. O blessed rest; O glorious state! Who would sell thee for dreams and shadows? Who would be enticed or affrighted from thee? Who would not strive, and fight, and watch, and run, and that with violence, even to the last breath, in order to obtain thee? Surely none but those that know thee not, and believe not thy glory."

5. The last affection to be exercised in heavenly contemplation, is *joy*. Love, desire, hope, and courage all tend to raise our joy. This is so desirable to every man by nature, and so essentially necessary to constitute our happiness, that I hope I need not say much to persuade you to any thing that would make your life delightful. Supposing you, therefore, already convinced that the pleasures of the flesh are brutish and perishing, that your

solid and lasting joy must be from heaven, instead
of persuading, I shall proceed in directing.   Reader, if thou hast managed well the former work
thou art got within sight of thy rest; thou believest
the truth of it; thou art convinced of its excellencies; thou hast fallen in love with it; thou
longest after it; thou hopest for it; and thou art
resolved to venture courageously for obtaining it.
But is here any work for joy in this?   We delight
in the good we possess; it is present good that is
the object of joy; and thou wilt say, "Alas, I am
yet without it."   But think a little further with
thyself.   Is it nothing to have a deed of gift from
God?   Are his infallible promises no ground of
joy?   Is it nothing to live in daily expectation of
entering into the kingdom of God?   Is not my
assurance of being hereafter glorified a sufficient
ground for inexpressible joy?   Is it not a delight
to the heir of a kingdom to think of what he must
soon possess, though at present he little differs from
a servant?   Have we not both command and
example for "rejoicing in the hope of the glory of
God?"

Here then, reader, take thy heart once more and
carry it to the top of the highest mount; show it
the kingdom of Christ and the glory of it; and say
to it, "All this will thy Lord give thee, who hast
believed in him, and been a worshipper of him.
'It is the Father's good pleasure to give thee this

kingdom.' Seest thou this astonishing glory which is above thee? All this is thine own inheritance. This crown is thine, these pleasures are thine—this company, this beautiful place, all are thine, because thou art Christ's, and Christ is thine; when thou wast united to him, thou hadst all these with him." Thus take thy heart into the land of promise; show it the pleasant hills and fruitful valleys; show it the clusters of grapes which thou hast gathered, to convince it that it is a blessed land, flowing with better than milk and honey. Enter the gates of the holy city, walk through the streets of the "New Jerusalem, walk about Zion, and go round about her; tell the towers thereof; mark well her bulwarks; consider her palaces, that thou mayest tell it to" thy soul. Has it not "the glory of God," and is not "her light like unto a stone most precious, even like a jasper stone, clear as crystal?" See the "twelve foundations of her walls, and in them the names of the twelve apostles of the Lamb. The walls of it are of jasper; and the city is pure gold, like unto clear glass; and the foundations are garnished with all manner of precious stones; and the twelve gates are twelve pearls, every several gate is of one pearl, and the street of the city is pure gold, as it were transparent glass. There is no temple in it, for the Lord God Almighty and the Lamb are the temple of it. It hath no need of the sun, neither of the moon in it, for the glory of God doth lighten it, and the Lamb is the light thereof; and the nations of them which are saved shall walk in the light of it. These sayings are faithful and true; and the Lord God of the holy prophets sent his angels," and his own Son, "to show unto his servants the things which must shortly be done." Say now to all this, " This is thy rest, O my soul; and this must be the place of thy everlasting habitation." Let all the sons of "Zion rejoice; let the daughters of Jerusalem be glad; for great is the Lord, and greatly to be praised in the city of our God, in the mountain of his holiness. Beautiful for situation, the joy of the whole earth, is mount Zion. God is known in her palaces for a refuge."

Yet proceed on: the soul that loves ascends frequently, and runs familiarly through the streets of the heavenly Jerusalem, visiting the patriarchs and prophets, saluting the apostles, and admiring the armies of martyrs; so do thou lead on thy heart as from street to street; bring it into the palace of the great King; lead it, as it were, from chamber to chamber. Say to it, "Here must I lodge; here must I live; here must I praise; here must I love and be beloved. I must shortly be one of this heavenly choir, and be better skilled in the music. Among this blessed company must I take my place my voice must join to make up the melody. My tears will then be wiped away; my groans be turned to another tune; my cottage of clay be changed to this palace; my prison rags to these splendid robes; and my sordid flesh shall be put off, and such a sunlike, spiritual body be put on; 'for the former things are here passed away.' 'Glorious things are spoken of thee, O city of God!' When I look upon this glorious place, what a dung-hill and dungeon methinks is earth. O what difference between a man, feeble, pained, groaning, dying, rotting in the grave, and one of these triumphant, shining saints. Here shall I 'drink of the river of pleasures, the streams whereof make glad the city of God.' Must Israel, under the bondage of the law, 'serve the Lord with joyfulness, and with gladness of heart, for the abundance of all things?' Surely I shall serve him with joyfulness and gladness of heart for the abundance of glory. Did persecuted saints 'take joyfully the spoiling of their goods?' And shall not I take joyfully such a full reparation of all my losses? Was it a celebrated 'day wherein the Jews rested from their enemies,' because it 'was turned unto them from sorrow to joy, and from mourning into a good day?' What a day, then, will that be to my soul, whose rest and change will be inconceivably greater! 'When the wise men saw the star' that led to Christ, 'they rejoiced with exceeding great joy;' but I shall shortly see him who is himself 'the bright and morning Star.' If the disciples 'departed from the sepulchre with great joy,' when they had but heard that their Lord 'was risen from the dead,' what will be my joy when I shall see him reigning in glory, and myself raised to a blessed communion with him? Then shall I indeed have 'beauty for ashes, the oil of joy for mourning, and the garment of praise for the spirit of heaviness, and Zion shall be made an eternal excellency, a joy of many generations.' Why, then, do I not arise from the dust, and cease my complaints? Why do I not trample on vain delights, and feed on the foreseen delights of glory? Why is not my life a continual joy, and the savor of heaven perpetually upon my spirit?"

Let me here observe that there is no necessity to exercise these affections, either exactly in this order, or all at one time. Sometimes one of thy affections may need more exciting, or may be more lively than the rest; or, if thy time be short, one may be exercised one day and another the next; all which must be left to thy prudence to determine. Thou hast also an opportunity, if inclined to make use of it, to exercise opposite and more mixed affections, such as hatred of sin, which would deprive thy soul of these immortal joys; godly fear, lest thou shouldst abuse thy mercy; godly shame and grief, for having abused it; unfeigned repentance; self-indignation; jealousy over thy heart; and pity for those who are in danger of losing these immortal joys.

Thirdly, we are also to take notice how heavenly contemplation is promoted by SOLILOQUY and PRAYER. Though consideration be the chief instrument in this work, yet by itself it is not so likely to affect the heart. In this respect contemplation is like preaching, where the mere explaining of truths and duties is seldom attended with such success as the lively application of them to the conscience; and especially when a divine blessing is earnestly sought to accompany such application.

1. By *soliloquy*, or a pleading the case with thyself, thou must in thy meditation quicken thy own heart. Enter into a serious debate with it. Plead with it in the most moving and affecting language, and urge it with the most powerful and weighty arguments. It is what holy men of God have practised in all ages. Thus David, "Why art thou cast down, O my soul; and why art thou disquieted within me? Hope thou in God; for I shall yet praise him who is the health of my countenance, and my God." And again, "Bless the Lord, O my soul; and all that is within me, bless his holy name. Bless the Lord, O my soul, and forget not all his benefits." This soliloquy is to be made use of according to the several affections of the soul, and according to its several necessities. It is a preaching to one's self; for as every good master or father of a family is a good preacher to his own family, so every good Christian is a good preacher to his own

soul. Therefore the very same method which a minister should use in his preaching to others, every Christian should endeavor after in speaking to himself. Observe the matter and manner of the most heart-affecting minister; let him be as a pattern for your imitation, and the same way that he takes with the hearts of his people do thou also take with thy own heart. Do this in thy heavenly contemplation; explain to thyself the things on which thou dost meditate; confirm thy faith in them by Scripture, and then apply them to thyself, according to their nature and thy own necessity. There is no need to object against this from a sense of thy own inability. Doth not God command thee to "teach the Scriptures diligently unto thy children, and talk of them when thou sittest in thine house, and when thou walkest by the way, and when thou liest down, and when thou risest up?" And if thou must have some ability to teach thy children, much more to teach thyself; and if thou canst talk of divine things to others, why not also to thy own heart?

2. Heavenly contemplation is also promoted by speaking to God in *prayer*, as well as by speaking to ourselves in soliloquy. Ejaculatory prayer may very properly be mixed with meditation as a part of the duty. How often do we find David, in the same psalm, sometimes pleading with his soul and sometimes with God. The apostle bids us "speak

to ourselves in psalms and hymns and spiritual songs," and no doubt we may also speak to God in them. This keeps the soul sensible of the divine presence, and tends greatly to quicken and raise it. As God is the highest object of our thoughts, so our viewing him, speaking to him, and pleading with him, more elevates the soul and excites the affections than any other part of meditation. Though we remain unaffected while we plead the case with ourselves, yet, when we turn our speech to God, it may strike us with awe; and the holiness and majesty of him whom we speak to, may cause both the matter and words to pierce the deeper. When we read that "Isaac went out to meditate in the field," the margin says, "to pray," for the Hebrew word signifies both. Thus, in our meditations, to intermix soliloquy and prayer, sometimes speaking to our own hearts and sometimes to God, is, I apprehend, the highest step to which we can advance in this heavenly work. Nor should we imagine it will be as well to take up with prayer alone and lay aside meditation, for they are distinct duties, and must both of them be performed. We need one as well as the other, and therefore shall wrong ourselves by neglecting either. Besides, the mixture of them, like music, will be more engaging, as the one serves to put life into the other. And our speaking to ourselves in meditation should go before our speaking to God in prayer. For want of attending to this due order, men speak to God with far less reverence and affection than they would speak to an angel if he should appear to them, or to a judge if they were speaking for their lives. Speaking to the God of heaven in prayer, is a weightier duty than most are aware of.

CHAPTER XV

HEAVENLY CONTEMPLATION ASSISTED BY SENSIBLE
OBJECTS, AND GUARDED AGAINST A TREACHEROUS
HEART

It is difficult to maintain a lively impression of heavenly
things: therefore, I. Heavenly contemplation may be assisted by sensible objects; 1. If we draw strong suppositions from sense; and, 2. If we compare the objects of
sense with the objects of faith. II. Heavenly contemplation may also be guarded against a treacherous heart, by
considering, 1. The great backwardness of the heart to
this duty; 2. Its trifling in it; 3. Its wandering from it;
and, 4. Its too abruptly putting an end to it.

THE most difficult part of heavenly contemplation is to maintain a lively sense of heavenly things
upon our hearts. It is easier merely to think of
heaven a whole day, than to be lively and affectionate in those thoughts a quarter of an hour.
Faith is imperfect, for we are renewed but in part,
and goes against a world of resistance ; and being
supernatural, is prone to decline and languish, unless it be continually excited. Sense is strong according to the strength of the flesh ; and being
natural, continues while nature continues. The
objects of faith are far off, but those of sense are
nigh. We must go as far as heaven for our joys.
To rejoice in what we never saw, nor ever knew

the man that did see, and this upon a mere promise
of the Bible, is not so easy as to rejoice in what we
see and possess.   It must, therefore, be a point of
spiritual prudence to call in sense to the assistance
of faith.   It will be a good work if we can make
friends of these usual enemies, and make them
instruments for raising us to God, which are so often
the means of drawing us from him.   Why hath God
given us either our senses or their common objects,
if they might not be serviceable to his praise?
Why doth the Holy Spirit describe the glory of the
new Jerusalem in expressions that are even grateful to the flesh?   Is it that we might think heaven
to be made of gold and pearl; or that saints and
angels eat and drink?   No; but to help us to conceive of them as we are able, and to use these borrowed phrases as a glass, in which we must see the
things themselves imperfectly represented till we
come to an immediate and perfect sight.   Besides
showing how heavenly contemplation may be assisted by sensible objects, this chapter will also
show how it may be preserved from a wandering
heart.

First, in order that heavenly contemplation may
be ASSISTED BY SENSIBLE OBJECTS, let me only advise
to draw suppositions from sense, and to compare the
objects of sense with the objects of faith.

1. For the helping of thy affections in heavenly
contemplation, draw as *strong suppositions* as pos-

sible from thy senses. Think on the joys above as
boldly as Scripture hath expressed them. Bring
down thy conceptions to the reach of sense. Both
love and joy are promoted by familiar acquaintance.
When we attempt to think of God and glory without the Scripture's manner of representing them, we
are lost, and have nothing to fix our thoughts upon;
we set them so far from us that our thoughts are
strange, and we are ready to say, what is above us
is nothing to us. To conceive of God and glory
only as above our conception, will beget but little
love; or above our love, will produce little joy.
Therefore put Christ no further from you than he
hath put himself, lest the divine nature be again
inaccessible. Think of Christ as in our own glorified nature. Think of glorified saints as men made
perfect. Suppose thyself a companion with John
in his survey of the new Jerusalem, and viewing
the thrones, the majesty, the heavenly hosts, the
shining splendor which he saw. Suppose thyself
his fellow-traveller into the celestial kingdom, and
that thou hadst seen all the saints in their white
robes, with "palms in their hands," and that thou
hadst heard those "songs of Moses and of the Lamb."
If thou hadst really seen and heard these things, in
what a rapture wouldst thou have been. And the
more seriously thou puttest this supposition to thyself, the more will thy meditation elevate thy heart.
Do not, like the Papists, draw them in pictures, but

get the liveliest picture of them in thy mind that thou possibly canst, by contemplating the scripture account of them, till thou canst say, "Methinks I see a glimpse of glory. Methinks I hear the shouts of joy and praise, and even stand by Abraham and David, Peter and Paul, and other triumphant souls. Methinks I even see the Son of God appearing in the clouds, and the world standing at his bar to receive their doom, and hear him say, 'Come, ye blessed of my Father;' and see them go rejoicing into the joy of their Lord. My very dreams of these things have sometimes greatly affected me; and should not these just suppositions much more affect me? What if I had seen, with Paul, those 'unutterable things?' Or, with Stephen, had seen 'heaven opened, and Christ sitting at the right hand of God?' Surely that one sight was worth his storm of stones. What if I had seen, as Micaiah did, 'the Lord sitting upon his throne, and all the host of heaven standing on his right hand and on his left?' Such things did these men of God see; and I shall shortly see far more than ever they saw, till they were loosed from the flesh as I must be." Thus you see how it excites our affections in this heavenly work, if we make strong and familiar suppositions from our bodily senses concerning the state of blessedness, as the Spirit hath in condescending language expressed it.

2. The other way in which our senses may

promote this heavenly work, is by *comparing the objects of sense with the objects of faith*. As for instance, you may strongly argue with your heart, from the corrupt delights of sensual men to the joys above. Think with thyself, " Is it such a delight to a sinner to do wickedly ; and will it not be delightful indeed to live with God ? Hath the drunkard such delight in his cups, that the fears of damnation will not make him forsake them ? Will the licentious man rather part with his credit, estate, and salvation, than with his brutish delights ? If the way to hell can afford such pleasure, what then are the pleasures of the saints in heaven? If the covetous man hath so much pleasure in his wealth, and the ambitious man in places of power and titles of honor, what then have the saints in everlasting treasures, and in heavenly honors, where we shall be set above principalities and powers, and be made the glorious spouse of Christ? How delightfully do the voluptuous follow their recreations from morning till night, or sit at their cards and dice nights and days together. O the delight we shall have, when we come to our rest, in beholding the face of the living God, and in singing forth praises unto him and the Lamb."

Compare also the delights above with the lawful and moderate delights of sense. Think with thyself, " How sweet is food to my taste when I am hungry, especially if it be, as Isaac said, 'such as I

love,' which my temperance and appetite incline
to. What delight then must my soul have in feeding upon 'Christ, the living bread,' and in 'eating
with him at his table in his kingdom.' Was a mess
of pottage so sweet to Esau in his hunger, that he
would buy it at so dear a rate as his birthright ?
How highly then should I value this never-perish-
ing food. How pleasant is drink in the extremity
of thirst—scarcely to be expressed—enough to make
the 'strength of Sampson revive.' O how delightful will it be to my soul to drink of that 'fountain
of living water, which whoso drinketh shall thirst
no more.' How delightful are grateful odors to the
smell, or music to the ear, or beautiful sights to the
eye. What fragrance, then, hath 'the precious ointment which is poured on the head' of our glorified
Saviour, and which must be poured on the head of
all his saints, and will fill all heaven with its odor.
How delightful is the music 'of the heavenly host.'
How pleasing will be those real beauties above.
How glorious the 'building not made with hands,'
the house that God himself dwells in, the walks
and prospects in 'the city of God' and the celestial
paradise.''

Compare also the delights above with those we
find in *natural knowledge*. These are far beyond
the delights of sense ; but how much further are
the delights of heaven. Think, then, ''can an
Archimedes be so taken up with his mathematical

invention, that the threats of death cannot disengage him, but he will die in the midst of his contemplations? Should not I be much more taken up with the delights of glory, and die with these contemplations fresh upon my soul, especially when my death will perfect my delights, while those of Archimedes die with him? What exquisite pleasure is it to dive into the secrets of nature, and find out the mysteries of arts and sciences, especially if we make a new discovery in any one of them. What high delights are there then in the knowledge of God and Christ. If the face of human learning be so beautiful as to make sensual pleasures appear base and brutish, how beautiful then is the face of God. When we meet with some choice book, how could we read it day and night, almost forgetful of meat, drink, or sleep. What delights are there then at God's right hand, where we shall know in a moment all that is to be known."

Compare also the delights above with the delights of *morality* and of *the natural affections*. What delight had many sober heathen in the rules and practice of moral duty, so that they took him alone for an honest man who did well through the love of virtue, and not merely for fear of punishment; yea, so much valued was this moral virtue, that they thought a man's chief happiness consisted in it. Think, then, "What excellency will there be in our heavenly perfection, and in that uncreated perfection of God which we shall behold. What sweetness is there in the exercise of natural love, whether to children, parents, yoke-fellows, or intimate friends. Does David say of Jonathan, 'Thy love to me was wonderful, passing the love of women?' Did the 'soul of Jonathan cleave to David?' Had Christ himself one 'disciple whom he especially loved, and who was wont to lean on his breast?' If then the delights of close and cordial friendship be so great, what delight shall we have in the friendship of the Most High, and in our mutual intimacy with Jesus Christ, and in the dearest love of the saints. Surely this will be a stricter friendship than these, more lovely and desirable friends than ever the sun beheld; and both our affections to our Father and Saviour, and especially theirs to us, will be such as we never knew here. If one angel could destroy a host, the affections of spirits must also be proportionably stronger, so that we shall then love a thousand times more ardently than we can now. As all the attributes and works of God are incomprehensible, so is this of love; he will love us infinitely beyond our most perfect love to him. What then will there be in this mutual love!"

Compare also the excellencies of heaven with those glorious *works of creation* which our eyes now behold. What wisdom, power, and goodness are manifested therein. How does the majesty of the

Creator shine in this fabric of the world. "His works are great, sought out of all them that have pleasure therein." What divine skill in forming the bodies of men or beasts. What excellency in every plant. What beauty in flowers. What variety and usefulness in herbs plants, fruits, and minerals. What wonders are contained in the earth and its inhabitants; the ocean of waters, with its motions and dimensions; and the constant succession of spring and autumn, of summer and winter. Think, then, "If these things, which are but servants to sinful man, are so full of mysterious worth, what is that place where God himself dwells, and which is prepared for just men made perfect with Christ? What glory is there in the least of yonder stars. What a vast resplendent body is yonder moon, and every planet. What an inconceivable glory has the sun. But all this is nothing to the glory of heaven. Yonder sun must there be laid aside as useless. Yonder sun is but darkness to the lustre of my Father's house. I shall myself be as glorious as that sun. This whole earth is but my Father's footstool. This thunder is nothing to his dreadful voice. These winds are nothing to the breath of his mouth. If the 'sending rain, and making the sun to rise on the just and on the unjust' be so wonderful, how much more wonderful and glorious will that Sun be which must shine on none but saints and angels?"

Compare also the enjoyments above with *the wonders of Providence* in the church and the world. Would it not be an astonishing sight to see "the sea stand as a wall on the right hand and on the left, and the dry land appear in the midst, and the people of Israel pass safely through, and Pharaoh and his host drowned; or to have seen the ten plagues of Egypt; or the rock gushing forth streams; or manna and quails rained from heaven; or the earth opening and swallowing up the wicked? But we shall see far greater things than these; not only sights more wonderful, but more delightful; there shall be no blood, nor wrath, intermingled; nor shall we cry out, as the men of Beth-shemesh, "Who is able to stand before this holy Lord God?" How astonishing to see the sun stand still in the firmament, or "the dial of Ahaz go back ten degrees." But we shall see when there shall be no sun; or rather, shall behold for ever a Sun of infinitely greater brightness. What a life should we have, if we could have drought or rain at our prayers; or have fire from heaven to destroy our enemies, as Elijah had; or raise the dead, as Elisha; or miraculously cure diseases, and speak all languages, as the apostles. Alas, these are nothing to the wonders we shall see and possess with God; and all of them wonders of goodness and love. We shall ourselves be the subjects of more wonderful mercies than any of these. Jonah was raised but from a three days' burial in the belly of a fish, but we shall be raised from many years' decay and dust; and that dust exalted to the glory of the sun; and that glory perpetuated through eternity. Surely, if we observe but common providences, as the motions of the sun, the tides of the sea, the standing of the earth, the watering it with rain as a garden, the keeping in order a wicked, confused world, with many others, they are all admirable. But what are these to the Zion of God, the vision of the divine Majesty, and the order of the heavenly host?

Add to these those particular providences which thou hast *thyself* enjoyed and recorded through thy life, and compare them with the mercies thou shalt have above. Look over the mercies of thy youth and riper age, of thy prosperity and adversity, of thy several places and relations; are they not excellent and innumerable, rich and engaging? How sweet was it to thee when God resolved thy doubts, scattered thy fears, prevented the inconveniences into which thy own counsel would have cast thee, eased thy pains, healed thy sickness, and raised thee up, as from death and the grave. Think, then, "Are all these so sweet and precious, that without them my life would have been a perpetual misery? Hath his providence on earth lifted me so high, 'and his gentleness made me so great?' How sweet, then, will his glorious presence be.

How high will his eternal love exalt me. And how great shall I be made in communion with his greatness. If my pilgrimage and warfare have such mercies, what shall I find in my home and in my triumph; If God communicates so much to me while I remain a sinner, what will he bestow when I am a perfected saint? If I have had so much at such a distance from him, what shall I have in his immediate presence, where I shall ever stand before his throne?"

Compare the joys above with the comforts thou hast here received in *ordinances*. Has not the Bible been to thee as an open fountain, flowing with comforts day and night? What suitable promises have come into thy mind; so that, with David, thou mayest say, "Unless thy law had been my delight, I should then have perished in mine affliction." Think, then, "If his word be so full of consolation, what overflowing springs shall we find in God himself? If his letters are so comfortable, what will the glory of his presence be? If the promise is so sweet, what will the performance be? If the testament of our Lord and our charter for the kingdom be so comfortable, what will be our possession of the kingdom itself?"

Think further, "What delights have I also found in the word preached. When I have sat under a heavenly, heart-searching teacher, how has my heart been warmed. Methinks I have felt myself almost in heaven. How often have I gone to the congregation troubled in spirit, and returned joyful. How often have I gone doubting, and God hath sent me home persuaded of his love in Christ. What cordials have I met with to animate me in every conflict. If the face of Moses shine so gloriously, what glory is there in the face of God. If 'the feet of them that publish peace, that bring good tidings of salvation, be beautiful,' how beautiful is the face of the Prince of peace. If this treasure be so precious in earthen vessels, what is that treasure laid up in heaven. Blessed are the eyes that see what is seen there, and the ears that hear the things that are heard there. There shall I hear Elijah, Isaiah, Jeremiah, John, Peter, Paul— not preaching to gainsayers, in imprisonment, persecution, and reproach, but triumphing in the praises of Him who hath raised them to honor and glory."

Think also, "What joy is it to have access and acceptance in prayer; that I may always go to God, and open my case and unbosom my soul to him, as to my most faithful friend. But it will be a more unspeakable joy, when I shall receive all blessings without asking, and all my necessities and miseries will be removed, and when God himself will be the portion and inheritance of my soul."

As for the Lord's supper, "What a privilege is it to be admitted to sit at his table, to have his covenant sealed to me there. But all the life and comfort there is to assure me of the comforts here-after. O the difference between the last supper of Christ on earth, and the marriage supper of the Lamb at the great day. Then his room will be the glorious heavens; his attendants all the hosts of angels and saints : no Judas, no unfurnished guest comes there ; but the humble believers must sit down by him, and their feast will be their mutual loving and rejoicing."

Concerning the communion of saints, think with thyself, "What a pleasure is it to live with intelli-gent and heavenly Christians. David says of such, they were 'all his delight.' O what a delightful society, then, shall I have above! Had I but seen Job on the dunghill, what a mirror of patience ; and what will it be to see him in glory? How de-lightful to have heard Paul and Silas singing in the stocks ; how much more to hear them sing praises in heaven. What melody did David make on his harp ; but how much more melodious to hear that sweet singer in the heavenly choir. What would I have given for an hour's free converse with Paul, when he was just come down from the third heav-en. But I must shortly see those things myself, and possess what I see."

Once more, think of praising God in concert with his saints : "What if I had been in the place of those shepherds who saw and heard the heavenly host singing, 'Glory to God in the highest, and on earth peace, good will towards men!' But I shall see and hear more glorious things. How blessed should I have thought myself, had I heard Christ in his thanksgivings to his Father; how much more when I shall hear him pronounce me blessed. If there was such joy at bringing back the ark, or at rebuilding the temple, what will there be in the new Jerusalem? If the earth rent when the people rejoiced at Solomon's coronation, what a joyful shout will there be at the appearing of the King of the church. If, 'when the foundations of the earth were laid, the morning stars sang together, and all the sons of God shouted for joy,' what a joyful song will there be when the world of glory is both founded and finished, when the top-stone is laid, and when 'the holy city is adorned as the bride, the Lamb's wife!'"

Compare the joys thou shalt have in heaven with what *the saints have found in the way to it*, and in the foretastes of it. When did God ever reveal the least of himself to any of his saints, but the joy of their hearts corresponded to the revelation? In what an ecstasy was Peter on the mount of transfiguration. "Master," says he, "it is good for us to be here: let us make three tabernacles; one for thee, and one for Moses, and one for Elias." As if he had said, "O let us not go down again to yonder persecuting rabble; let us not return to our mean

and suffering state. Is it not better to stay here,
now we are here? Is not here better company and
sweeter pleasure?" How was Paul lifted up with
what he saw. How did the face of Moses shine
when he had been talking with God. These were
all extraordinary foretastes; but little to the full
beatific vision. How often have we read and heard
of dying saints who have been full of joy; and when
their bodies have felt the extremity of sickness and
pain, have had so much of heaven in their spirits
that their joy has far exceeded their sorrows. If a
spark of this fire be so glorious even amidst the sea
of adversity, what then is glory itself? O the joy
that the martyrs have felt in the flames. They
were flesh and blood, as well as we; it must therefore be some excellent thing that filled their spirits
with joy while their bodies were burning. Think,
reader, in thy meditations, " Sure it must be some
wonderful foretaste of glory that made the flames
of fire easy, and the king of terrors welcome. What
then is glory itself? What a blessed rest, when the
thoughts of it made Paul desire to depart and be with
Christ; and make the saints never think themselves
well till they are dead. Shall Saunders embrace
the stake, and cry, ' Welcome, cross!' and shall I
not more delightfully embrace my blessedness, and
cry, ' Welcome, crown?' Shall Bradford kiss the
fagot, and shall I not kiss the Saviour? Shall another poor martyr rejoice to have her foot in the

same hole of the stocks in which Mr. Philpot's had been before her; and shall not I rejoice that my soul shall live in the same pláce of glory where Christ and his apostles are gone before me? Shall fire and fagot, prisons and banishment, cruel mockings and scourgings, be more welcome to others than Christ and glory to me? God forbid."

Compare the glory of the heavenly kingdom with *the glory of the church on earth, and of Christ in his state of humiliation.* If Christ's suffering in the room of sinners had such excellency, what is Christ at his Father's right hand? If the church, under her sins and enemies have so much beauty, what will she have at the marriage of the Lamb? How wonderful was the Son of God in the form of a servant. When he is born, a new star must appear, and conduct the strangers to worship him in a manger, heavenly hosts with their songs must celebrate his nativity; while a child, he must dispute with doctors; when he enters upon his office, he turns water into wine, feeds thousands with a few loaves and fishes, cleanses the lepers, heals the sick, restores the lame, gives sight to the blind, and raises the dead. How wonderful, then, is his celestial glory. If there be such cutting down of boughs, and spreading of garments, and crying Hosanna, for one that comes into Jerusalem riding on an ass, what will there be when he comes with his angels in his glory? If they that heard him "preach the

gospel of the kingdom" confess, "Never man spake
like this man," they that then behold his majesty
in his kingdom will say, "There was never glory
like this glory." If, when his enemies came to
apprehend him, they fell to the ground—if, when
he is dying, the earth quakes, the veil of the temple
is rent, the sun is eclipsed, the dead bodies of the
saints arise, and the standers-by acknowledge, "Truly this was the Son of God"—O what a day will it
be when the dead must all arise and stand before
him; when he "will once shake, not the earth only,
but the heavens also;" when this sun shall be
taken out of the firmament, and be everlastingly
darkened with his glory; and when every tongue
shall confess him to be the Lord and King! If,
when he rose again, death and the grave lost their
power; if angels must "roll away the stone," terrify the keepers till they are "as dead men," and
send the tidings to his disciples; if he ascend to
heaven in their sight, of what power, dominion,
and glory is he now possessed, and which we must
for ever possess with him! When he is gone, can
a few poor fishermen and tent-makers cure the
lame, blind, and sick, open prisons, destroy the
disobedient, raise the dead, and astonish their ad-
versaries? what a world will that be where every
one can do greater works than these. If the preaching of the gospel be accompanied with such power
as to discover the secrets of the heart, humble the

proud sinner, and make the most obdurate tremble ;
if it can make men burn their books, sell their lands,
and bring in the price and lay it down at the preacher's feet ; if it can convert thousands, and turn the
world upside down ; if its doctrine, from the prisoner at the bar, can make the judge on the bench
tremble ; if Christ and his saints have this power
and honor in the day of their abasement, and in
the time appointed for their suffering and disgrace,
what then will they have in their absolute dominion and full advancement in their kingdom of
glory ?

Compare the glorious change thou shalt have at
last, with *the gracious change* which the Spirit
hath here wrought on thy heart.   There is not the
smallest sincere grace in thee, but is of greater
worth than the riches of the Indies ; not a hearty
desire after Christ, but is more to be valued than
the kingdoms of the world.   A renewed nature is
the very image of God ; Christ dwelling in us, and
the Spirit of God abiding in us ; it is a beam from
the face of God ; the seed of God remaining in us ;
the only inherent beauty of the rational soul : it
ennobles man above all nobility ; fits him to understand his Maker's pleasure, do his will, and receive
his glory.   If this grain of mustard-seed be so precious, what is "the tree of life in the midst of the
paradise of God."   If a spark of life, which will
but strive against corruptions, and flame out a few

desires and groans, be of so much worth, how glorious, then, is the fountain of this life. If we are
said to be like God when we are pressed down with
a body of sin, surely we shall be much more like
God when we have no such thing as sin within us.
Is the desire after, and love of heaven so excellent,
what then is the thing itself? Is our joy in fore-
seeing and believing so sweet; what will be the
joy of full possession? How glad is a Christian
when he feels his heart begin to melt and be dissolved with the thoughts of sinful unkindness.
Even this sorrow yields him joy. O what then
will it be when we shall know and love and rejoice and praise in the highest perfection? Think
with thyself, "What a change was it to be taken
from that state wherein I was born, and in which
I was riveted by custom, when thousands of sins
lay against me; and if I had so died, I had been
damned for ever. What an astonishing change, to
be justified from all these enormous crimes, and
freed from all these fearful plagues, and made an
heir of heaven. How often, when I have thought
of my regeneration, have I cried out, O blessed day,
and blessed be the Lord that ever I saw it! How,
then, shall I cry out in heaven, O blessed eternity,
and blessed be the Lord that brought me to it.
Did the angels of God rejoice to see my conversion?
surely they will congratulate my felicity in my
salvation. Grace is but a spark raked up in the

ashes, covered with flesh from the sight of the world, and sometimes covered with corruption from my own sight; but my everlasting glory will not be so clouded, nor my light be 'under a bushel, but upon a hill,' even upon mount Zion, the mount of God."

Once more, compare the joys which thou shalt have above, with those *foretastes* of it which the Spirit hath given thee here.   Hath not God sometimes revealed himself extraordinarily to thy soul, and let a drop of glory fall upon it?   Hast thou not been ready to say, "O that it might be thus with my soul continually?"   Didst thou never cry out with the martyr, after thy long and mournful expectations, "He is come, he is come?"   Didst thou never, under a lively sermon of heaven, or in thy retired contemplations on that blessed state, perceive thy drooping spirits revive, and thy dejected heart lift up thy head, and the light of heaven dawn on thy soul?   Think with thyself, "What is this earnest to the full inheritance?   Alas, all this light, that so amazeth and rejoiceth me, is but a candle lighted from heaven to lead me thither through this world of darkness.   If some godly men have been overwhelmed with joy till they have cried out, 'Hold, Lord, stay thy hand; I can bear no more!' what then will be my joys in heaven, when my soul shall be so capable of seeing and enjoying God, that though the light be ten thousand times greater than the sun, yet my eyes shall be able for ever to behold it?" Or, if thou hast not yet felt these sweet foretastes—for every believer hath not felt them—then make use of such delights as thou hast felt, in order the better to discern what thou shalt hereafter feel.

Secondly, I am now to show how heavenly contemplation may be PRESERVED FROM A WANDERING HEART. Our chief work here is to discover the danger, and that will direct to the fittest remedy. The heart will prove the greatest hinderance in this heavenly employment, either by backwardness to it or by trifling in it, or by frequent excursions to other objects, or by abruptly ending the work before it is well begun. As you value the comfort of this work, these dangerous evils must be faithfully resisted.

1. Thou wilt find thy heart as *backward* to this, I think, as to any work in the world. O what excuses will it make ; what evasions will it find out ; what delays and demurs, when it is ever so much convinced. Either it will question whether it be a duty or not; or if it be so to others, whether to thyself. It will tell thee, "This is a work for ministers that have nothing else to study, or for persons that have more leisure than thou hast." If thou be a minister, it will tell thee, "This is the duty of the people ; it is enough for thee to meditate for their instruction, and let them meditate on what they have heard." As if it was thy duty

only to cook their meat and serve it up, and they alone must eat it, digest it, and live upon it. If all this will not do, thy heart will tell thee of other business, or set thee upon some other duty; for it had rather go to any duty than this. Perhaps it will tell thee, " Other duties are greater, and therefore this must give place to them, because thou hast no time for both. Public business is more important; to study and preach for the saving of souls must be preferred before these private contemplations." As if thou hadst not time to care for thy own salvation, for looking after that of others; or thy charity to others were so great, that it obliges thee to neglect thy own eternal welfare; or as if there was any better way to fit us to be useful to others, than making this proof of our doctrine ourselves. Certainly heaven is the best fire to light our candle at, and the best book for a preacher to study; and if we would be persuaded to study that more, the church would be provided with more heavenly lights; and when our studies are divine and our spirits divine, our preaching will also be divine, and we may be called divines indeed. Or, if thy heart have nothing to say against the work, it will trifle away the time in delays, and promise this day and the next, but still keep off from the business. Or it will give thee a flat denial, and oppose its own unwillingness to thy reason. All this I speak of the heart, so far as it is still carnal; for I know, so far as it is spiritual, it will judge this the sweetest work in the world.

What is now to be done? Wilt thou do it if I tell thee? Wouldst thou not say in a like case, "What should I do with a servant that will not work, or with a horse that will not travel? Shall I keep them to look at?" Then faithfully deal thus with thy heart; persuade it to the work, take no denial, chide it for its backwardness, use violence with it. Hast thou no command of thy own thoughts? Is not the subject of thy meditations a matter of choice, especially under the guidance of thy judgment? Surely God gave thee, with thy new nature, some power to govern thy thoughts. Art thou again become a slave to thy depraved nature? Resume thy authority. Call in the Spirit of Christ to thine assistance, who is never backward to so good a work, nor will deny his help in so just a cause. Say to him, "Lord, thou gavest my reason the command of my thoughts and affections; the authority I have received over them is from thee; and now, behold, they refuse to obey thine authority. Thou commandest me to set them to the work of heavenly meditation; but they rebel and stubbornly refuse the duty. Wilt thou not assist me to exercise that authority which thou hast given me? O send down thy Spirit, that I may enforce thy commands, and effectually compel them to obey thy will." Thus thou shalt see thy heart will submit, its resistance be overcome, and its backwardness be turned into cheerful compliance.

2. Thy heart will also be likely to betray thee by *trifling*, when it should be effectually meditating. Perhaps, when thou hast an hour for meditation, the time will be spent before thy heart will be serious. This doing of duty as if we did it not, ruins as many as the omission of it. Here let thine eye be always upon thy heart. Look not so much to the time it spends in the duty, as to the quantity and quality of the work that is done. You can tell by his work whether a servant has been diligent. Ask yourself, "What affections have yet been exercised? How much nearer am I to heaven?" Think not, since thy heart is so trifling, it is better to let it alone; for by this means thou wilt certainly banish all spiritual obedience; because the best hearts, being but sanctified in part, will resist so far as they are carnal. But rather consider well the corruptions of thy nature, and that its sinful indispositions will not supersede the commands of God, nor one sin excuse another; and that God has appointed means to excite our affections. This self-reasoning, self-considering duty of heavenly meditation, is the most effective means both to excite and increase love. Therefore neglect not the duty till thou feelest thy love constrain thee, any more than thou wouldst stay from the fire till thou feel-

est thyself warm; but engage in the work till love
is excited, and then love will constrain thee to further duty.

3. Thy heart will also be *making excursions*
from thy heavenly meditation to other objects. It
will be turning aside, like a careless servant, to talk
with every one that passes by. When there should
be nothing in thy mind but heaven, it will be thinking of thy calling, or thy afflictions, or of every bird,
or tree, or place thou seest. The cure is here the
same as before: use watchfulness and violence.
Say to thy heart, "What, did I come hither to think
of my worldly business, of persons, places, news, or
vanity, or of any thing but heaven, be it ever so
good? 'Canst thou not watch one hour?' Wouldst
thou leave this world and dwell for ever with Christ
in heaven, and not leave it one hour to dwell with
Christ in meditation? 'Is this thy love to thy
friend?' Dost thou love Christ and the place of thy
eternal blessed abode no more than this?" If the
ravening fowls of wandering thoughts devour the
meditations intended for heaven, they devour the
life and joy of thy thoughts; therefore drive them
away from thy sacrifice, and strictly keep thy heart
to the work.

4. *Abruptly ending* thy meditation before it is
well begun, is another way in which thy heart will
deceive thee. Thou mayest easily perceive this in
other duties. In secret prayer, is not thy heart

urging thee to cut it short, and frequently making a motion to have done? So in heavenly contemplation, thy heart will be weary of the work, and will stop thy heavenly walk before thou art well warm. But charge it in the name of God to stay, and not do so great a work by halves. Say to it, "Foolish heart, if thou beg a while, and goest away before thou hast thine alms, is not thy begging a lost labor? If thou stoppest before the end of thy journey, is not thy travel lost? Thou camest hither in hope to have a sight of the glory which thou must inherit; and wilt thou stop when thou art almost at the top of the hill, and turn back before thou hast taken thy survey? Thou camest hither in hope to speak with God; and wilt thou go before thou hast seen him? Thou camest to bathe thyself in the streams of consolation, and to that end didst unclothe thyself of thy earthly thoughts; and wilt thou only touch the bank and return? Thou camest to 'spy out the land of promise;' go not back without 'one cluster of grapes to show thy brethren' for their encouragement. Let them see that thou hast tasted of the wine by the gladness of thy heart; and that thou hast been anointed with the oil, by the cheerfulness of thy countenance; and hast fed of the milk and honey, by the mildness of thy disposition and the sweetness of thy conversation. This heavenly fire would melt thy frozen heart, and refine and spiritualize it; but it must have time to operate." Thus pursue the work till something be done, till thy graces be in exercise, thy affections raised, and thy soul refreshed with the delights above ; or if thou canst not attain these ends at once, be the more earnest at another time. "Blessed is that servant, whom his Lord, when he cometh, shall find so doing."

CHAPTER XVI

HEAVENLY CONTEMPLATION EXEMPLIFIED, AND THE WHOLE WORK CONCLUDED

The reader's attention excited to the following example of
meditation : 1. The excellencies of heavenly rest; 2. Its
nearness; 3. Dreadful to sinners; 4. And joyful to saints;
5. Its dear purchase; 6. Its difference from earth; 7. The
heart pleaded with; 8. Unbelief banished; 9. A careless
world pitied; 10. Heavenly rest the object of love; 11. And
joy; 12. The heart's backwardness to heavenly joy lamented; 13. Heavenly rest the object of desire.

AND now, reader, according to the above directions, make conscience of daily exercising thy
graces in meditation as well as prayer. Retire into
some secret place at a time the most convenient to
thyself, and laying aside all worldly thoughts, with
all possible seriousness and reverence look up towards heaven; remember there is thine everlasting
rest; study its excellency and reality; and rise
from sense to faith by comparing heavenly with
earthly joys. Then mix ejaculations with thy
soliloquies, till, having pleaded the case reverently
with God and seriously with thy own heart, thou
hast pleaded thyself from a clod to a flame; from
a forgetful sinner and a lover of the world, to an
ardent lover of God; from a fearful coward to a
resolved Christian; from an unfruitful sadness to a

joyful life : in a word, till thou hast pleaded thy
heart from earth to heaven ; from conversing below
to walking with God ; and till thou canst lay thy
heart to rest, as in the bosom of Christ, by some
such meditation of thy everlasting rest as is here
added for thy assistance.

1. "*Rest*! How sweet the sound. It is melody
to my ears. It lies as a reviving cordial to my
heart, and from thence sends forth lively spirits,
which beat through all the pulses of my soul.
Rest! not as the stone that rests on the earth, nor
as this flesh shall rest in the grave, nor such a rest
as the carnal world desires. O blessed rest, when
we 'rest not day and night, saying, Holy, holy, holy,
Lord God Almighty !' when we shall rest from sin,
but not from worship ; from suffering and sorrow,
but not from joy. O blessed day, when I shall rest
with God ; when I shall rest in the bosom of my
Lord ; when I shall rest in knowing, loving, rejoicing, and praising ; when my perfect soul and
body shall together perfectly enjoy the most perfect
God ; when God, who is love itself, shall perfectly
love me, and rest in his love to me, as I shall rest
in my love to him ; and rejoice over me with joy,
and joy over me with singing, as I shall rejoice in
him.

2. "How *near* is that most blessed, joyful day.
It comes apace. 'He that shall come, will come,
and will not tarry.' Though my Lord seems to

delay his coming, yet a little while and he will be here. What is a few hundred years when they are over? How surely will his sign appear. How suddenly will he seize upon the careless world, even 'as the lightning cometh out of the east and shineth unto the west.' He who is gone hence shall so come. Methinks I hear his trumpet sound. Methinks I see him coming in clouds, with his attending angels, in majesty and glory.

3. "O, *secure sinners*, what now will you do; where will you hide yourselves; what shall cover you? Mountains are gone; the heavens and the earth, which were, are passed away; the devouring fire hath consumed all, except yourselves, who must be the fuel for ever. O that you could consume as soon as the earth, and melt away as did the heavens. Ah, these wishes are now but vain. The Lamb himself would have been your friend; he would have loved you and ruled you, and now have saved you; but you would not then, and now it is too late. Cry not, 'Lord, Lord!' it is too late, too late. Why dost thou look about; can any save thee? Whither dost thou run; can any hide thee? O wretch, that hast brought thyself to this.

4. " Now, *blessed saints*, that have believed and obeyed, this is the end of faith and patience. This is it for which you prayed and waited. Do you now repent your sufferings and sorrows, your self-denial and holy walking? Are your tears of repentance

now bitter or sweet? See how the Judge smiles upon you; there is love in his looks; the titles of Redeemer, Husband, Head, are written in his amiable, shining face. Hark, he calls you; he bids you stand here on his right hand; fear not, for there he sets his sheep. O joyful sentence, 'Come, ye blessed of my Father, inherit the kingdom prepared for you from the foundation of the world.' He takes you by the hand, the door is open, the kingdom is his, and therefore yours; there is your place before his throne. The Father receives you as the spouse of his Son, and bids you welcome to the crown of glory. Ever so unworthy, you must be crowned. This was the project of free redeeming grace, the purpose of eternal love. O blessed grace; O blessed love. O how love and joy will rise. But I cannot express it, I cannot conceive it.

5. "This is that joy which was *procured by sorrow*, that crown which was procured by the cross. My Lord wept, that now my tears might be wiped away; he bled, that I might now rejoice; he was forsaken, that I might not now be forsaken; he then died, that I might now live. O free mercy, that can exalt so vile a wretch. Free to me, though dear to Christ. Free grace, that hath chosen me when thousands were forsaken. When my companions in sin must burn in hell, I must here rejoice in rest. Here must I live with all these saints. O comfortable meeting of my old acquaintance, with

whom I prayed and wept and suffered, and spoke often of this day and place. I see the grave could not detain you; the same love hath redeemed and saved you also.

6. "This *is not like* our cottages of clay, our prisons, our earthly dwellings. This voice of joy is not like our old complaints, our impatient groans and sighs; nor this melodious praise like the scoffs and revilings, or the oaths and curses which we heard on earth. This body is not like that we had, nor this soul like the soul we had, nor this life like the life we lived. We have changed our place and state, our clothes and thoughts, our looks, language, and company. Before, a saint was weak and despised—so proud and peevish, we could often scarce discern his graces; but now, how glorious is a saint. Where is now their body of sin which wearied themselves and those about them? Where are now our different judgments, reproachful names, divided spirits, exasperated passions, strange looks, uncharitable censures? Now we are all of one judgment, of one name, of one heart, house, and glory. O sweet reconciliation. Happy union. Now the gospel shall no more be dishonored through our folly. No more, my soul, shalt thou lament the sufferings of the saints or the church's ruins; nor mourn thy suffering friends, nor weep over their dying beds or their graves. Thou shalt never suffer thy old temptations from Satan, the world, or

thy own flesh. Thy pains and sickness are **all**
cured; thy body shall no more burden thee with
weakness and weariness; thy aching head and
heart, thy hunger and thirst, thy sleep and labor
are all gone.   O what a mighty change is this,
from the dunghill to the throne; from persecuting
sinners to praising saints; from a vile body to this
which 'shines as the brightness of the firmament;'
from a sense of God's displeasure to the perfect
enjoyment of him in love; from all my doubts
and fears to this possession which puts me out of
doubt; from all my fearful thoughts of death to
this joyful life. Blessed change! Farewell sin and
sorrow for ever; farewell my rocky, proud, unbelieving heart—my worldly, sensual, carnal heart;
and welcome now my most holy, heavenly nature.
Farewell repentance, faith, and hope; and welcome
love and joy and praise. I shall now have my harvest without ploughing or sowing, my joy without
a preacher or a promise; even all from the face of
God himself. Whatever mixture is in the streams,
there is nothing but pure joy in the fountain. Here
shall I be encircled with eternity, and ever live, and
ever, ever praise the Lord; my face will not wrin-
kle, nor my hair be gray; 'for this corruptible shall
have put on incorruption, and this mortal, immortality; and death shall be swallowed up in victory.
O death, where is now thy sting? O grave, where
is thy victory?' The date of my lease will no more

expire, nor shall I trouble myself with thoughts of death, nor lose my joys through fear of losing them. When millions of ages are passed, my glory is but beginning; and when millions more are passed, it is no nearer ending. Every day is all noon, every month is harvest, every year is a jubilee, every age is full manhood; and all this is one eternity. O blessed eternity, the glory of my glory, the perfection of my perfection!

7. "Ah, drowsy, earthly heart, how *coldly* dost thou think of this reviving day. Hadst thou rather sit down in dirt than walk in the palace of God? Art thou now remembering thy worldly business, or thinking of thy lusts, earthly delights, and merry company? Is it better to be here, than above with God? Is the company better? Are the pleasures greater? Come away; make no excuse nor delay; God commands and I command thee; gird up thy loins; ascend the mount; look about thee with faith and seriousness. Look not back upon the way of the wilderness, except it be to compare the kingdom with that howling desert, more sensibly to perceive the wide difference. Yonder is thy Father's glory; yonder, O my soul, must thou remove when thou departest from this body; and when the power of thy Lord hath raised it again and joined thee to it, yonder must thou live with God for ever. There is the glorious new Jerusalem, the gates of pearl, the foundation of pearl, the streets and pavements

of transparent gold.   That sun which lighteth all
this world will be useless there; even thyself shall
be as bright as yonder shining sun; God will be the
sun and Christ the light, and in his light shalt thou
have light.

8. "O my soul, dost thou 'stagger at the promises of God through *unbelief?*' I much suspect
thee.   Didst thou believe indeed, thou wouldst be
more affected with it.   Is it not under the hand
and seal and oath of God?   Can God lie?   Can he
that is truth itself be false?   What need hath God
to flatter or deceive thee?   Why should he promise
thee more than he will perform?   Dare not to
charge the wise, almighty, faithful God with this.
How many of the promises have been performed to
thee in thy conversion.   Would God so powerfully
concur with a feigned word?   O wretched heart of
unbelief, hath God made thee a promise of rest,
and wilt thou come short of it?   Thine eyes, thine
ears, and all thy senses may prove delusions sooner
than a promise of God can delude thee.   Thou
mayest be surer of that which is written in the
word, than if thou didst see it with thine eyes, or
feel it with thine hands.   Art thou sure thou art
alive, or that this is earth thou standest on, or that
thine eyes see the sun?   As sure is all this glory to
the saints; as sure shall I be higher than yonder
stars, and live for ever in the holy city, and joyfully
sound forth the praises of my Redeemer, if I be not

shut out by this 'evil heart of unbelief,' causing me to 'depart from the living God.'

9. "And is this rest so sweet and so sure? Then what mean *the careless world?* Know they what they neglect? Did they ever hear of it, or are they yet asleep, or are they dead? Do they certainly know that the crown is before them, while they thus sit still, or follow trifles? Undoubtedly they are beside themselves, to mind so much their provision by the way, when they are hasting so fast to another world, and their eternal happiness lies at stake. Were there left one spark of reason, they would never sell their rest for toil, nor their glory for worldly vanities, nor venture heaven for sinful pleasure. Poor men. O that you would once consider what you hazard, and then you would scorn these tempting baits. Blessed for ever be that love which hath rescued me from this bewitching darkness.

10. "Draw yet nearer, O my soul, with thy *most fervent love.* Here is matter for it to work upon, something worth thy loving. O see what beauty presents itself. Is not all the beauty in the world united here? Is not all other beauty but deformity? Dost thou now need to be persuaded to love? Here is a feast for thine eyes and all the powers of thy soul: dost thou need entreaties to feed upon it? Canst thou love a little shining earth, a walking piece of clay; and canst thou not love that God

that Christ, that glory, which are so truly and un-measurably lovely? Thou canst love thy friend, because he loves thee; and is the love of a friend like the love of Christ? Their weeping or bleed-ing for thee does not ease thee, nor stay the course of thy tears or blood; but the tears and blood that fell from thy Lord have a sovereign, healing virtue. O my soul, if love deserves and should beget love, what incomprehensible love is here before thee. Pour out all the store of thy affections here, and all is too little. O that it were more—O that it were many thousand times more. Let him be first served, that served thee first. Let him have the first-born and strength of thy soul, who parted with strength and life and love for thee.

"O my soul, dost thou love for *excellency*? Yon-der is the region of light; this is the land of dark-ness. Yonder twinkling stars, that shining moon, and radiant sun, are all but lanterns hung out of thy Father's house, to light thee while thou walk-est in this dark world. But how little dost thou know the glory and blessedness that are within.

"Dost thou love for *suitableness*? What person more suitable than Christ? His godhead and hu-manity, his fulness and freeness, his willingness and constancy, all proclaim him thy most suitable friend. What state more suitable to thy misery than mercy, or to thy sin and pollution than honor and perfection? What place more suitable to thee than heaven? Does this world agree with thy desires? Hast thou not had a sufficient trial of it, or dost thou love for interest and near relation? Where hast thou better interest than in heaven, or nearer relation than there?

"Dost thou love for *acquaintance and familiarity?* Though thine eyes have never seen thy Lord, yet thou hast heard his voice, received his benefits, and lived in his bosom. He taught thee to know thyself and him; he opened thee that first window, through which thou sawest into heaven. Hast thou forgotten since thy heart was careless, and he awakened it; hard, and he softened it; stubborn, and he made it yield; at peace, and he troubled it; whole, and he broke it; and broken till he healed it again? Hast thou forgotten the times when he found thee in tears; when he heard thy secret sighs and groans, and left all to come and comfort thee; when he took thee, as it were, in his arms, and asked thee, 'Poor soul, what ails thee? Dost thou weep, when I have wept so much? Be of good cheer; thy wounds are saving, and not deadly; it is I have made them, who mean thee no hurt; though I let out thy blood, I will not let out thy life.' I remember his voice. How gently did he take me up; how carefully did he dress my wounds. Methinks I hear him still saying to me, 'Poor sinner, though thou hast dealt unkindly with me and cast me off, yet I will not do so by thee. Though thou hast set light by me and all my mercies, yet they and myself are all thine. What wouldst thou have that I can give thee; and what dost thou want that I cannot give thee? If any thing I have will give thee pleasure, thou shalt have it. Wouldst thou have pardon? I freely forgive thee all the debt. Wouldst thou have grace and peace? thou shalt have both. Wouldst thou have myself? behold, I am thine, thy Friend, thy Lord, thy Brother, Husband, and Head. Wouldst thou have the Father? I will bring thee to him, and thou shalt have him, in and by me.' These were my Lord's reviving words.

"After all, when I was doubtful of his love, me-thinks I yet remember his overcoming arguments . 'Have I done so much, sinner, to testify my love, and yet dost thou doubt? Have I offered thee myself and love so long, and yet dost thou question my willingness to be thine? At what dearer rate should I tell thee that I love thee? Wilt thou not believe my bitter passion proceeded from love? Have I made myself in the gospel a lion to thine enemies and a lamb to thee, and dost thou overlook my lamb-like nature? Had I been willing to let thee perish, what need I have done and suffered so much? What need I follow thee with such patience and importunity? Why dost thou tell me of thy wants; have I not enough for me and thee? or of thy unworthiness; for, if thou wast thyself

worthy, what shouldst thou do with my worthi
ness? Did I ever invite or save the worthy and
righteous; or is there any such upon earth? Hast
thou nothing; art thou lost and miserable, helpless
and forlorn? Dost thou believe I am an all-suffi-
cient Saviour, and wouldst thou have me? Lo, I
am thine; take me; if thou art willing, I am; and
neither sin nor Satan shall break the bond.' These,
O these were the blessed words which his Spirit
from his gospel spoke unto me, till he made me
cast myself at his feet, and cry out, ' My Saviour,
and my Lord, thou hast broken, thou hast revived
my heart; thou hast overcome, thou hast won my
heart; take it, it is thine : if such a heart can
please thee, take it; if it cannot, make it such as
thou wouldst have it.' Thus, O my soul, mayest
thou remember the sweet familiarity thou hast had
with Christ; therefore, if acquaintance will cause
affection, let out thy heart unto him. It is he that
has stood by thy bed of sickness, has eased thy
pains, refreshed thy weariness, and removed thy
fears. He has been always ready, when thou hast
earnestly sought him; has met thee in public and
private; has been found of thee in the congregation, in thy house, in thy closet, in the field, in thy
waking nights, in thy deepest dangers.

"If *bounty and compassion* be an attractive of
love, how unmeasurably, then, am I bound to love
him. All the mercies that have filled up my life, all

the places that ever I abode in, all the societies and persons I have been conversant with, all my employ- ments and relations, every condition I have been in, and every change I have passed through, all tell me that the fountain is overflowing goodness. Lord, what a sum of love am I indebted to thee. And how does my debt continually increase. How should I love again for so much love. But shall I dare to think of requiting thee, or of recompensing all thy love with mine? Will my mite requite thee for thy golden mines; my faint wishes, for thy constant bounty; mine, which is nothing, or not mine, for thine, which is infinite, and thine own? Shall I dare to contend in love with thee, or set my borrowed, languid spark against the sun of love? Can I love as high, as deep, as broad, as long as Love itself; as much as he that made me, and that made me love, and gave me all that little which I have? As I cannot match thee in the works of power, nor make, nor preserve, nor rule the worlds, no more can I match thee in love. No, Lord, I yield, I am overcome. O blessed con- quest. Go on victoriously, and still prevail, and triumph in thy love. The captive of love shall proclaim thy victory: when thou leadest me in triumph from earth to heaven, from death to life, from the tribunal to the throne, myself and all that see it shall acknowledge thou hast prevailed, and all shall say, ' Behold, how he loved him.' Yet let me. love in subjection to thy love; as thy redeemed captive, though not thy peer. Shall I not love at all, because I cannot reach thy measure? O that I could feelingly say, 'I love thee,' even as I love my friend and myself. Though I cannot say, as the apostle, 'Thou knowest that I love thee;' yet I can say, Lord, thou knowest that I would love thee. I am angry with my heart that it doth not love thee; I chide it, yet it doth not mend; I reason with it, and would fain persuade it, yet I do not perceive it stir; I rub and chafe it in the use of ordinances, and yet I feel it not warm within me.

"Unworthy soul, is not thine eye now upon the only lovely object? Art thou not now beholding the ravishing glory of the saints? And dost thou not love? Art thou not a rational soul, and should not reason tell thee that earth is a dungeon to the celestial glory? Art thou not thyself a spirit, and shouldst thou not love God, 'who is a spirit, and the Father of spirits?' Why dost thou love so much thy perishing clay, and love no more the heavenly glory? Shalt thou love when thou comest there—when the Lord shall take thy body from the grave, and make thee shine as the sun in glory for ever and ever—shalt thou then love, or shalt thou not? Is not the place a meeting of lovers? Is not the life a state of love? Is it not the great marriage-day of the Lamb? Is not the em-

ployment there the work of love, where the souls
with Christ take their fill? O then, my soul, begin
it here. 'Be sick with love' now, that thou mayest be well with love there. 'Keep thyself' now
'in the love of God,' and let 'neither life nor death
nor any thing separate thee from it;' and thou
shalt be kept in the fulness of love for ever, and
nothing shall imbitter or abate thy pleasure; for
the Lord hath prepared a city of love, a place for
communicating love to his chosen, 'and they that
love his name shall dwell therein.'

11. "*Awake*, then, O my drowsy soul! To sleep
under the light of grace is unreasonable, much more
in the approach of the light of glory. Come forth,
my dull, congealed spirit; thy Lord bids thee '*rejoice, and again rejoice.*' Thou hast lain long
enough in thy prison of flesh, where Satan has been
thy jailer, cares have been thy irons, fears thy
scourges, and thy food the bread and water of affliction; where sorrows have been thy lodgings,
and thy sin and foes have made thy bed, and an
unbelieving heart has been the gates and bars that
have kept thee in: the angel of the covenant now
calls thee, and bids thee 'arise and follow him.'
Up, O my soul, and cheerfully obey, and thy bolts
and bars shall all fly open: follow the Lamb
whithersoever he goeth. Shouldst thou fear to
follow such a guide? Can the sun lead thee to a
state of darkness? Will He lead thee to death

who died to save thee from it? Follow him, and
he will show thee the paradise of God; he will
give thee a sight of the new Jerusalem, and a taste
of the tree of life.   Come forth, my drooping soul,
and lay aside thy winter dress; let it be seen, by
thy 'garments of joy and praise,' that the spring is
come ; and as thou now seest thy comforts green,
thou shalt shortly see them 'white and ripe for
harvest,' and then thou shalt be called to reap, and
gather, and take possession.   Should I suspend and
delay my joys till then?   Should not the joys of
the spring go before the joys of harvest?   Is title
nothing before possession?   Is the heir in no better
a state than a slave?   My Lord has taught me to
rejoice in hope of his glory, and how to see it
through the bars of a prison ; for, when persecuted
for righteousness' sake, he commands me to 'rejoice
and be exceeding glad,' because 'my reward in
heaven is great.'

"I know he would have my joys exceed my
sorrows ; and as much as he delights in 'the humble and contrite,' he yet more delights in the soul
that 'delights in him.'   Hath my Lord spread me
a table in this wilderness, and furnished it with the
promises of everlasting glory, and set before me
angels' food?   Doth he frequently and importunately invite me to sit down and partake, and
spare not?   Hath he to that end furnished me
with reason, and faith, and a joyful disposition ;

and is it possible that he should be unwilling to
have me rejoice? Is it not his command to 'delight thyself in the Lord,' and his promise, to 'give
thee the desires of thine heart?' Art thou not
charged to 'rejoice evermore;' yea, to 'sing aloud
and shout for joy?' Why should I, then, be discouraged? My God is willing, if I were but willing. He is delighted in my delights. He would
have it my constant frame and daily business to be
near him in my believing meditations, and to live
in the sweetest thoughts of his goodness. O blessed
employment, fit for the sons of God. But thy feast,
my Lord, is nothing to me without an appetite.
Thou hast set the dainties of heaven before me,
but alas, I am blind and cannot see them. I am
sick, and cannot relish them; I am so benumbed
that I cannot put forth a hand to take them. I
therefore humbly beg this grace, that as thou hast
opened heaven to me in thy word, so thou wouldst
open mine eyes to see it, and my heart to delight
in it; else heaven will be no heaven to me. O
thou Spirit of life, breathe upon thy graces in me;
take me by the hand, and lift me from the earth,
that I may see what glory 'thou hast prepared for
them that love thee.'

"Away, then, ye soul-tormenting cares and fears,
ye heart-vexing sorrows. At least, forbear a little
while: stand by; stay here below, till I go up and
see my rest. The way is strange to me, but not

to Christ. There was the eternal abode of his glorious Deity ; and thither hath he also brought his glorified flesh. It was his work to purchase it ; it is his to prepare it, and to prepare me for it, and bring me to it. The eternal God of truth hath given me his promise, his seal and oath, that, 'believing in Christ, I shall not perish, but have everlasting life.' Thither shall my soul be speedily removed, and my body very shortly follow. And can my tongue say that I shall shortly and surely live with God, and yet my heart not leap within me ? Can I say it with faith, and not with joy ? Ah, faith, how sensibly do I now perceive thy weakness. But though unbelief darken my light, and dull my life, and suppress my joys, it shall not be able to conquer and destroy me ; though it envy all my comforts, yet some, in spite of it, I shall even here receive ; and if that did not hinder, what abundance might I have. The light of heaven would shine into my heart, and I might be almost as familiar there as I am on earth. Come away, then, my soul, stop thine ears to the ignorant language of infidelity ; thou art able to answer all its arguments ; or if thou art not, yet tread them under thy feet. Come away ; stand not looking on that grave, nor turning those bones, nor read ing thy lesson now in the dust ; those lines will soon be wiped out. But lift up thy head and look to heaven, and see thy name written in golden letters 'in the book of life of the Lamb that was slain.'

"What if an angel should tell thee that there is a mansion in heaven prepared for thee, that it shall certainly be thine for ever; would not such a message make thee glad? And dost thou make light of the infallible word of promise, which was delivered by the Spirit, and even by the Son himself? Suppose thou hadst seen a fiery chariot come for thee, and take thee up to heaven, like Elijah; would not this rejoice thee? But thy Lord assures thee that the soul of a Lazarus hath a convoy of angels to carry it into Abraham's bosom. Shall a drunkard be so merry among his cups, or the glutton in his delicious fare, and shall not I rejoice, who must shortly be in heaven? Can meat and drink delight me when I hunger and thirst? Can I find pleasure in walks and gardens and convenient dwellings? Can beautiful objects delight my eyes, or grateful odors my smell, or melody my ears; and shall not the forethought of celestial bliss delight me? Methinks among my books I could employ myself in sweet content, and bid the world farewell, and pity the rich and great that know not this happiness; what then will my happiness in heaven be, where my knowledge will be perfect? If 'the queen of Sheba came from the utmost parts of the earth to hear the wisdom of Solomon,' and see his glory, how cheerfully should I pass from earth to heaven, to see the glory of the eternal majesty, and attain the height of wisdom, compared with which the most learned on earth are but fools and idiots.   What if God had made me commander of the earth ; what if I could ' remove mountains, heal diseases with a word or a touch, or cast out devils,' should I not rejoice in such privileges and honors as these ; and shall I not much more rejoice that my name is written in heaven ?   I cannot here enjoy my parents, or my near and beloved friends, without some delight ; especially when I have given my whole heart to my friend, how sweet was that exercise of my love.   O what will it then be to live in the perpetual love of God ?   ' For brethren to dwell together in unity here, how good and how pleasant it is.'   To see a family live in love ; husband and wife, parents, children, and servants doing all in love to one another ; to see a town live together in love, without any envyings, brawlings, or contentions, law-suits, factions, or divisions, but every man loving his neighbor as himself, thinking they can never do too much for one another, but striving to go beyond each other in love ; how happy, how delightful a sight is this !   O then, what blessed society will the family of heaven be, and those peaceful inhabitants of the new Jerusalem, where there is no division nor differing judgments, no disaffection nor strangeness, no deceitful friendship, no, not one unkind expression, not an

angry look or thought; but all are one in Christ,
who is one with the Father, and all live in the love
of him who is love itself! The soul is not more
where it lives than where it loves. How near,
then, will my soul be united to God, when I shall
so heartily, strongly, and incessantly love him.
Ah, wretched, unbelieving heart, that can think of
such a day and work and life as this with such
low and feeble joys. But my future enjoyments
will be more lively.

"How delightful is it to me to behold and study
these inferior works of creation. What a beautiful
fabric do we here dwell in; the floor so dressed
with herbs and flowers and trees, and watered with
springs and rivers; the roof so widely expanded, so
admirably adorned. What wonders do sun, moon,
and stars, seas and winds contain. And hath God
prepared such a house for corruptible flesh, for a
soul imprisoned; and doth he bestow so many millions of wonders upon his enemies? O what a
dwelling must that be which he prepares for his
dearly beloved children; and how will the glory
of the new Jerusalem exceed all the present glory
of earth. Arise then, O my soul, in thy contemplation, and let thy thoughts of that glory as far
exceed in sweetness thy thoughts of the excellencies
below. Fear not to go out of this body and this
world, when thou must make so happy a change;
but say, as one did when he was dying, 'I am

glad, and even leap for joy, that the time is come in which that mighty Jehovah, whose majesty in my search of nature I have admired, whose goodness I have adored, whom by faith I have desired and panted after, will now show himself to me face to face.'

"How wonderful also are the works of Providence. How delightful to see the great God interest himself in the safety and advancement of a few humble, praying, but despised persons; and to review those special mercies with which my own life has been adorned and sweetened. How often have my prayers been heard, my tears regarded, my troubled soul relieved. How often hath my Lord bid me be of good cheer. What a support are these experiences, these clear testimonies of my Father's love, to my fearful, unbelieving heart. O then what a blessed day will that be when I shall have all mercy, perfection of mercy, and fully enjoy the Lord of mercy; when I shall stand on the shore and look back on the raging seas I have safely passed; when I shall review my pains and sorrows, my fears and tears, and possess the glory which was the end of all. If one drop of lively faith was mixed with these considerations, what a heaven-ravishing heart should I carry within me. Fain would 'I believe; Lord, help my unbelief.'

"How sweet, O my soul, have ordinances been to thee. What delight hast thou had in prayer and thanksgiving, under heavenly sermons and in the society of saints, and to see 'the Lord adding to the church such as should be saved.' How then can my heart conceive the joy which I shall have to see the perfected church in heaven; and to be admitted into the celestial temple, and with the heavenly host praise the Lord for ever? Was the word of God sweeter to Job than his necessary food, and to David than honey and the honeycomb, and was it the joy and rejoicing of Jeremiah's heart? how blessed a day will that be when we shall fully enjoy the Lord of this word, and shall no more need these written precepts and promises, nor read any book but the face of the glorious God. If they that heard Christ speak on earth 'were astonished at his wisdom and answers, and wondered at the gracious words that proceeded out of his mouth,' how shall I then be affected to behold him in his majesty.

"Can the prospect of his glory make others welcome the cross and even refuse deliverance; and cannot it make thee cheerful under lesser sufferings? Can it sweeten the flames of martyrdom, and not sweeten thy life, or thy sickness, or thy natural death? Is it not the same heaven which they and I must live in? Is not their God, their Christ, their crown and mine the same? And shall I look upon it with an eye so dim, a heart so dull, a countenance so dejected? Some small foretastes of it have I myself had; and how much more delightful have they been than any earthly things ever were. What then will the full enjoyment be?

"What a beauty is there here in the imperfect graces of the Spirit. Alas, how small are these to what we shall enjoy in our perfect state. What a happy life should I here live, could I but love God as much as I would—could I be all love and always loving. O my soul, what wouldst thou give for such a life? Had I such apprehensions of God, such knowledge of his word as I desire; could I fully trust him in all my straits; could I be as lively as I would in every duty; could I make God my constant desire and delight, I would not envy the world their honors or pleasures. What a blessed state, O my soul, wilt thou shortly be in, when thou shalt have far more of these than thou canst now desire, and shalt exercise thy perfected graces in the immediate vision of God, and not in the dark and at a distance, as now.

"Is the sinning, afflicted, persecuted church of Christ so much more excellent than any particular gracious soul? What then will the church be when it is fully gathered and glorified; when it has ascended from the valley of tears to mount Zion; when it shall sin and suffer no more? The glory of the old Jerusalem will be darkness and deformity to the glory of the new. What cause shall we have then to shout for joy, when we shall see how glorious the heavenly temple is, and remember the meanness of the church on earth.

12. "But, alas, *at what a loss am I* in the midst of my contemplations. I thought my heart had all the while attended, but I see it hath not. What life is there in empty thoughts and words without affections? Neither God nor I find pleasure in them. Where hast thou been, unworthy heart, while I was opening to thee the everlasting treasures? Art thou not ashamed to complain so much of an uncomfortable life, and to murmur at God for filling thee with sorrows, when he in vain offers thee the delights of angels? Hadst thou now but followed me close, it would have made thee revive and leap for joy, and forget thy pains and sorrows. Did I think my heart had been so backward to rejoice?

13. "Lord, thou hast reserved my perfect joys for heaven ; therefore, *help me to desire* till I may possess, and let me long when I cannot, as I would, rejoice. O my soul, thou knowest to thy sorrow that thou art not yet at thy rest. When shall I arrive at that safe and quiet harbor where there are none of these storms, waves, and dangers ; when I shall never more have a weary, restless night or day? Then my life will not be such a mixture of hope and fear, of joy and sorrow ; nor shall flesh and spirit be combating within me ; nor faith and unbelief, humility and pride, maintain a

continual conflict. O when shall I be past these
soul-tormenting fears and cares and griefs? When
shall I be out of this soul-contradicting, ensnaring,
deceitful flesh; this corruptible body, this vain,
vexatious world? Alas, that I must stand and
see the church and cause of Christ tossed about in
contention, and made subservient to private interests or deluded fancies. There is none of this disorder in the heavenly Jerusalem; there I shall find
a harmonious concert of perfected spirits obeying
and praising their everlasting King. O how much
better to be a door-keeper there, than the commander
of this tumultuous world. Why am I no more
weary of this weariness? Why do I so forget my
resting-place? Up then, O my soul, in thy most
raised and fervent desires. Stay not till this flesh
can desire with thee; expect not that sense should
apprehend thy blessed object, and tell thee when
and what to desire.

"Doth not the dulness of thy desires after rest
accuse thee of most detestable ingratitude and
folly? Must thy Lord procure thee a rest at so
dear a rate, and dost thou no more value it? Must
he go before to prepare so glorious a mansion for
such a wretch, and art thou loath to go and possess
it? Shall the Lord of glory be desirous of thy
company, and thou not desirous of his? Must
earth become a very hell to thee before thou art
willing to be with God? Behold the most lovely

creature, or the most desirable state, and tell me, where wouldst thou be if not with God? Poverty is a burden; riches a snare; sickness unpleasing; health unsafe; the frowning world bruises thy heel; the smiling world stings thee to the heart; so much as the world is loved and delighted in, it hurts and endangers the lover; and if it may not be loved, why should it be desired? If thou art applauded, it proves the most contagious breath; if thou art vilified, or unkindly used, methinks this should not entice thy love. If thy successful labors and thy godly friends seem better to thee than a life with God, it is time for God to take them from thee. If thy studies have been sweet, have they not also been bitter? And at best, what are they to the everlasting view of the God of truth? Thy friends here have been thy delight, and have they not also been thy vexation and grief? They are gracious, and are they not also sinful? They are kind, and are they not soon displeased? They are humble, but, alas, how proud also. Their graces are sweet, and their gifts helpful; but are not their corruptions bitter, and their imperfections hurtful? And art thou so loath to go from them to thy God?

"O my soul, look above this world of sorrows. Hast thou so long felt the smarting rod of affliction, and no better understood its meaning? Is not every stroke to drive thee hence? Is not its voice like that to Elijah, 'What doest thou here?' Dost thou forget thy Lord's prediction? 'In the world ye shall have tribulation; in me ye shall have peace.' Ah, my dear Lord, I feel thy meaning; it is written in my flesh, engraved in my bones. My heart thou aimest at; thy rod drives; thy silken cord of love draws; and all to bring it to thyself. Lord, can such a heart be worth thy having? Make it worthy, and then it is thine; take it to thyself, and then take me. This clod hath life to stir, but not to rise. As the feeble child to the tender mother, it looketh up to thee, and stretcheth out the hands, and fain would have thee take it up. Though I cannot say, 'My soul longeth after thee,' yet I can say, I long for such a longing heart. 'The spirit is willing, the flesh is weak.' My spirit cries, 'Let thy kingdom come,' or let me come to thy kingdom; but the flesh is afraid thou shouldst hear my prayer, and take me at my word. O blessed be thy grace, which makes use of my corruptions to kill themselves; for I fear my fears, and sorrow for my sorrows, and long for greater longings; and thus the painful means of attaining my desires increase my weariness, and that makes me groan to be at rest.

"Indeed, Lord, my soul itself is in a strait, and what to choose I know not; but thou knowest what to give: 'to depart and be with thee is far better;' but 'to abide in the flesh' seems needful. Thou knowest I am not weary of thy work, but of sorrow

and sin; I am willing to stay while thou wilt
employ me, and despatch the work thou hast put
into my hands; but I beseech thee, stay no longer
when this is done; and while I must be here, let
me be still amending and ascending; make me still
better, and take me at the best. I dare not be so
impatient as to importune thee to cut off my time,
and snatch me hence unready; because I know my
everlasting state so much depends on the improvement of this life. Nor would I stay when my work
is done, and remain here sinning, while my brethren are triumphing. Thy footsteps bruise this
worm, while those stars shine in the firmament of
glory. Yet I am thy child as well as they. Christ
is my head as well as theirs; why is there then so
great a distance? But I acknowledge the equity
of thy ways; though we are all children, yet I am
the prodigal, and therefore more fit, in this remote
country, to feed on husks, while they are always
with thee, and possess thy glory. They were once
themselves in my condition, and I shall shortly be
in theirs. They were of the lowest form before
they came to the highest; they suffered before they
reigned; they 'came out of great tribulation, who
are now before thy throne;' and shall I not be content to come to the crown as they did, and to 'drink
of their cup, before I sit with them in the kingdom?' Lord, I am content to stay thy time, and
go thy way, so thou wilt exalt me also in thy

season, and take me into thy barn when thou seest me ripe. In the meantime, I may desire, though I am not to repine; I may believe and wish, though not make any sinful haste; I am willing to wait for thee, but not to lose thee; and when thou seest me too contented with thine absence, then quicken my languid desires, and blow up the dying spark of love; and leave me not until I am able unfeignedly to cry out, 'As the heart panteth after the water-brooks, so panteth my soul after thee, O God. My soul thirsteth for God, for the living God; when shall I come and appear before God? My conversation is in heaven, from whence I look for a Saviour. My affections are set on things above, where Christ sitteth and my life is hid. I walk by faith, and not by sight, willing rather to be absent from the body and present with the Lord.'

"What interest hath this empty world in me; and what is there in it that may seem so lovely as to entice my desires from my God, or make me loath to soar away? Methinks, when I look upon it with a deliberate eye, it is a howling wilderness, and too many of its inhabitants are untamed monsters. I can view all its beauty as deformity, and drown all its pleasures in a few penitent tears; or the wind of a sigh will scatter them away. O let not this flesh so seduce my soul as to make it pre-fer this weary life before the joys that are about thy throne. And though death itself be unwelcome to

nature, yet let thy grace make thy glory appear to
me so desirable that the king of terrors may be the
messenger of my joy. Let not my soul be ejected by
violence, and dispossessed of its habitation against
its will; but draw it to thyself by the secret power
of thy love, as the sunshine in the spring draws
forth the creatures from their winter cells; meet it
half way, and entice it to thee as the loadstone
doth the iron, and as the greater flame attracts the
less. Dispel therefore the clouds that hide thy
love from me, or remove the scales that hinder
mine eyes from beholding thee; for the beams
that stream from thy face, and the foretastes of thy
great salvation, and nothing else, can make a soul
unfeignedly say, 'Now let thy servant depart in
peace.' But it is not thy ordinary discoveries that
will here suffice; as the work is greater, so must
thy help be. O turn these fears into strong desires;
and this loathness to die into longings after thee.
While I must be absent from thee, let my soul as
heartily groan as my body doth under its want of
health. If I have any more time to spend on
earth, let me live as without the world in thee,
as I have sometimes lived as without thee in the
world. While I have a thought to think, let me
not forget thee; or a tongue to move, let me mention thee with delight; or breath to breathe, let it
be after thee, and for thee; or a knee to bend, let
it daily bow at thy footstool; and when by sickness

thou confinest me, do thou 'make my bed, number my pains, and put all my tears into thy bottle.'

"As my flesh desired what my spirit abhorred, so now let my spirit desire that day which my flesh abhorreth ; that my friends may not with so much sorrow wait for the departure of my soul, as my soul with joy shall wait for its own departure. Then 'let me die the death of the righteous, and let my last end be like his;' even a removal to that glory which shall never end. Then let thy convoy of angels bear my departing soul among the perfected spirits of the just, and let me follow my dear friends who have died in Christ before me ; and while my sorrowing friends are weeping over my grave, let my spirit be reposed with thee in rest ; and while my body shall lie mouldering in the dust, let my soul have 'the inheritance of the saints in light.' O thou that numberest the very hairs of my head, number all the days that my body lies in the dust ; and thou that 'writest all my members in thy book,' keep an account of my scattered bones. O my Saviour, hasten the time of thy return ; send forth thy angels, and let that dreadful, joyful trumpet sound. Delay not, lest the living give up their hope ; delay not, lest earth should grow like hell, and thy church by division be all crumbled to dust ; delay not, lest thy enemies get advantage of thy flock, and lest pride, hypocrisy, sensuality, and unbelief prevail against that little remnant, and

share among them thy whole inheritance, and
when thou comest, thou find not faith on the
earth; delay not, lest the grave should boast of
victory, and having learned rebellion of its guest,
should refuse to deliver thee up thy due. O hasten
that great resurrection-day, when thy command
shall go forth, and none disobey; when 'the sea
and the earth shall yield up their hostages, and all
that sleep in the grave shall awake, and the dead
in Christ shall rise first;' when the seed which thou
sowest corruptible, shall come forth incorruptible;
and graves that received rottenness and dust, shall
return thee glorious stars and suns. Therefore
dare I lay down my body in the dust, intrusting it
not to a grave, but to thee; and therefore my flesh
shall rest in hope, till thou shall raise it to the possession of everlasting rest. 'Return, O Lord, how
long? O let thy kingdom come.' Thy desolate
'bride saith, Come !' for thy Spirit within her saith,
Come, and teacheth her thus to 'pray with groan-
ings which cannot be uttered; yea, the whole creation saith, Come—waiting to be delivered from the
bondage of corruption into the glorious liberty of
the children of God.' Thou thyself hast said,
'Surely I come quickly. Amen. Even so, come,
Lord Jesus.' "

CONCLUSION

THUS, reader, I have given thee my best advice for maintaining a heavenly conversation. If thou canst not thus meditate methodically and fully, yet do it as thou canst; only be sure to do it seriously and frequently. Be acquainted with this heavenly work, and thou wilt, in some degree, be acquainted with God; thy joys will be spiritual, prevalent, and lasting, according to the nature of their blessed object; thou wilt have comfort in life and death. When thou hast neither wealth nor health nor the pleasures of this world, yet wilt thou have comfort. Without the presence or help of any friend, without a minister, without a book, when all means are denied thee or taken from thee, yet mayest thou have vigorous, real comfort. Thy graces will be mighty, active, and victorious; and the daily joy which is thus drawn from heaven will be thy strength. Thou wilt be as one that stands on the top of an exceeding high mountain; he looks down on the world as if it were quite below him; fields and woods, cities and towns seem to him but little spots. Thus despicably wilt thou look on all things here below. The greatest princes will seem but as grasshoppers; the busy, contentious, covetous world, but as a heap of ants. Men's threatenings will be no terror to thee, nor the honors of this world any strong enticement; temptations will be more harmless, as having lost their strength; and afflictions less grievous, as having lost their sting; and every mercy will be better known and relished. It is now, under God, in thy own choice, whether thou wilt live this blessed life or not; and whether all this pains I have taken for thee shall prosper or be lost. If it be lost through thy neglect, thou thyself wilt prove the greatest loser. O man, what hast thou to mind but God and heaven? Art thou not almost out of this world already? Dost thou not look every day, when one disease or another will release thy soul? Does not the grave wait to be thine house, and worms to feed upon thy face and heart? What if thy pulse must beat a few strokes more? What if thou hast a little longer to breathe, before thou breathe out thy last—a few more nights to sleep, before thou sleepest in the dust? Alas, what will this be when it is gone? And is it not almost gone already? Very shortly thou wilt see thy glass run out, and say to thyself, "My life is done; my time is gone; it is past recalling. There is nothing now but heaven or hell before me." Where, then, should thy heart be now but in heaven? Didst thou know what a dreadful thing it is to have a doubt of heaven when a man is dying, it would raise thee up. And what else but doubt can that man then do, that never seriously thought of heaven before?

Some there be that say, "It is not worth so much time and trouble to think of the greatness of the joys above; if we can make sure they are ours, we know they are great." But as these men obey not the command of God, which requires them to have their "conversation in heaven, and to set their affections on things above;" so they wilfully make their own lives miserable, by refusing the delights which God hath set before them. And if this were all, it were a small matter : but see what abundance of other mischiefs follow the neglect of these heavenly delights. This neglect will damp, if not destroy, their love to God; will make it un pleasant to them to think or speak of God, or en gage in his service ; it tends to pervert their judgment concerning the ways and ordinances of God ; it makes them sensual and voluptuous; it leaves them in the power of every affliction and temptation, and is a preparative to total apostasy ; it will also make them fearful and unwilling to die; for who would go to a God or a place he hath no delight in? Who would leave his pleasure here, if he had not better to go to ? Had I only proposed a course of melancholy and fear and sorrow, you might reasonably have objected. But you must have heavenly delights, or none that are lasting. God is willing you should daily walk with him, and draw consolations from the everlasting fountain : if you are unwilling, even bear the loss ; and when you are dying, seek for comfort where you can get it, and see whether fleshly delights will remain with you. Then conscience will remember, in spite of you, that you were once persuaded to a way for more excellent pleasures—pleasures that would have followed you through death, and have lasted to eternity.

As for you whose hearts God has weaned from all things here below, I hope you will value this heavenly life, and take one walk every day in the new Jerusalem. God is your love and your desire; you would fain be more acquainted with your Saviour; and I know it is your grief, that your hearts are not nearer to him, and that they do not more feelingly love him and delight in him. O try this life of meditation on your heavenly rest. Here is the mount on which the fluctuating ark of your souls may rest. Let the world see by your heavenly lives, that religion is something more than opinions and disputes, or a task of outward duties. If ever a Christian is like himself, and conformable to his principles and profession, it is when he is most serious and lively in this duty. As Moses, before he died, went up into mount Nebo to take a survey of the land of Canaan, so the Christian ascends the mount of contemplation, and by faith surveys his rest. He looks upon the glorious mansions, and says, " Glorious things are'" deservedly "spoken of thee, thou city of God." He hears, as it were, the melody of the heavenly choir, and says, "Happy is the people that is in such a case; yea, happy is that people whose God is the Lord." He looks upon the glorified inhabitants, and says, "Happy art thou, O Israel; who is like unto thee, O people, saved by the Lord, who is the shield of thy help and the sword of thine excellency?" When he looks upon the Lord himself, who is their glory, he is ready, with the rest, to "fall down and worship Him that liveth for ever and ever, and say, Holy, holy, holy, Lord God Almighty, who was, and is, and is to come! Thou art worthy, O Lord, to receive glory and honor and power." When he looks on the glorified Saviour, he is ready to say *Amen* to that "new song, Blessing and honor and glory and power be unto Him that sitteth upon the throne, and unto the Lamb, for ever and ever. For thou wast slain, and hast redeemed us to God by thy blood, out of every kindred and tongue and people and nation, and hast made us unto our God kings and priests." When he looks back on the wilderness of this world, he blesses the believing, patient, despised saints; he pities the ignorant, obstinate, miserable world; and for himself he says, as Peter, "It is good to be here;" or as Asaph, "It is good for me to draw near to God; for lo, they that are far from thee shall perish." Thus as Daniel, in his captivity, daily opened his window towards Jerusalem, though far out of sight, when he went to God in his devotions, so may the believing soul, in this captivity of the flesh, look towards "Jerusalem which is above." And as Paul was to the Colossians, so may the believer be with the glorified spirits, "though absent in the flesh, yet with them in the spirit, joying and beholding their heavenly order." And as the lark sweetly sings while she soars on high, but is suddenly silenced when she falls to the earth; so is the frame of the soul most delightful and divine while fixed in the views of God by heavenly contemplation. Alas, we make there too short a stay, fall down again, and lay by our music.

But "O thou, the merciful Father of spirits, the attraction of love and ocean of delights, draw up these drossy hearts unto thyself, and keep them there till they are spiritualized and refined; and second thy servant's weak endeavors, and persuade those that read these lines to the practice of this delightful, heavenly work. O suffer not the soul of thy most unworthy servant to be a stranger to those joys which he describes to others; but keep me, while I remain on earth, in daily breathings after thee, and in a believing, affectionate walking with thee. And when thou comest, let me be found so doing—not serving my flesh, nor asleep, with my lamp unfurnished, but waiting and longing for my Lord's return. Let those who shall read these heavenly directions, not merely read the fruit of my studies, but the breathing of my active hope and love; that if my heart were open to their view, they might there read the same most deeply engraven with a beam from the face of the Son of God; and not find vanity or lust or pride within, when the words of life appear without; that so these lines may not witness against me; but proceeding from the heart of the writer, may be effectual, through thy grace, upon the heart of the reader, and so be the savor of life to both.   Amen."

"*Glory be to God in the highest; on earth peace, good will towards men.*"